Guys, Gangs, and Girlfriend Abuse

Guys, Gangs, and Girlfriend Abuse

Mark D. Totten

broadview press

Canadian Cataloguing in Publication Data

Totten, Mark Douglas, 1962–
     Guys, gangs, and girlfriend abuse

Includes bibliographical references.
ISBN 1-55111-341-4

1. Male juvenile delinquents — Psychology.   2. Violence in children.   3. Young women — Abuse of.   4. Minorities — Abuse of.   5. Gangs.   I. Title.

HV9069.T67 2000   364.36   C00-930578-5

Broadview Press Ltd., is an independent, international publishing house, incorporated in 1985.

North America:
P.O. Box 1243, Peterborough, Ontario, Canada K9J 7H5
3576 California Road, Orchard Park, NY 14127
TEL: (705) 743-8990; FAX: (705) 743-8353;
E-MAIL: customerservice@broadviewpress.com

United Kingdom:
Turpin Distribution Services Ltd.,
Blackhorse Rd., Letchworth, Hertfordshire SG6 1HN
TEL: (1462) 672555; FAX (1462) 480947; E-MAIL: turpin@rsc.org

Australia:
St. Clair Press, P.O. Box 287, Rozelle, NSW 2039
TEL: (02) 818-1942; FAX: (02) 418-1923

www.broadviewpress.com

Broadview Press gratefully acknowledges the financial support of the Ministry of Canadian Heritage through the Book Publishing Industry Development Program.

Text design and composition by George Kirkpatrick

PRINTED IN CANADA

THIS BOOK is dedicated to my three great kids — 13-year-old Daniel, 11-year-old Kaila, and 9-year-old Leah — and their great Mom, Sharon Dunn. Together, you have taught me that which is most important in life, and have given me the inspiration to carry on, especially when the going got tough. I will always love you and cherish your gifts.

MT

contents

acknowledgements

This research was financially supported, in part, by generous funding from the Youth Services Bureau of Ottawa-Carleton and my wonderful grandmother, Alice Carol McLurg. I would like to thank the following persons for their assistance in supporting this project: Florence Kellner, Don Whyte, Tullio Caputo, Katharine Kelly, Robert Stebbins, and Colleen Lundy for their helpful reviews and guidance around my doctoral work at Carleton University; Dan Paré, Executive Director of the Youth Services Bureau of Ottawa-Carleton, for his strong encouragement, vision, and patience; Mary Wehrle and Barbara Bole, extraordinary word processors at YSB, and all of the other YSB staff who supported me in this project; the adolescents who participated in this study, both the young abusers and the survivors of their often brutal violence; and Betsy Struthers, my great editor, and Michael Harrison, Vice-President, at Broadview Press. Finally, my loving partner, Sharon Dunn, deserves special mention. Sharon provided me with unwavering support and the courage to complete this project. This book and my Ph.D. are just as much the fruition of her dedication and efforts as they are of mine.

introduction

S HE'S pissed me off, and she won't stop. I've grabbed her
arm, squeezed her, and slapped her. I've punched her
after she put me down in front of my friends. My ex-
girlfriend used to cry after we had fights. I had to punch her to
get her to stop.... I mean, when she nags me for nothing, I'll
tell her to "Shut up bitch," or I'll call her a slut.... Almost every
week I'll say to her "Stop it or I'll hit you." I punch her in the
arm or the leg – not in her face. I'll never punch a girl in the
face unless she punches me first. Sometimes she nags, and she
won't stop. Once I punched this girl in the face and knocked
her out. She grabbed my hair at a dance. When she pisses me
off, sometimes instead of hitting her, I'll push her or shove her
down. I've busted pretty much all of her stuff: lamps, I kicked
her radio, smashed her mirror, punched her walls – I've
destroyed her things. I know it scares her, and I think that's
why I keep doing it. She always does what I tell her to do. I
don't like punching her in the face because it leaves bruises.
Once I punched her in the leg and gave her a big purple mark.
Once at a party she wouldn't leave. I grabbed my girlfriend
and dragged her outside to give her shit. My friends saw it all
and didn't say anything.... I don't know what to do. It's like I
know what I should be as a man, I mean – strong, lots of

money, a good job, and a beautiful wife. But my life isn't like that. I'm not really much of a man without a good job and lots of money. She makes me so angry when she won't do what I want her to do. It's not supposed to be that way. A girl is supposed to get along with a man. She's supposed to respect him and listen to him. But that never happens to me. I feel like a piece of shit around my girlfriends. Sometimes it's them who has to pay for things because they've got the job. It's like they're more important than me and they think they can make the decisions because they've got the money. It's not right. It makes me feel like a wimp or a pussy. That's not the way things are supposed to be.[1]

Male violence against women[2] is a major problem in western, post-industrial societies. Statistics Canada's Violence Against Women Survey (VAWS) estimates that 51 per cent of Canadian women have experienced at least one incident of physical or sexual assault since the age of 16; 10 per cent of the women participating in this random sample survey had been victims of violence in the 12-month period preceding it. Wife assault poses a major threat to women's health and well-being and is present in all significant demographic and social groups. Girlfriend abuse is a significant social problem as well. A large body of survey data suggests that male-to-female physical, sexual, and psychological assaults in dating relationships are common on Canadian and American university and college campuses. These assaults pose a significant threat to the health and well-being of these young women.[3]

Walter S. DeKeseredy and Katharine Kelly have provided the only national representative sample survey incidence and prevalence data on the physical, sexual, and psychological victimization of women in Canadian university and college dating relationships.[4] They found that 45 per cent of female respondents reported being physically abused, 35 per cent reported being sexually abused, and 86 per cent reported being psychologically abused since leaving high school. Statistics Canada's 1993 VAWS used the legal definitions of physical and sexual assault contained in the Canadian Criminal Code on a random sample of 12,300 adult women. Using telephone interviews, the VAWS found that for single women in the 18-24 age group, the rate of women ever assaulted by dates was 24 per cent (15 per cent sexually assaulted; 14 per cent physically assaulted). This figure was almost 50 per cent higher than the national rate of all women 18 years and older who had been sexually or physically assaulted (12 per cent sexually assaulted; 7 per cent physically assaulted; overall rate 16 per cent). The VAWS estimates that 25 per cent of all women who were attending school at the time of the study in 1993 had been sexually assaulted (17 per cent) or physically assaulted (12 per cent) by a male date or a boyfriend. DeKeseredy and Kelly's findings and the results of the VAWS are consistent with the data generated in comparable American studies. Data on the extent of girlfriend abuse in high school and/or elementary school dating relationships suggests that girlfriend abuse is likewise a serious problem in these settings.[5]

While statistics on this issue are available, there is an absence of research which provides theoretical analysis and qualitative understanding of this phenomenon. Further, although some studies suggest that the prevalence and incidence of violent interpersonal assaults vary inversely with social class and age (those with the least resources are suggested to be both the most frequent perpetrators and victims, especially the younger people),[6] there is an absence of girlfriend abuse research amongst those who are less privileged. This project attempts to address these gaps.

The rationale for this study is political; social change is a goal of my research. Like other feminist researchers, I am open about my commitment to ending woman abuse. As Susan Schechter has stated:

> Woman abuse is viewed here as a historical expression of male domination manifested within the family and currently reinforced by the institutions, economic arrangements and sexist divisions of labour within capitalist society. Only by analyzing this total context of battering will women and men be able to devise a long-range plan to eliminate it.[7]

The Study

The purpose of this study is to explore how male youth who are abusive make sense of their behaviour, and how we can understand their behaviour as a social phenomenon; that is, how we, as outside observers, can better understand their world from their viewpoint.

Abusive behaviour is best understood from a sociological perspective, since a problem of this magnitude cannot be effectively understood through psychological or biological perspectives. It has been suggested that at maximum 10 per cent of woman abuse cases can be explained by mental disorders in the perpetrator.[8] Therefore, non-sociological analyses of male violence against women are ineffective because they

> ... ignore the question of power. They cannot answer the question of why allegedly mentally ill men beat their wives and not their bosses, nor why impulse ridden, out of control husbands contain their rage until they are in the privacy of their homes, at which time they bruise their wives but less frequently kill them.[9]

Instead, there is a need for an integrative perspective which combines individual and societal-level factors in the explanation of girlfriend abuse. Through the exploration of the intentions, meanings, and motives associated with this behaviour, we can better comprehend this phenomenon in a social context.

Key concepts of familial patriarchal ideology, masculine identity, and male peer group/gang affiliations allow for a better understanding of girlfriend abuse in the context of the existing research by focussing on the development and impact of familial and gender ideologies upon the masculine identities of marginal male youth. Families and peer groups/gangs are highlighted as two primary sites of ideological influence.

What is a "girlfriend"? For this study the term defines any female aged 13-17 years with whom the male youth has had any current and past short-term (including "one night stands") and longer-term sexual relationships. The breadth of this definition covers both brief sexual relationships and steady, intimate ones of some duration. Relationships with females in which there was no sexual intimacy are not considered to be "dating" relationships. "Sexual intimacy" includes any form of sexual touching, including oral, anal, and vaginal intercourse and penetration by other objects.

The study was conducted in two parts. First, structured interviews held in 1993 with a purposive, non-representative sample of 90 male youth, aged 13-17 years achieved a number of objectives:

1) the schedule of interview questions was developed and assessed, and the usefulness of the questions was confirmed; 2) key concepts from the literature were tested with pre-constructed scales; 3) a sample of marginal, abusive male youth for in-depth interviews was produced; and 4) definitions of abuse, girlfriend, and marginal male youth were developed. The interviews are reported verbatim. Like the actions and feelings they describe, the words these young men use are coarse, explicit, and, at times, disturbing.

From the screening sample, 30 marginal youth were selected with whom to conduct a second set of in-depth, follow-up interviews, in which the key concepts identified in the screening interviews were developed, and which answered the two central research questions which emerged from this initial set of interviews: how do these males make sense of their participation in their abusive behaviour? What insights can be derived from using the key concepts to analyze the participants' behaviour in a broader social context? These interviews were conducted during January and February 1994.

The in-depth interviews benefitted from my ability to develop trust and investigate the participants' feelings, motives, justifications, and understanding through conversation. I realize that because I alone assumed the duties of observer, recorder, theorist, interpreter, and counsellor, certain limitations are placed upon my study. S. Reinharz, in addressing this issue, recommends that:

> since research is a personal activity, research reports should contain a vivid description of the experience of the researching. In these reports the value positions of the researcher should be faced squarely and addressed fully.[10]

My personal motivation and position as a social worker and manager in the social services field for the past 17 years contribute to the fact that this is not detached, objective research.

One of my primary objectives in conducting this project was to increase the safety of abused women. By learning more about how male youth understand their abusive behaviour, I hope that a contribution towards the elimination of woman abuse can be made. Notwithstanding this lofty objective, a number of immediate problems were encountered. How could the safety of the girlfriends being abused by research participants be enhanced without escalating the participants' abusive behaviour? How would disclosures of life-threatening criminal behaviour of the participants be treated? Could confidentiality and anonymity of the participants be ensured? How could the participants be challenged to accept responsibility for their abusive behaviour without introducing bias into the data? The way in which these questions were addressed was informed by Ontario's child welfare legislation and Youth Services Bureau of Ottawa-Carleton (YSB) policies and procedures.

To begin, I decided that an ethical way I could heighten the safety of the participants' girlfriends without escalating abusive behaviour was to conduct in-depth interviews only with those youth who agreed to allow me to have phone contact with their current or ex-girlfriends. This would allow me to support safety planning, explain legal rights, offer referrals to local services for abused females, and explain my research. I did not attempt to verify with these young women the male participant's accounts of his abusive behaviour because I believed that this may have put them at further risk of assault. In order to ensure that the participants fully understood the implications of this, a statement about contact was included on the interview consent form. In addition, I decided that an ethical way for me to handle participants' disclosures of abusive behaviour and not contaminate the data was to confront the participants at the end of the interview and identify any abusive behaviour as such. Existing literature on adult male abusers verifies the importance of holding men accountable for their abusive behaviour. Failure to label this behaviour as abusive and make men accountable can be interpreted by these men as tacit approval.[11]

YSB policy and procedures dealt with any disclosure by participants of perpetration of life-threatening criminal activity (for example death threats, physical and sexual assaults involving knives or guns, or serious injuries resulting from physical and sexual assaults). I informed participants of my obligation to report any such acts or threats immediately to the police, probation officer, and/or Children's Aid Society (CAS) worker. The risk I took in being direct with the participants about this issue was that it might inhibit participants from talking about abuse perpetration or from participating in the study altogether. Of the 30 in-depth interview participants, 8 told me about incidents which I classified as disclosures of perpetration of life-threatening physical and sexual assaults. In these cases, I contacted either the police, CAS, probation, school, or shelter staff to follow up this disclosure.

Two other issues precluded me from ensuring the complete anonymity and confidentiality of participants: disclosures of child abuse/neglect and suicidal behaviour. Ontario's child welfare legislation, the Child and Family Services Act (CFSA 1984), stipulates that any professional who has suspicions of child abuse or neglect of a young person under the age of 16 years must report these immediately to the local CAS. Again, I included my legal reporting obligations regarding suspicions of child abuse and neglect on the interview consent form. Given the fact that 24 of the in-depth interview participants reported having been beaten by father-figures, and many were under the age of 16 years, I had to report a significant number of these cases to the CAS which, in most instances, was already involved with these families.

Prior to the start of the interviews, I assumed that some participants would already have at some point in their lives attempted suicide and/or currently be engaging in suicidal behaviours; I decided to address the limitations of confidentiality concerning this issue also. I informed all participants that in the best interests of their own safety, I could not keep confidential the name of anyone I assessed to be at high risk of attempting suicide. I was clear with the participants that should this situation occur, I would take immediate action to secure the appropriate intervention, including calling an ambulance or advising parents.

Defining Abuse

In the 90 screening interviews the participants told me about their sexual experiences and methods of resolving conflict with their girlfriends. Their reported behaviour was classified into the categories of physical, sexual, and emotional abuse based upon the illegality of some of the specific behaviour and the definitions of abuse offered in the literature. These include emotional and psychological abuse, a broad range of forced sexual acts, and legal definitions of physical and sexual assault.[12] However, as Richard J. Gelles and Claire P. Cornell have indicated, "lumping all forms of malevolence and harm-doing may muddy the water so much that it might be impossible to determine what causes abuse."[13] As well, Douglas J. Besharov has stated that definitions should be the "basic building blocks" of research in family violence, and should be carefully measured.[14] Accordingly, definitions of physical and sexual abuse in this study are limited to the Canadian Criminal Code definitions of physical and sexual assault. Emotional abuse is limited to the most severe forms of emotional control and threats of physical violence. Only those incidents of emotional, physical, and sexual abuse that occurred since the participants' thirteenth birthday were assessed for the purpose of this study.

Measures of abusive behaviour were based upon questions derived from two standard scales. The Conflict Tactics Scale (CTS), developed by Murray Straus and Richard Gelles and based upon a "family conflict" model, is made up of 18 items directed at measuring two methods of dealing with interpersonal conflict in family relationships: psychological abuse and physical violence. The items are placed upon a continuum ranging from "verbal reasoning" (from discussing the issue calmly to requesting the assistance of a third party to facilitate problem resolution) to "verbal aggression" (from insulting and swearing to throwing, smashing, hitting, or kicking something) and "physical aggression" (throwing something at to using a knife or gun on another person). Sexual abuse is not addressed in the scale. The physical abuse component of the CTS is made up of nine violence items used by Straus and Gelles, with the last six items making up the severe violence index.

To place respondents on the CTS, they are asked how many times they have been victimized or have inflicted a violent act in the course of settling a conflict with a partner, child or sibling. The incidence and prevalence rates of violence perpetration and victimization for males and females are based upon these self-reports. These scales are widely used in studies on violence against women and they are found to be reliable and have concurrent and construct validity.[15]

However, the CTS has been soundly criticized for its shortcomings. In particular, it can be problematic in measuring abusive behaviour due to its silence regarding issues related to the context, intensity, meaning, and consequences of acts. By categorizing abuse on a continuum of severity, the CTS suggests that psychological assaults are not as bad as physical assaults; many abused women dispute this assumption. It also suggests that throwing something, pushing, grabbing, shoving, and slapping (minor violence sub-scale) are not as serious as the items contained in the severe violence sub-scale. However, when additional questions are included to probe the outcome of abuse (for example injuries, medical and police intervention), "minor" acts of violence can have "severe" consequences.[16] As well, several types of abuse are not included (sexual assaults, burning, suffocating, squeezing).

More seriously, the CTS is unable to explore the context and meaning of abusive behaviour. Feminists have noted that this is a significant issue given that many studies employing the CTS suggest that women are just as physically abusive when compared to men. However, when intensity and consequences of abusive behaviour are explored, data indicate that many women use violence in self-defence against attacks by men. Men are most likely to use the most severe types of violence and repetitive violence; women sustain more injuries than men. As well, many studies indicate that men underreport their abusive behaviour when compared to the reports of their wives and often fail to report that their actions caused severe injury or hospitalization of their wives.[17]

Finally, the CTS limits abusive behaviour to situations of interpersonal conflict and ignores other contextual factors at the interpersonal level, as well as the social and ideological factors (for example, class, patriarchy, ethno-racial origin) that may be linked to abusive behaviour.[18] In response to these criticisms, the CTS was modified for the purposes of this study.

A modification of Mary Koss and Cheryl Oros' Sexual Experiences Survey (SES) was used to assess sexually abusive behaviours. The SES is a valid and reliable measure and has been extensively used in North America.[19] In the original scale, the eight items are subdivided into four types of behaviour: unwanted sexual contact, sexual coercion, attempted rape, and rape.[20]

Physical Abuse

The criterion used to classify physical abuse is the presence of a minimum of five separate incidents of minor violence (throwing objects, pushing, grabbing, shoving, slapping) and/or one incident of severe violence (kicking, punching, hitting with objects, beating, choking, threatening with a knife or gun, and using a knife or gun on them). These items make up Straus and Gelles's physical abuse component of the CTS. All of these physically abusive behaviours could be classified under the Criminal Code of Canada as either common assault (Section 265), aggravated assault (Section 268), or assault with a weapon or assault causing bodily harm (Section 267).

Emotional Abuse

The definition of emotional abuse is based on a modification of the verbal aggression sub-scale of the CTS, which consists of six modified items of Straus and Gelles's verbal aggression sub-scale. Two new items first utilized in Statistics Canada's VAWS have been added.[21]

The criterion used to classify emotional abuse is the presence of "threatened to hit or throw something at her" and/or "threw, smashed or kicked something" on at least five separate occasions in the relationship in addition to the presence of "put her down in front of friends or family" and/or "accused her of screwing around" during the majority of time spent together. For "threw, smashed or kicked something," only those reported incidents in which there was a deliberate attempt to frighten the girlfriend are categorized as emotionally abusive. "Insulted or swore at" and "did or said something to get back at her"[22] were not categorized as abusive behaviour, since it is questionable whether or not there was a deliberate attempt by participants to harm their girlfriends or any serious consequences of these acts.

In addition, a number of other acts not contained in the emotional abuse sub-scale are categorized as emotional abuse. Many participants reported doing the following to their girlfriends: threatening to use other forms of physical violence (not including hitting or throwing something at them) or threatening to murder them;[23] stalking and monitoring their routine activities; beating up their new and old boyfriends in their presence; and threatening to kill themselves or their girlfriends if they left them. Due to the seriousness of these acts, the presence of only one of these items was required in order to be categorized as emotional abuse, because the intent was to threaten physical violence (defined as assault in the Canadian Criminal Code), to control, and/or repeatedly to humiliate girlfriends. Most of the participants reported engaging in these activities a number of times.

Sexual Abuse

The criterion used to classify sexual abuse is an affirmative response to one or more items on the modified Sexual Experiences Survey in the categories of unwanted sexual contact and rape.[24] Sexual acts subsequent to the use of verbal pressure are not counted as sexual abuse in order to maintain a clear definition. The categorization of sexually abusive behaviour against girlfriends is limited to sexual touching subsequent to the use of threats of physical force or actual physical force (what Koss and Oros refer to as unwanted sexual contact); and oral, anal, or vaginal penetration against consent through the use of force, threat of physical violence, or intentional incapacitation (what Koss and Oros refer to as rape). Therefore, only those behaviours that could be classified under the Canadian Criminal Code as sexual assault (Section 271), aggravated sexual assault (Section 273) or sexual assault with a weapon or causing bodily harm (Section 272) were included in the definition of sexual abuse.

Conclusion

This study is exploratory. Existing research on girlfriend abuse does not examine any of these central research questions. Simply put, there are no published, qualitative studies on girlfriend abuse exploring the development and impact of familial and gender ideologies (in families and peer groups/gangs) upon the masculine identities of marginal male youth. This multi-method approach addresses some of the shortcomings of existing quantitative studies that have primarily surveyed samples of university/college and high school students. Most of the existing work on girlfriend abuse is survey research, with the collection of incidence and prevalence data as the primary goal here.[25] The qualitative data from the 30 in-depth interviews provides material for a systematic search for patterns, explanations, and meanings in the narrative text.

So, this study addresses the question of woman abuse almost at its inception. Surveys and longitudinal studies show that girlfriend abuse precedes wife abuse. It is relevant to programs and policy because information concerning its motivation, justification, and conditions can inform the content of programs designed to alleviate it.

The following chapter provides a discussion of the literature and theoretical work related to the general concepts of this study. Chapter 2 provides an overview of the data from the 90 screening interviews and contextualizes the in-depth interviews. This is followed by three chapters that address the research questions, including the insights derived from the key concepts.

The presentation of the findings is organized around three major themes. Chapter 3 explores the development of familial and gender ideologies in the home, along with the specific assumptions associated with these ideologies. The impact of many of the participants' early childhood experiences of being beaten, emotionally abused, and witnessing the abuse of their mothers by father-figures is key to understanding how these young men make sense of their abusive upbringing. It also helps us analyze the participants' interpretation of their childhood. Chapter 4 explores the development of familial and gender ideologies outside the home, the methods by which these young men struggled with fears and anxieties about their own masculine identities, and the ways in which they negotiated their identities. Most protested against and compensated for their perceived masculine deficits. Chapter 5 looks at the group/gang affiliations of the participants as important sites of ideological influence, by assessing socialization into the group/gang and the role played by these affiliations in girlfriend abuse. The similar ways in which many of these young men engaged in group/gang assaults on females and on males perceived to be woman abusers are also explored.

In each of these chapters examples of the participants' experiences are analyzed in light of both how the participants made sense of these experiences and how we can understand their behaviour as a social phenomenon; that is, how we, as outside observers, can better comprehend the participants' world from their viewpoint. Particular attention is paid to differences within this sample of 30 young men, differences which help explain the variations in the degree to which they embraced patriarchal/authoritarian models of family and gender. As well, these differences account for the variation in the types and severity of abuse inflicted.

The last chapter summarizes the empirical problem, method, research questions, and findings. Theoretical, social policy, and practice implications are addressed, and areas for future research are also proposed.

Notes

1. Interview with Serge, a 16-year-old street kid. All the interviews in this book are from the transcripts of in-depth interviews conducted with the participants in this study. See below pp. 14-15, and Chapters 3 and 4 for details on how these interviews were set up and conducted.

2. The term "male violence against women" is used here to denote physical and sexual violence against females by males. The terms "woman abuse" and "girlfriend abuse" are used to denote physical, sexual, and emotional abuse. The former term refers to abuse by males against adult females, whereas the latter term refers to the abuse by male youth against their female dates.

3. Thorne-Finch, 1992; Johnson, 1996; O'Neill and Harway, 1997; Dobash and Dobash, 1979; Okun, 1986; Smith, 1990b; Stets and Straus, 1989; Stets and Henderson, 1991; White and Koss, 1991; Barnes et al., 1991; Elliot et al., 1992; DeKeseredy and Schwartz, 1998.

   Studies of girlfriend abuse in dating relationships on Canadian university and college campuses are not as common as those on American university and college settings. Instead, Canadian literature focuses primarily on male-to-female physical and psychological assaults on married, cohabiting, and separated/divorced women (Ellis and Wright, 1987; Lupri, 1990; Smith, 1990[a], 1990[b]). Apart from DeKeseredy and Kelly's 1993(b) study, the VAWS (Johnson, 1996) provides the only other national, random sample data on dating violence in Canada.

   See also Coffey et al., 1996; Frazier and Seales, 1997; Sappington et al., 1997; Shapiro and Schwartz, 1997.

4. DeKeseredy and Kelly, 1993b.

5. Johnson, 1996, pp. 112-13; White and Koss, 1991; projects reviewed by Sugarman and Hotaling, 1989; Bergman, 1992; Jaffe et al., 1992; and DeKeseredy and Schwartz, 1994.

6. Studies indicating a higher incidence of physical wife assault in lower income groups include Smith, 1986, 1990b; Kennedy and Dutton, 1989; Lupri, 1990; Rodgers, 1994; Johnson, 1996; and McKendy, 1997. Broidy and Agnew (1997), among others, provide an interesting analysis on this topic by using

general strain theory. See also, Messerschmidt, 1986, 1993; McKendy, 1997; O'Keefe, 1998.

7. Schechter, 1982, p. 209.

8. See Pagelow, 1981; Thorne-Finch, 1992; Johnson, 1996; and Gelles and Straus, 1988.

9. Bograd, 1988, p. 17.

10. Reinharz, 1979.

11. See Adams, 1988; Totten, Manton, and Baker, 1995; and Ptacek, 1988, for further discussion related to this issue.

12. Koss and Oros, 1982; Straus and Gelles, 1986; Johnson, 1996; DeKeseredy and Kelly, 1993b; Koss and Gidycz, 1985.

13. Gelles and Cornell, 1985, p. 23.

14. Besharov, 1990.

15. Straus, 1990a.

16. See DeKeseredy and McLean, 1990; Dobash et al., 1992; Johnson, 1996; Breines and Gordon, 1983; Walker, 1979; and Smith, 1987.

17. Brinkerhoff and Lupri, 1988; Lupri, 1990; Kennedy and Dutton, 1989; Steinmetz, 1981; Stets, 1990; Szinovacz, 1983; Straus, 1990a; Gelles and Straus, 1988; Browne, 1987; Dobash and Dobash, 1988; Makepeace, 1986; Saunders, 1988, 1989; Walker, 1989; Edleson and Brygger, 1986; Smith, 1987; Brush, 1990; Dobash et al., 1992; Browning and Dutton, 1986; Totten and Reed, 2000.

18. Browning and Dutton, 1986; Saunders, 1988; Brush, 1990; DeKeseredy and MacLean, 1990; Dobash et al., 1992.

19. Koss et al., 1987; Koss and Gidycz, 1985.

20. Appendix A, 38.

21. Appendices A and B, 39 a-f.

22. Appendices A and B, 39 a, d. The reader should note that the wording on items 39c and 39d was slightly modified in the in-depth interview based upon feedback from the screening interviews.

23. Uttering threats of physical violence and death are contrary to Section 264 of the Criminal Code of Canada.

24. Koss and Oros, 1982. The reader should note that the wording for the questions on sexually abusive behaviour (Appendices A and B, 38) was changed in the in-depth interviews based upon feedback from the screening interviews.

25. For example, see Makepeace, 1986; Koss et al., 1987; Stets and Henderson, 1991; White and Koss, 1991; DeKeseredy and Kelly, 1993b; Johnson, 1996.

one

A Theoretical Survey: The Study of Male Violence

ALTHOUGH the academic study of male violence and male violence against women includes very little research on the specific topic of girlfriend abuse, it does have some bearing on the subject. This chapter briefly examines the wide range of literature and theoretical work related to familial patriarchal ideology, masculine identity, and male youth involvement in peer groups/gangs, drawing attention to the relationship between these key concepts and violent marginal males. These theories point to the need to explore the development and impact of familial and gender ideologies on marginal male youth. While families and male peer groups/gangs are two primary sites of ideological influence, witnessing abuse against mothers and being abused as a child are also related to girlfriend abuse. The relationship between economic/social marginalization and certain types of male physical and sexual violence against females needs to be qualified by focussing on familial and gender ideologies.

The theoretical approach of this study is an integrative perspective that draws on social learning, sex/gender roles and socialization, lifestyle/routine activities, social construction of masculinity, youth subcultures, and peer group/gang theories and models. This integrative approach, based upon elements of psycho-social – or what Ron Thorne-Finch has termed social constructionist theories – is best able to explain the complex phenomenon of male violence against women.[1]

Early attempts to explain male violence against women have been limited by a narrow focus on typically one of the following areas: societal, psychological, interpersonal, or biological.[2] As a result of this rigidity in thinking, few models have been proposed which can explain the multiplicity of causes of male violence against women. Instead, existing explanations tend to focus on one factor alone. This does not mean that physiological and intrapsychic theories are not relevant to the study of woman abuse. However, if there is not an expressed linkage between the central concepts of these theories and the social context in which the individual is situated, their applicability to the explanation of why males abuse women is limited.

Physiological Theories

Sociobiological theories on woman abuse centre on genetic factors to explain the social differences between males and females, and evolutionary theory is used to explain social behaviours, including violence. Male violence is not criminal, but biologically necessary. Sociobiological theorists suggest that humans have no control over their social environment and that genes determine interpersonal relations between men and women. Meanwhile, biosocial theory attempts to contextualize biological factors within broader society and the environment. Both brain structure and testosterone have been linked to woman abuse, although the evidence is not overwhelming.[3]

Physiological theories suggest parts of the brain and testosterone may be correlated with male violence and aggression. However, as Thorne-Finch notes, social factors, which have not been fully explored by this research, play a very important mediating role. They also cannot explain why most men are not violent despite having certain brain structures and hormones believed to be related to violence, nor why many men are selective in their targets for violent behaviour; for example, many men choose to abuse their female intimates and not their co-workers or supervisors. Until the relationship between physiological and social factors has been more fully explored, there will always be the risk that simple or inaccurate interpretations of this research may be reached.[4] This can result in the legitimization of woman abuse and a failure to make men accountable for their abusive behaviours.

Intrapsychic Theories

Intrapsychic theories on male violence against women focus on the attributes of individual personality. In a major break from the physiological theorists, researchers and clinicians proposed that psychological problems were at the root of violent behaviour. Thorne-Finch notes that these problems included: "immature personalities, personality disorders, poor impulse control, low frustration tolerance, dependency, depression, developmental trauma leading to misogyny or other ego functioning problems, fear of intimacy or abandonment, jealousy, addiction, and other psychiatric illnesses."[5] However, there is a large body of research suggesting that only a small minority of abusive men have psychological or psychiatric problems. The problem of woman abuse is so widespread that causative explanations cannot focus solely at the individual level of analysis. As well, intrapsychic studies on this issue have been fraught with methodological problems.[6]

The body of psycho-social theoretical work on the causes of and risk factors associated with male violence against women can be divided roughly into two camps. As Holly Johnson[7] and Thorne-Finch have identified, some approaches have a psychological focus and centre on the individual make-up of perpetrators and survivors. These include social learning, sex/gender roles and socialization, and situational factors. Others have a sociological focus, focussing on the social context of abusers and survivors of violence. Although both groups of theories examine to a greater or lesser degree the role played by society in developing violent males, none of these models or theories on their own can fully explain why males abuse females. Instead, all offer different insights into this complex social phenomenon. Johnson and Thorne-Finch offer excellent analyses of many of these different theories and models.

Social Learning Theory

Being abused by parents, witnessing parental marital abuse, and exposure to repeated images of violence outside the home, such as those portrayed in the media, are risk factors that may contribute to abuse perpetration in dating relationships. Many authors have suggested a link between witnessing and/or experiencing abuse at home and perpetrating and/or being victimized by abuse later on in life.[8]

The consequences of being abused as a child by parent(s) can be serious. Victimization by child abuse is associated with a vast number of mental health and behavioural problems by numerous researchers, including depression, low self-esteem, self-destructive and delinquent behaviour, and violence perpetration. Overall, most of these studies suggest that severity, frequency, and duration of child abuse are crucial factors in the extent of emotional and behavioural difficulties these youth experience in their lives.[9]

The consequences of witnessing parental marital violence can be serious as well. According to Statistics Canada's national survey on violence against women (VAWS), 2.6 million women in Canada have been assaulted by a marital partner, and in 39 per cent of these cases, children witnessed this violence. As Johnson notes, this means that at least two million children (many of whom are now adults) in Canada have been exposed to some disturbing messages about the legitimacy of using violence to settle problems in intimate relationships. Previous researchers have suggested that intergenerational transmission of family violence occurs in roughly 30 per cent of children and youth who experience and/or witness violence in their families of origin.[10]

J.W. Fantuzzo and C.V. Lindquist, in a review of 29 papers on witnessing parental violence, report that these children are at risk for a host of externalizing behaviour including elevated levels of aggression at home, school, and in the community. Child witnesses are reported to have high levels of behavioural problems and low levels of social competence and higher levels of internalizing behaviour (such as anxiety and psychosocial deficits) compared to children who have not witnessed marital violence.[11]

Recently, researchers are reporting gender-specific findings regarding the impact of witnessing parental violence. Most of this research suggests that male and female children who witness wife assault cope in distinct ways. Whereas female children tend to be at greater risk for further victimization through abuse in dating and marital relationships, male adolescents are more likely to be violent towards girlfriends, mothers, sisters, and male peers.[12] These children have learned that violence is a positive way to solve conflict.

Men who experience violence at home while growing up are much more likely to use violence against their wives in their adult lives. The VAWS found that men who witnessed their mothers being abused were three times as likely to be physically violent with their own wives compared to men who grew up in homes where violence was not present. Johnson reports that these men were also significantly more likely to perpetrate more severe and repeated violence on their wives. As well, women who witnessed violence committed against their own mothers had been victimized by higher rates of violence by their own husbands than women who lived in non-violent families. These Statistics Canada data point to the relevancy of parental modelling in understanding how abusive behaviour is learned.[13]

A significant number of researchers have argued that poverty, with the associated stresses of unemployment, low status jobs and lack of resources, is a major contributing factor to violence. For example, recently it has been found that low socio-economic status (SES), exposure to community and school violence, acceptance of violence in dating relationships, and low self-esteem were key mediators of girlfriend abuse. These factors differentiated young males who had witnessed high levels of inter-parental violence and were perpetrating violence in dating relationships from male youth who had likewise witnessed similar violence in their families but had violence-free dating relationships.[14] However, many authors dispute the relationship between poverty and abuse, arguing that low-income families do not have the resources to hide violence in the home and that survivors have few avenues open for support, excluding shelters and the police. In fact, these researchers maintain that middle-income men are even more seriously impacted by unemployment because of a heightened threat to self-identity.

There are significant factors outside of the family unit which contribute to violence being learned as an effective tool to achieve desired ends. Television, music videos, video games, movies, pornography, sports, and the military (to name but a few) all contribute to popular images of violence in society. Young people are living in a society in which violence is glorified in many of these agents of socialization. Violence against women is a common theme in many leisure activities. For some people, frequent exposure to these violent images can result in the modelling of violent and aggressive behaviour. Summarizing the findings related to the media and violence, Johnson explains that the closer an individual's real life situation approaches that shown in the movie or television show, the greater the likelihood of the behaviour being copied.[15] The greater the personal identification with the sports star or movie star displaying violent behaviour, for example, the greater the chance of the viewer using these images to inform his or her behaviour. Desensitization to violence can occur in children and youth repeatedly exposed to situations in which violent behaviour is portrayed in a positive fashion. This can lead to changes in the attitudes and behaviour of these young people. One American study has demonstrated that young people who view images of violence in the media can become uncertain about what constitutes healthy dating relationships. These negative effects of exposure to violent messages in the media can be amplified in the absence of long-term, healthy relationships with caring adults.[16]

This glorification of violence in North American society supports and gives legitimacy to the use of violent means to resolve family conflict. Murray Straus asserts that although violence occurs in only a minority of families, abusive behaviour is far too prevalent. As an example, the regular physical punishment of children by their parents results in these children learning four lessons: love is associated with violence, and those that love you also have the right to hurt you; physical punishment is used to train the child, which establishes the moral rightness of hitting other family members; when something is really important, it justifies the use of physical force; and when one is under stress, tense, or angry, hitting is understandable and, to a certain extent, legitimate.[17] During maturation, these children can apply this learning to the resolution of problems in their peer and adult relationships.

Johnson writes that one of the most crucial determinants of whether or not violence will be perceived as being an effective tool to resolve problems is the concept of reinforcement. Violence will increase in frequency if the perpetrator gets what he or she wants (for example, feelings of power and control for the perpetrator; desired behaviour of the abused person), and if the sanctions against violent behaviour are perceived to be weak or non-existent (for example, if there is little support for wife assault survivors, or the wife batterer rarely is confronted as a result of his behaviour).[18]

Social learning theory has been criticized for its lack of empirical support, its gender insensitivity, its failure to distinguish witnessing from experiencing child abuse, and its failure to fully explain how youth may learn to become violent in extra-familial contexts.[19] Despite the compelling nature of this theory on violent behaviour, social learning cannot explain on its own the complexities of woman abuse.

Sex/Gender Roles and Socialization

Perhaps the most significant issue that social learning theory does not address in any substantive way is the issue of gender. As Johnson argues, the significance of gender lies in its ability to explain such issues as how some men perceive violence against female intimates as acceptable, whereas violence against other adults is not, and how a significant number of boys and men learn that it is acceptable to harass and abuse women.[20] The importance of sex role theory lies in its incorporation into social learning theory an understanding of the gendered complexities of interpersonal relationships.

Gender role socialization in patriarchal capitalism is theorized to associate aggression, dominance, independence, and violence with masculinity and power. Femininity and powerlessness are believed to be associated with passivity, dependence, nurturance, and non-violence. Most girls are taught to focus on the maintenance of social relationships and the importance of serving others. Most boys grow up believing that they are entitled to power and privilege because they are males.[21] These cultural messages regarding the appropriateness of gendered behaviour during childhood and adolescence are complex and delivered by most of society's institutions. Through such socializing agents as the family, media (television, music videos, movies, advertisements, pornography), military, sports, and the peer group (including school), women are often portrayed as less powerful and inferior to men.

Lifestyle/Routine Activities Theory

Recently, theoretical accounts of victim–offender relationship dynamics have been put forth to explain variation in violence victimization rates among different segments of the population. Lifestyle (how and in what proportion people spend their time engaging in work, leisure, and recreational activities) is the major focus of this work. These explanations are commonly referred to as lifestyle, routine activities, or exposure theories.

Socio-demographic characteristics like marital status, employment status, income, and age result in lifestyle variations, which are related to violence victimization and perpetration. For example, young single women are more likely to be targets of male violence compared to older married women. Young single women have a high rate of victimization of sexual assault because they tend to associate with young single men at bars, parties, and on university and college campuses. Young single men have the highest rates of sexual assault perpetration.[22] Both young single men and women usually have begun the process of separation from their families, and the peer group has become the primary reference point for them. They spend the majority of their leisure time apart from their families in settings where violence may occur.

Data from Statistics Canada's VAWS supports these assumptions by routine activities theory. Twenty per cent of assaults by dating partners in the survey occurred in a car, 28 per cent in the woman's home, 22 per cent in the man's home, and 10 per cent in another place of residence. Only 20 per cent of these reported assaults occurred in a public place. Sexual assaults were more likely to occur in a car, whereas physical assaults were most likely to take place in the man or woman's place of residence.[23]

Many researchers have written about the ambiguous nature of the dating event and how this confusion can contribute to misunderstanding by the male about a woman's level of motivation to have sex. In the highly charged, sexual context of dating, it has been found that students who adhere to traditional sex role attitudes and the adversarial nature of male-female relationships were more likely to justify rape scenarios in specific situations.[24]

Lifestyle theorists also point to alcohol abuse as a main factor associated with violence. Alcohol is present in a significant number of dating activities, and many abused women recall how their partners drank heavily during episodes of violence. For example, the VAWS found that alcohol was involved in 51 per cent of the assaults by offenders against their female dates. However, the relationship between alcohol and violence is complex, and likely not a simple causative correlation.[25] Alcohol increases the chance of sexual assault occurring for a number of reasons.

1. Many men use alcohol abuse to legitimize and excuse their violent behaviour.[26] Female survivors of violence by male partners also use their partner's alcohol abuse to rationalize and justify the violence.

2. Alcohol can serve to lower the social constraints around violence and change emotional reactions to perceived disrespectful behaviour in certain people.

3. Excessive drinking can lead to faulty perceptions and miscommunication by both parties, resulting in an increased likelihood that messages about sexual relations will be misinterpreted.[27]

4. Women who are intoxicated on a date are not as able to fight off or get away from a sexual attack, and can be perceived as legitimate victims by their attacker and wider society.

In Canada, there have been a number of recent cases where extreme drunkenness has been used by the defence to successfully acquit a number of men charged with crimes of violence against women. In response to this issue, in 1995 Parliament passed amendments to the Criminal Code to prohibit the defence of extreme drunkenness in the majority of situations of violence against women and children.

Resource Theory

Resource theory suggests that, throughout history, men have had higher status and power than women in the home and extra-familial settings. Men have traditionally had the legislative and normative authority to hold power and control over their wives and children in all societal settings. Largely through schooling and employment outside of the home, men have been able to gain greater income, respect, expertise, and authority. This has resulted in an unequal balance of power in the family, with women for the most part being unable to match the power and force of their male partners. Resource theorists suggest that the greater the degree of power and control men are able to exhibit, the lesser the risk that they will use violence to control their female intimates. When these men perceive that their superiority is being eroded, they are most likely to use violence and the threat of violence to regain this sense of authority.[28]

Similar to sex role theory, resource theorists such as David Finkelhor argue that prolonged unemployment, low-income or low-status jobs result in elevated rates of stress and conflict in the home and pose a significant challenge to the male breadwinner's authority in the family.[29] As a result of this perceived decrease in power and authority, these men can resort to abusive behaviour against female partners to regain control.

Resource theory may have particular relevance in the analysis of girlfriend abuse by marginal male youth. These youth may be at heightened risk to react with violence to perceived imbalances in privilege and status in their dating relationships. Physically abusive behaviour may be used to lash out against and punish females perceived to be "liberated." If these young men are likely to adhere to rigid models of family and gender, they may experience greater confusion than more privileged male adolescents between roles and expectations in dating relationships.

Social Control and General Systems Theories

Social control and general systems theories maintain that adequate control mechanisms are necessary to avoid socially inappropriate behaviour, and that the avoidance of punishment and pursuit of reward mould human action. For example, for many abusive men, perceived control is a primary reward for their behaviour. These theorists argue that people abuse "because they can." The unequal balance of power within the family, its relative isolation, and cultural ideals which legitimize the dominance of men all contribute to the minimal social controls over and the costs of using violence in the family. The dominance of men over women and children is explained by the physical size and strength of men compared to other family members, and the elevated social standing which is attributed to them. Given the minimal consequencing of violence in the family and in dating relationships by larger society, men are relatively free to use violence to get their own way with children and female intimates. Social controls such as the police and the courts have limited impact on this issue due to social norms supporting the privacy of the home and intimate relationships. Abusive men are rewarded for their behaviour in part by the powerful masculine images in wider society supporting male dominance and control.[30] Female partners are reluctant to physically abuse their male partners because of the physical and economic superiority of their spouses.[31]

The general systems theory of family violence suggests that violence is the result of the family system. It is argued that families are composed of interdependent parts, balanced through mechanisms of action and reaction. Key attributes of families at risk of violence include amount of time spent together by family members, the emotional degree of involvement, tension between the desires and needs of family members, and the relative control some members hold over other members.[32]

The general systems theory of family violence has been attacked by feminists as failing to incorporate issues of power and control inequalities. There can be a tendency to blame abuse survivors as causing or deserving the abuse and a failure to hold the abuser accountable for his behaviour. As well, this theory has been criticized for not fully exploring the impact of the gendered relations of inequality in the family. In general, it is men who commit the most serious and frequent types of abuse which result in the more extreme forms of injuries. Many researchers have concluded that much of women's violence is used in self-defence or in anticipation of another assault by the man.

Feminist Theories

Feminist theories combine many of the concepts of the theories reviewed so far, but focus as well on the historical and institutional context of male privilege and female subservience. Although other theories maintain that male status is a significant variable that can explain male violence against women, feminist theorizing on this issue contextualizes sex role acquisition and male power and control in the historical patriarchal organization of capitalist society. Feminists argue that gender role socialization into stereotypical feminine and masculine sex roles occurs in the context of laws and cultural practices that at all levels award greater power and authority to males. Male violence against women is a logical extension of this patriarchal ordering of social relations.

The concept of patriarchy implies both a structure, in which men have more power and privilege than women, and an ideology that legitimizes male dominance. Many men are situated in social structures which support their privileged status. The ideology portrays these social structures as just and accords legitimacy to the status quo of stratified gender relations.[33] Radical feminist theorists argue that male power and privilege is the fundamental cause of stratified gender relations. They suggest that patriarchal social relations constitute the foundation of all social inequalities and determine class relations. Perceived threats to patriarchal power are believed to be a key motive for woman abuse.[34] Marxist-feminists, such as Herman and Julia Schwendinger, suggest that the structural conditions in the economy are the root cause of male power and control. Capitalism is the primary oppressive system, within which is situated gender inequality.[35]

Familial and gender ideologies play a central role in the social problem of woman abuse. Feminists have written extensively on the relationship between familial and gender ideologies and the social construction of gender and sexuality. Michelle Barrett and Mary McIntosh note that the contemporary family can be analyzed on two levels: as a social and economic institution, which is organised primarily by the division of labour between the main breadwinner and primary child rearer, and as an ideology, in which the family is culturally represented as stereotypically nuclear and heterosexual. They argue that the institution and the ideology are inextricably linked.[36] With its sexual division of labour, the family plays a central role in the ideological construction and acquisition of masculinity and femininity (gender ideologies). As such, the family is presented to be one of the primary sites of the oppression of women. The familial sexual division of labour is suggested to be reflective of women's experiences in the labour market as well. Those women who work outside of the home still make significantly less than men and continue to be ghettoized in stereotypically feminine, unstable, low-paying jobs. Familial patriarchal ideology has been defined as a set of beliefs that legitimize male power and authority over women in a marriage-like arrangement.[37]

Feminist work on woman abuse contains many useful elements for this project. While Marxist research highlights the material factors which are related to abusive behaviour and suggests that low-income males are at greater risk for perpetrating certain types of abuse than middle- and upper-income males, it does not explore non-economic factors, such as patriarchy. Radical feminist researchers suggest that males who adhere to familial patriarchal beliefs are at higher risk for physically abusing females than are males who do not hold these beliefs. However, existing research on girlfriend abuse focuses mainly on middle-income college/university populations and high school students. There has been no qualitative or quantitative girlfriend abuse research conducted on low-income male youth. It is not known if marginal male youth adhere to an ideology of familial patriarchy. As well, the existing body of work on patriarchy and woman abuse in the adult population is based upon the reports of female survivors of male violence, primarily in victimization surveys. Radical feminist theory assumes that all men in patriarchal societies have roughly an equal potential to abuse women. This assumption is not supported by current empirical data on the incidence and prevalence of abuse. This "universal risk theory" of assault for all women in patriarchal societies downplays important class and race variations.

The primary implications of feminist research include testing the concept of familial patriarchal ideology with a sample of marginal adolescent males to explore how familial patriarchal beliefs are acquired, and the nature of the relationship of these beliefs to abusive behaviour. It is possible that because low-income adolescent males both experience the highest rates of unemployment and perceive their economic future to be hopeless, many may not be able to attain the superior economic position to which they feel entitled.[38] Economic marginalization and patriarchal power may therefore increase the potential for physical and sexual violence against women by some of these youth.

Social Construction of Masculinity Theories

Despite the contributions of feminist theories to understanding the causative factors underlying male violence against women, there are significant limitations to this body of work, and there is a need to integrate these important theories with the other theories reviewed here. Perhaps, as Johnson suggests, the most significant problem with both sex role and feminist theorizing on this topic lies in their inability to explain the fact that many men who have undergone traditional gender role socialization are not abusive. Furthermore, those who are abusive do not exhibit identical types of abuse perpetration.[39] Sex role and feminist theorizing on this issue paints all men and women with the same patriarchal brush, suggesting that most, if not all, men have comparable "traditional" gender identities. The same assumption is made for women. However, there is a growing body of evidence suggesting that masculinity and femininity are constructed differently according to the social conditions in which people are situated.

The major break that social construction of masculinity theorists such as James Messerschmidt have made with other researchers is that they consider masculinity to be malleable, constructed and reconstructed daily in relationships with other people, rather than a fixed trait developed in childhood and adolescence. Men in different "structural spaces" may employ different forms of violence based on the resources available to them to achieve their gender.

Masculinity theorists argue that masculinity is rooted in a particular socio-historical context, structured by the social relations of class, race, and gender as well as individual and group behaviour. They maintain that dominant and subordinate masculinity types are formed through practices that perpetuate stratified relationships between males, and between males and females. The individual and collective practice of oppressive gender relations occurs within the context of social structures. As such, Wil Coleman maintains, role/socialization and social constructionist theories of masculinity, if not integrated, offer inadequate accounts on the construction and practice of masculinity. He summarizes the limitations of these theories:

There are but two ways of answering the question: either masculinity is constructed and sustained by hidden but discoverable forces, discourses, ideologies, structures and the like (in which case its contingent and moment-to-moment accomplishment is unconscious, the actor being unaware, and necessarily unaware, of all that he does), or else it is constructed, bricoleur-fashion, by the actor and sustained by conscious monitoring and impression-management.[40]

The research and theoretical work on masculine identity is important for this project for a number of reasons. It suggests that many factors impact upon the construction and practice of masculine identity and that dominant and subordinate identity types may exist at any given point in time. It points to the importance of testing the concept of masculine identity in a sample of marginal males, because these males may exhibit identifiable patterns of behaviour related to negotiating their masculine identities. Some of these young men may have perceived deficits resultant from blocked access to traditional male entitlements of power and privilege. This literature also suggests that group behaviour may play an important role in expressing and confirming masculinity.

Male Peer Groups/Gangs and Youth Subculture Theory

Male Peer Groups/Gangs

A large body of diverse research on youth gangs, prisons, hockey players, and soccer "hooligans" suggests that interpersonal violence may result from interactions with male peers. Research on woman abuse in marital relationships and in dating relationships in college and universities shows how social exchanges with male friends can encourage and legitimate physical, sexual, and psychological assaults on women. This has been referred to as the "male peer support model."[41] Yet, these studies – unqualitative and age and class biased – do not answer the questions which interest us here. Do marginalized male youth belong to groups similar to those found in college/university samples? How do these youth understand their participation in peer groups/gangs? Do these groups/gangs commit collective acts of physical, sexual, and emotional abuse against females? Is masculinity collectively practised and constructed in these groups/gangs? Are these collectivities patriarchal?

It is unlikely that patriarchal male peer groups whose members hold attitudes supportive of abusive behaviour are formed only in university/college settings. Instead, they are most likely formed in high school.[42] Although there is no previous research which documents the emergence of patriarchal, pro-abuse peer groups, related research suggests that marginal male youth are more likely to gravitate towards these groups than are middle-income youth.

The male peer support model is limited. Although it is helpful in explaining the dynamics of woman abuse, it is one-dimensional. Youth participate in groups/gangs for a number of reasons, many of which have little to do with male peer support. The literature suggests that same-sex peer groups are important agents of socialization. The transition from family towards developing independence is in part mediated through peer groups. Peer groups present an opportunity for youth moving from adolescence into adulthood to meet a number of needs not being met by family or school. These groups are also a key space for socializing, hanging out, and having fun.[43]

Youth Subcultures

There is a significant body of literature on marginal, delinquent male youth subcultures in the context of male peer groups/gangs. Some of these studies suggest that juvenile delinquents employ techniques of neutralization which allow them to carry on with their lives while engaging in deviant behaviour. Many of these males do not identify their behaviour as being wrong. Instead, they portray their values and actions to be morally right and superior to those societal values in their mundane, everyday reality. Their accounts are characterized by the use of a vocabulary of adjustment, in which their socially unacceptable behaviour is denied through the sophisticated use of justifications. Male youth with few resources find excitement and adventure in violent crime, simultaneously finding an outlet to express their anger and rage. The less-powerful can be controlled through physical and sexual violence. Girls, gays, and racial minorities typically occupy the bottom rungs of this power hierarchy. The literature on the routine activities of working class and marginal male youth indicate that the lives of many of these adolescents are characterized by substance abuse, crime, violence, and boredom (hanging out).[44]

Conclusion

This brief survey of the theories concerning male violence and male violence against women has provided three central concepts to test in the interviews. The limitations of these theories point to the need to explore the relationship between economic/social marginalization and certain types of male violence (physical and sexual) against females. Families and/or peer groups/gangs are two primary sites of ideological influence which, along with witnessing abuse against mothers and being abused as a child, are related to girlfriend abuse. The development and impact of familial and gender ideologies on marginal male youth will be examined in the following chapters.

Notes

1. Thorne-Finch, 1992. I am aware of the vast theoretical and empirical body of work on the self and its development (symbolic interactionalist perspective), including Sarbin and Rosenberg, 1995; Mead, 1934; and Cooley, 1922. Including this literature might have increased the scope of this project so as to make it unmanageable.

2. O'Neil and Harway, 1997.

3. See Barash, 1987; Wilson and Daly, 1985; Thorne-Finch, 1992, p. 49; Shibley Hyde, 1980, p. 240. For discussion of brain and limbic structure effects on violence see Elliot, 1982, 1977; Stearns, 1972; Thiessen, 1976; Grossman, 1988; Franken, 1988; and Thorne-Finch, 1992, p. 49. For discussions of testosterone and violence, see Persky et al., 1971; Kreuz and Rose, 1972.

4. Thorne-Finch, 1992, p. 51.

5. Thorne-Finch, 1992, p. 52.

6. Gelles and Straus, 1988; Maiuro et al., 1988; Dutton, 1984.

7. Johnson, 1996.

8. For example, see De Maris, 1987; Gwartney-Gibbs et al., 1987; Marshall and Rose, 1987, 1988; Breslin et al., 1990; Foo and Margolin, 1995; Johnson, 1996; O'Keefe, 1997.

9. Readers interested in this segment of the literature review should refer to Foo and Margolin, 1995; Lane and Gwartney-Gibbs, 1995; Langhinrichsen-Rohling and Neidig, 1995; O'Keefe, 1997; and Sappington, 1997.

10. For example, see Peled, 1997a, 1997b; Statistics Canada, 1993; Kaufman and Zigler, 1987.

11. Fantuzzo and Lindquist, 1989; Rosenbaum and O'Leary, 1981; Hershorn and Rosenbaum, 1985; Wolfe et al., 1985, 1986; Holden and Ritchie, 1991; Fantuzzo et al., 1991; Forsstrom-Cohen and Rosenbaum, 1985; Jaffe, Wolfe, and Wilson, 1990.

12. Hughes, 1988; Jaffe et al., 1990; Mangold and Koski, 1990; Johnson, 1996; O'Keefe, 1997; Sappington et al., 1997; Wofford, Mihalic, and Elliott, 1997; James Madison University Department of Psychology, 1997; O'Keefe, 1998.

13. Straus, Gelles, and Steinmetz, 1980; Straus, 1990a; Kalmuss, 1984; Hotaling and Sugarman, 1986; Rodgers, 1994; Johnson, 1996, especially p. 6; Statistics Canada, 1993.

14. O'Keefe, 1998.

15. Johnson, 1996, p. 3.

16. Bandura, 1977; Huesmann and Malamuth, 1986; Wolf et al., 1995. This issue will be more fully explored in the next section on Sex/Gender Roles and Socialization, below p. 31.

17. Straus, 1990b, p. 185.

18. Johnson, 1996, pp. 5-6.

19. For example, see Kaufman and Zigler, 1993, and Langhinrichsen-Rohling et al., 1995.

20. Johnson, 1996, p. 7.

21. Brownmiller, 1976; Rubin, 1983; Messerschmidt, 1986, 1993, 1997; Johnson, 1996.

22. Johnson, 1996, p. 16.

23. Johnson, 1996.

24. Sacco and Kennedy, 1994; Muehlenhard and Linton, 1987; Calhoun et al., 1997; Koss and Cleveland, 1997.

25. For example, see Dobash and Dobash, 1979; Martin, 1981; O'Keefe, 1997; Statistics Canada, 1994; Johnson, 1996, p. 11.

26. Ptacek, 1988; Scully, 1990.

27. Benson, Charlton, and Goodhart, 1992.

28. Johnson, 1996, pp. 17-18; Bersani and Chen, 1988.

29. Finkelhor, 1983.

30. Gelles, 1983; Gelles and Straus, 1988; Tolman, Edleson, and Fendrich, 1996.

31. For discussion on how society does not censure "date rape," see Alvi and Selbee, 1997 and Koss and Cleveland, 1997; also Johnson, 1996, pp. 19-20.

32. Gelles, 1979; Margolin, Sibner, and Gleberman, 1988.

33. Dobash and Dobash, 1979; Eisenstein, 1979; Walby, 1990.

34. For example, see Daly, 1978.

35. H. and J. Schwendinger, 1983.

36. Chodorow, 1978; Barrett, 1980; Rich, 1980; Barrett and McIntosh, 1982.
37. Smith, 1990a.
38. Messerschmidt, 1986, 1993.
39. Johnson, 1996, pp. 22–23.
40. Coleman, 1990, p. 197.
41. See DeKeseredy, 1988 for a review. Also see Koss and Cleveland, 1997; DeKeseredy and Schwartz, 1991.
42. Kanin, 1967.
43. Brownfield and Thompson, 1991; Caputo, 1994.
44. Sykes and Matza, 1957; Matza, 1964; Kanin, 1967; Chambliss, 1973; Willis, 1977; Messerschmidt, 1983, 1993; Schwendinger and Schwendinger, 1985; Connell 1991.

two

Laying the Foundations: The Screening Interviews

THE screening interviews yielded valuable data on the manner in which young abusers presented their behaviour. Their accounts were socially constructed, replete with a complex mixture of excuses, denial, and justifications. The quantitative methodology used to gather information helped to develop, evaluate, and confirm the semi-structured questions to be used in the in-depth interviews; made it possible to test the key concepts with pre-constructed scales; led to the exploration of familial and gender ideologies in two sites of ideological influence (the home and peer groups/gangs); produced a sample of thirty marginal, abusive male youth for the in-depth interviews; and defined the terms abuse, girlfriend, and marginal male youth.

The initial data set was gathered through structured interviews with a purposive, non-representative sample of 90 male youth, ages 13-17 years, during February and March 1993. These participants were selected from the YSB client list, members of a local Boys and Girls Club, Byward Market street youth, and youth congregating at a local mall. Two pieces of legislation informed the decision to include 13- to 17-year-old youth in the sample: the federal Young Offender's Act (YOA) and the provincial Child and Family Services Act (CFSA). The YOA establishes the age of criminal responsibility at 12 years, and stipulates that young criminals 12-17 years of age receive both rehabilitation and punishment separately from adult offenders; it attempts to balance both offender rehabilitation and protection of the public. The CFSA is Ontario's child welfare legislation, and permits youth 12 years of age and older to receive confidential counselling without knowledge of their parent(s). Unfortunately, I was not able to recruit any 12-year-olds who met the criteria for this study.

Sample Selection

Research participants who were not YSB clients were pre-selected at least 24 hours prior to each interview, from names of youth encountered at key areas in the downtown Byward Market (shopping mall, youth shelter, youth drop-in), a suburban shopping mall and a Boys and Girls Club. During this pre-selection stage of the research, I introduced myself as a YSB worker and a doctoral candidate researching problems in teenage dating relationships. The topic of girlfriend abuse was not raised at this time. I explained to the groups that each participant would be paid $10 for an interview, but that I had to randomize participant selection. I also described the limits of confidentiality as articulated on the participation consent form. Following this, the names, phone numbers and/or addresses (some youth had no phone) of each youth who wished to participate were recorded; at maximum, one-quarter of these youth (every fourth name, starting from the middle of the page) were selected. The following 60 participants were selected in this manner during a five-day period in February 1993: 15 out of 100 Boys and Girls Club members; 25 out of 100 Byward market street youth; and 20 out of 85 youth congregating at the mall.

The process for selecting participants from YSB casework, residential, and employment services clients was much easier. Using the YSB weekly client list of February 5, 1993, 30 male clients were randomly selected from a total of 160 clients. Clients were telephoned to explain the study and set up an interview time if they agreed to participate. Each interview took between one and one-half to two hours to complete, and each participant was paid $10 following the interview. Clients were assured that they were under no obligation to participate and that their participation (or lack thereof) would in no way negatively impact upon their status as a consumer of YSB services.

The interviews took place at three main locations: a Boys and Girls Club, a youth shelter, and YSB program sites (drop-ins, residences, employment office, young offender's unit). Audio-taping was not used given the sensitive nature of the research topic and the reluctance of the five participants in the pre-test sample to be audio-taped. This decision was supported by the literature on the reluctance of adult men to honestly discuss their abusive behaviour.[1]

Following each interview, participants were informed of the primary goals of the study and were given the opportunity to ask questions about girlfriend abuse. They were again guaranteed confidentiality and anonymity. Fifteen participants accepted referral information on substance abuse, individual or group counselling regarding their abusive behaviour, and employment counselling. No participant voiced concerns to me regarding the methodology or the research topic.

A number of participants disclosed severe physical and/or sexual abuse committed against girlfriends. In five of these cases, it was apparent to me that these girlfriends were at significant risk of further assaults. Accordingly, after gaining consent of the participant, I transferred this information over to their YSB worker (all five participants were YSB counselling, drop-in, employment, or young offender unit clients). I assessed one participant to be at risk for committing suicide, and this information was immediately transferred to his YSB worker with his consent.

Screening Sample Characteristics

Initially, I had intended to explore whether the social class of the family of origin of the participants affected their behaviour with their girlfriends. My assumption was that social class would be related to specific forms of girlfriend abuse, and I expected that youth from lower-income families might be more physically abusive, whereas youth from more affluent families might be more likely to use emotional control and threats of violence in their relationships with girlfriends. Although these initial assumptions were not supported by the data from the 90 screening interviews, discussion on this issue is warranted here.

I attempted to gain a sample that might provide me with the opportunity to compare differences between classes. Wallace

Clement has identified four main classes in capitalist society, each of which is defined in relation to the command of capital (the means of production) and the labour power of others (the source of value): capitalists/executives, the new middle class, the old middle class, and the working class.[2] Based upon this definition and adding another sub-group to the working class (the dependent poor), I categorized the 90 screening interview participants into three sub-groups of 30 youth – the dependent poor (DP), working class (WC), and middle class (MC) – by asking the following questions:

1. What was the main source of income in your family (welfare, alimony, disability, work)?

2. Who provided most of the income in your family while you were growing up?

3. When you were growing up, was your parent(s)/caregiver usually working? If no, why weren't they working?

4. If yes, was s/he self-employed or working for someone else? If self-employed, did s/he usually have paid employees working for her/him, or did s/he usually work by her/himself? If s/he usually worked for someone else, did s/he usually work as a manager or supervisor?

5. What is the highest level of school completed by your parent(s)/person(s) who brought you up?

6. What would the total income/earnings (before taxes) of your parent(s)/caretaker(s) be for last year?

7. What kind of place (residence) did you grow up in (apartment, public housing, owned home)?

Tables 2.1-2.4 describe the socio-demographic differences between abusers and non-abusers, and within the three social class sub-groups.

Youth who reported that their parent's income was based upon welfare, disability assistance, and/or alimony, and in addition that their parents never or very rarely worked (for two weeks or less yearly), were defined as dependent poor. The parents of these youth had only primary or high school education. In addition, almost all of these youth grew up in low-income housing communities.

Youth who reported that their parent's income was primarily based upon working for someone else in low-paying, service sector jobs or in the underground economy,[3] and whose net annual income for the past year was $30,000 or less, were defined as working class. Almost two-thirds of the parents of these youth had completed high school, and just under one-third had completed post-secondary education. One-half of these youth reported that their parents owned their own homes, with the remaining youth reporting that they grew up in rented townhouses or apartments.

Youth who reported that their parent's income was between $30,001-$50,000 and was based upon self-employment (with a minimum of two employees) or working for someone else as a manager or supervisor were defined as middle class. Over one-half of these youth reported that their parents had completed post-secondary schooling, and four-fifths reported that their parents owned their own homes.

Sixty-seven per cent of the 90 participants (60 youth) reported behaviour which was categorized as abusive according to the criteria defined in the Introduction. Their mean age was 15.8 years. Ethno-racial minorities made up 16 per cent of the sample (14 participants), and 93 per cent of the participants (84 youth) were heterosexual (2 participants reported that they were gay, 3 said that they were questioning their sexual orientation, and 1 participant said that he was bisexual). The mean school grade completed was 8.9. At the time of the interviews, one-half of the sample was living away from home in a young offender open custody facility, group home, rooming house/apartment, or in a shelter. Thirty-seven participants had received or were currently receiving counselling services, although none of these services focused on their own abuse perpetration.

When the 60 abusers are compared to the 30 non-abusers, there are no apparent differences with regards to mean age, mean school grade completed, sexual orientation, social class, and previous counselling history. However, more non-abusers were living at home (63 per cent) than abusers (42 per cent), and more of the non-abusers were ethno-racial minorities (23 per cent) than were the abusers (12 per cent) (see Table 2.1).

Table 2.1
Socio-
demographic
Characteristics of
Abusers and
Non-Abusers

	Abusers (N = 60)	Non-Abusers (N = 30)
Mean Age	16.1 yrs.	16.1 yrs.
% Ethno-Racial Minorities	12% (7)	23% (7)
Mean School Grade Completed	8.9	8.6
% Living At Home	42% (25)	65% (20)
% Gay/Bisexual/Questioning	7% (4)	8% (2)
% Dependant Poor (DP) (n = 30)	70% (21)	30% (9)
% Working Class (WC) (n = 30)	63.3% (19)	36.6% (11)
% Middle Class (MC) (n = 30)	66.6% (20)	33.3% (10)
% Received Previous Counselling	40% (24)	43% (13)

Dependent poor participants were more likely to be living at home and were least likely to be living in a YOA or group home or independently in a rented house or apartment. All classes had equal numbers of participants living on the streets (see Table 2.2).

Table 2.2
Living
Arrangement at
Time of
Interview

	YOA/GROUP HOME	SHELTER/ STREET	RENTED HOUSE/ APARTMENT	AT HOME
DP 33.3% (30)	6.6% (2)	20% (6)	6.6% (2)	66.6% (20)
WC 33.3% (30)	20% (6)	20% (6)	16.6% (5)	43.3% (13)
MC 33.3% (30)	10% (2)	20% (6)	33.3% (10)	40% (12)
TOTALS 100% (90)	11.2% (10)	20% (18)	18.8% (17)	50% (45)

Thirty-five participants had parents with post-high-school education. Not surprisingly, middle-class participants had the highest number of parents who had completed post-secondary education (see Table 2.3).

Twenty-six participants had grown up in low-income housing communities; 39 participants reported that their primary caregiver(s) owned their own homes. As could be expected, the vast majority of

	PRIMARY	HIGH SCHOOL	POST–HIGH	UNKNOWN
DP 33.3% (30)	13.3% (4)	33.3%(10)	30% (9)	23.3% (7)
WC 33.3% (30)	3.3% (1)	63.3%(19)	30% (9)	3.3% (1)
MC 33.3% (30)	0% (–)	40%(12)	56.6% (17)	3.3% (1)
TOTALS 100%(90)	5.5% (5)	45.5% (41)	38.8% (35)	10% (9)

Table 2.3
Parental Level
of Education
Completed

dependent poor participants grew up in subsidized housing, and almost all of the middle-class participants grew up in houses owned by their caregivers (see Table 2.4).

	OWNED	RENTED	SUBSIDIZED
DP 33.3% (30)	0% (–)	16.6% (5)	83.3% (25)
WC 33.3% (30)	50% (15)	46.6% (14)	3.3% (1)
MC 33.3% (30)	80% (24)	20% (6)	0% (–)
TOTALS 100%(90)	43.3%(39)	27.7% (25)	28.8% (26)

Table 2.4
Type of
Residence Grew
Up In

Abusive Behaviour

Table 2.5 describes abuse type by class and the total abuse types for the complete sample of 90 youth. Thirty-four per cent of the participants were emotionally, physically and sexually abusive; 22 per cent were emotionally and physically abusive; and 10 per cent were emotionally and sexually abusive. Social class does not appear to be related to the incidence, type, or severity of abuse in the screening sample.

Fifty-six per cent of the 90 participants (51 youth) reported behaviour with girlfriends classified as physically abusive.[4] These males had physically assaulted their girlfriends on at least one occasion since age 13. Thirty-three engaged in minor forms of physical abuse (throwing something, pushing, grabbing, shoving, slapping), and 18 reported having used one or more acts of severe violence (punching, kicking, beating, choking, using a knife or a gun) against their girlfriends. All of the participants who reported severe physical abuse also reported numerous acts of minor physical abuse.

Forty-four per cent of the 90 participants reported behaviour with girlfriends classified as sexually abusive.[5] These males had sexually assaulted their girlfriends on at least one occasion since the age of 13 years. Twenty-five reported acts categorized as forced sexual contact (sexual touching subsequent to the use of threats of physical force or actual physical force) and 15 reported acts categorized as forced intercourse (oral, anal, or vaginal penetration against consent through the use of physical force, threats of physical force, or intentional incapacitation through the use of drugs or alcohol). All of the participants who reported having forced intercourse also reported having committed many acts of forced sexual contact.

	PHYS/SEX/ EMOT.	PHYS/ EMOT.	SEX/ EMOT.	TOTALS
Dependent Poor (30)	30% (9) (4 severe violence and 4 forced intercourse)	23% (7) (2 severe violence)	17% (5) (no forced intercourse)	70% (21) (6 severe violence and 4 forced intercourse)
Working Class (30)	40% (12) (5 severe violence and 4 forced intercourse)	10% (3) (no severe violence)	13% (4) (1 forced intercourse)	63% (19) (5 severe violence and 5 forced intercourse)
Middle Class (30)	33% (10) (6 severe violence and 6 forced intercourse)	33% (10) (1 severe violence)	0% (0)	67% (20) (7 severe violence and 6 forced intercourse)
TOTALS (90)	34% (31) (15 severe violence and 14 forced intercourse)	22% (20) (3 severe violence)	10% (9) (1 forced intercourse)	67% (60) (18 severe violence and 15 forced intercourse)

Table 2.5 Abuse Type by Class

Familial and Gender Ideologies

The first key concept to be tested in the screening interviews was familial patriarchal ideology. Adherence to familial patriarchal beliefs and approval of using physical violence against girlfriends were assessed by using two slightly modified scales: Patriarchal Beliefs and Approval of Violence Against Wives.[6] Participants were categorized as adhering to patriarchal beliefs if they agreed with one or more of the following statements:

1. A male has the right to decide whether or not his wife/girlfriend should go out in the evening with her friends.

2. A male has the right to decide whether or not his wife/girlfriend should work outside the home.

3. Sometimes it is important for a male to show his wife/girlfriend that he is the head of the house.

4. A male has the right to have sex with his wife/girlfriend when he wants, even though she may not want to.

Participants were categorized as approving of physical violence against girlfriends if they reported agreeing with a male slapping his girlfriend in one or more of the following situations:

1. She won't do what he tells her to do.

2. She insults him when they are home alone.

3. She insults him in public.

4. She comes home drunk.

5. She is sobbing hysterically.

6. She won't have sex with him.

7. He learns that she is dating another male.

Sixty-two per cent of the abusers reported agreeing with at least one of the statements in the Patriarchal Beliefs Scale, whereas only 37 per cent of the non-abusers reported agreeing with one of these beliefs. Forty per cent of the abusers and 27 per cent of the non-abusers reported agreeing with at least one of the statements in the Approval of Violence Against Girlfriends Scale (see Table 2.6).[7] It is noteworthy that a substantial percentage of abusive participants (60 per cent) reported that they disapproved of a male slapping his girl-friend in these situations, yet were still abusive. There were no apparent class differences between dependent poor, working-class, and middle-class participants in their adherence to patriarchal beliefs and attitudes supporting violence against girlfriends.

The second key concept developed as a result of the screening interviews was the definition of masculine identity, which refers to both the subjective inner space and sense of self and to related individual behaviours. To assess the influence of masculine identity, participants were asked to provide ten quick answers to the question "What is the ideal man?"[8] A common pattern of masculine ideals, values, and anxieties was reported by abusers and non-abusers; Robert Connell has identified these as "protest," "complicit," and "negative" masculine identities in marginal male youth.[9]

In the group of abusers, there were indicators of a common pattern of values and beliefs consistent with a rigid definition of masculinity, related to the public, objective masculine space. These youth described to me elements of the main patterns of hegemonic masculinity described in the theory and research on marginal male youth:[10] subordination of women and gays and a connection to abusive behaviour and toughness (see Table 2.6). This identity was characterized by a public, objective display of power over gays, females, and other males. The traditional male role was pursued to an extreme through abusive behaviour, toughness, competitiveness, and dominance. This form of masculine identity, described as "protest" masculinity by Connell, was evident in 95 per cent of the 60 abusers who reported that the "ideal man" needs to be tough, aggressive, and muscular; heterosexual; has lots of money; agreed with at least one of the patriarchal beliefs described above; and/or approved of a male slapping his girlfriend in at least one of the situations noted previously.

In the group of non-abusers, there were indicators of a common set of values and beliefs consistent with what Connell describes as a "complicit" masculine identity. These participants appeared to participate in the subordination of females and gays without resorting to physical or sexual violence, but by using psychological control, manipulation, and male privilege. These males did not report that they were physically, sexually, or emotionally abusive. However, many of their behaviours with girlfriends could be considered as emotionally controlling. For example, many of them reported that they had been present when male peers had abused females, yet did nothing to intervene. As well, they said that they had often verbally humiliated their girlfriends and had not allowed them to "hang out" with other males. Neither of these actions were defined as emotionally abusive in this study. Complicit masculine identities, evident in 93 per cent of the 30 non-abusive participants, were defined as characteristic of non-abusers who reported that the "ideal man" needs to be tough, aggressive, and muscular; heterosexual; has lots of money; and agreed with at least one of the patriarchal beliefs noted above.

Finally, a third type of masculine identity, referred to by Connell as "negative" masculine identity, was evident in a small minority of the abusers and non-abusers. Four of the six gay/bisexual/questioning (g/b/q) participants provided evidence that they were practising behaviour contrary to those actions indicative of the traditional masculine identity. Negative masculine identity was defined as characteristic of those abusers and non-abusers who reported that they were g/b/q *and* who reported that the "ideal man" needs to be sensitive, caring, educated, and have a good job (in other words, they did not define this man as being heterosexual; having children and a wife; and being tough, aggressive, and muscular). Of these four youth with negative masculinity types, one was a gay girlfriend abuser, two were "questioning" girlfriend abusers, and one was a bisexual non-abuser. One bisexual abusive participant was categorized as having a protest masculinity because he defined the ideal man as being tough, muscular, and aggressive; he adhered strongly to patriarchal beliefs and strongly approved of violence against girlfriends. One bisexual non-abuser was categorized as having a complicit masculine type. Even though he did not report having physically or sexually abused a girlfriend, he defined the ideal man as being tough, muscular, and aggressive; adhered to familial patriarchal beliefs; and displayed the emotionally controlling behaviour described above as characteristic of the complicit masculinity type.

Finally, one heterosexual non-abuser described the ideal man in terms of being sensitive, caring, educated, and having a good job as well. He was also categorized as having a negative masculinity. He did not report adhering to patriarchal beliefs, nor did he approve of using violence against girlfriends. He indicated that he was committed to having egalitarian relationships with females and sexual minorities.

When I questioned the one gay girlfriend abuser and two "questioning" girlfriend abusers about the apparent inconsistency between their expressed desire to take a path out of the traditional male role and their abusive behaviour, they all responded in a similar fashion. These three youth reported that they had not "come out" to their peer group about their sexual orientation and were trying to demonstrate to their friends that they were heterosexual. They said that they feared being beaten up by their male peers if they disclosed their sexual orientation to them. They also indicated that, in choosing a sexual orientation different than their father's, they were making a clear break from their father's abusive behaviour. All three reported that their fathers had beat themselves and their mothers. The one bisexual abusive participant, who was categorized as having a protest masculinity, did not see his sexual orientation as a choice. He reported being beaten as a child and witnessing his mother being beaten, and indicated that there was nothing wrong with his abusive behaviour.

There were no apparent class differences in masculine identity between the dependent poor, working class, and middle class.

The final key concept was the peer group/gang affiliations of the participants. One of the goals of the screening interviews was to test DeKeseredy's male peer support model. DeKeseredy argues that woman abuse in dating relationships is related to a number of "support functions" performed by male peers. His male peer support model is derived from social support theory, which explains how social integration and interpersonal dynamics impact upon people's capabilities in dealing with stressful life events. He hypothesizes that social exchanges with male friends can encourage and legitimate girlfriend abuse.[11]

To assess the influence of any pro-abuse beliefs of male peers and family members, a modified version of Michael Smith's Approval of Violence Against Wives Scale was again used.[12] The influence of the male peer group in supporting and legitimating abusive behaviour and the influence of male family members in supporting and legitimating abusive behaviour (pro-abuse attitudes, pressure to have sex, routine activities, informational support, attachments to abusive peers) was assessed through a modified version of DeKeseredy and Kelly's peer support questions.[13]

The most frequent activities by abusive participants in the screening sample were drug/alcohol use, criminal activities (such as auto theft, drug-dealing, weapons offences, and aggravated assaults), and hanging out at malls and pool halls. Sixty-eight per cent of these 60 participants reported engaging in all three of these routine activities. Almost all reported that they had at least two peers who told them to abuse their girlfriends and who were abusive against females themselves.[14] Finally, 97 per cent of these same abusive screening interview participants reported that male friends had pressured them to have sex with their girlfriends. This latter finding is not surprising, given that having sex is a common aspect of adolescent male socialization.[15]

The most frequently engaged-in activities by non-abusive participants were sports, school, and working. Ninety per cent of these 30 participants reported that they went to school and/or worked and played sports regularly. Fifty-seven per cent reported that they had at least two peers who told them to abuse their girlfriends, and one-half said that they had peers who were abusive against females themselves (see Table 2.6). Like the abusers, the non-abusers reported that 97 per cent of their male peers had pressured them to have sex with their girlfriends.

Social class played a minor role in the routine activities reported by the participants. Working-class and middle-class males were approximately twice as likely as dependent poor males to routinely use drugs and alcohol, and to hang out at malls, arcades, and pool halls. This is not surprising given the economic resources necessary to engage in these activities. Further, dependent poor males were twice as likely as working- and middle-class males to play sports routinely. Given that most of these activities occur free of charge at the Boys and Girls Club and that this club is situated beside a large low-income housing community, this again is not surprising.

One of the most striking differences which differentiates the abusers from the non-abusers is the experiencing of abuse in the home. Whereas three-quarters of the abusers reported having been beaten by a male caregiver and having witnessed their mothers being beaten, just over one-third of the non-abusers reported similar experiences. As well, slightly more abusers than non-abusers reported having been told by family members to abuse females.[16] Although social class does not appear to play a role in the social support from family members to abuse females, this does not hold true for experiencing abuse at home. Over three-quarters of the dependent poor participants reported witnessing emotional abuse against females in their family, and almost two-thirds reported witnessing and being victimized by physical abuse. One-half of the working-class participants reported witnessing emotional abuse and just over one-third reported witnessing and being victimized by physical abuse. Of the middle-class participants, only 37 per cent reported witnessing emotional and physical abuse of females by males and being victimized by physical abuse in their families. In other words, there appear to be large class differences in the exposure of participants to the abuse of females by male family members. Whereas 77 per cent of the dependent poor and 50 per cent of the working class witnessed woman abuse and were victimized by abuse in their homes, only 37 per cent of the middle-class participants reported exposure to abuse in their families.

Participation in gang-related activities was another striking difference between the abusers and non-abusers. Whereas 35 per cent of the abusers reported belonging to a gang, only one of the 30 non-abusers said that he was a gang member. Many of these participants indicated that their gangs provided them with a place to meet unmet needs, including status, identity, and acceptance. Social class played a large role in the gang participation by the screening sample participants. Whereas 18 of the 22 gang members were dependent poor or working class (9 participants each), only four gang members came from middle-class families. The concept of a continuum of male peer groups/gangs, spanning from "groups of friends" to "hard-core criminal gangs" was tested.[17] The male peer groups/gangs identified by the participants were situated along this continuum based upon their degree of organization for criminal objectives. Based on their degree of participation in collective criminal activity, 30 of the participants were placed towards the hard-core gang end (including the 22 participants who were identified as hard-core gang members); 30 were located towards the middle; and the remaining 30 participants were placed towards the "group of friends" end.

	ABUSERS (N = 60)	NON–ABUSERS (N = 30)
Patriarchal Beliefs	62% (37)	37% (11)
Approval Slapping of Girlfriend	40% (24)	27% (8)
Experienced Abuse at Home	75% (45)	37% (11)
Family Support to Abuse	35% (21)	23% (7)
Abusive Peers	85% (51)	50% (15)
Peer Group Support to Abuse	88% (53)	57% (17)
Masculine Identity	95% (57) protest	93% (28) complicit
	5% (3) negative	7% (2) negative
Routine Activities	68% (41) crime/substance abuse/hang-out	90% (27) sport/school/ work
	35% (21) gang members	3% (1) gang member

Table 2.6 Familial and Gender Ideologies of Abusers and Non-Abusers

Marginalization

Due to the fact that social class played only a limited role in the participants' behaviour with their girlfriends, I decided to analyze the screening interview data from another angle: the social and economic marginalization of the participants. By exploring the data from this viewpoint, an opportunity was provided to incorporate the participants' present social class membership with the membership of their families of origin. As can be seen in Table 2.7, the comparison of abusive behaviour and familial and gender ideologies of the marginal and non-marginal participants reveals some large differences. Although all three classes were roughly equally represented in both groups, abusers made up 92 per cent of the marginal group and only 30 per cent of the non-marginal group. Almost all non-marginal participants were living at home and either in school or working at the time of the interviews, compared to only a small minority of the marginal youth. Many more marginal youth experienced abuse at home and family support to abuse and belonged to

		MARGINAL PARTICIPANTS (N = 53)	NON-MARGINAL PARTICIPANTS (N = 37)
	Social Class	DP 30% (16)	DP 38% (14)
		WC 38% (20)	WC 27% (10)
		MC 32% (17)	MC 35% (13)
	Abusers	92% (49)	30% (11)
	Living at Home	26% (14)	84% (31)
	In School/Working	15% (8)	84% (31)
	Experience Abuse at Home	79% (42)	38% (14)
	Family Support to Abuse	47% (25)	8% (3)
	Abusive Peers	89% (47)	51% (19)
	Peer Group Support to Abuse	89% (47)	62% (23)
	Masculine Identity	Protest 85% (45)	Protest 32% (12)
		Negative 9% (5)	Complicit 68% (25)
		Complicit 6% (3)	Negative 0% (0)
	Gang Member	42% (22)	0% (0)
	Patriarchal Beliefs	58% (31)	46% (17)
	Approval Slapping Girlfriend	51% (27)	14% (5)

Table 2.7 Abusive Behaviour and Familial/ Gender Ideologies of Marginal and Non-Marginal Participants

peer groups in which members were abusive. Finally, marginal participants were much more likely than non-marginal participants to have protest masculine identities, belong to gangs, and approve of slapping a girlfriend.

Related to familial and gender ideologies was the method used by participants to account for their behaviours. This has been referred to as "vocabulary of adjustment."[18] Almost all participants who reported having abused a girlfriend went to great lengths to excuse, justify, or deny their abusive behaviours. A number of common themes ran through their accounts, and it is useful to categorize these themes as Scully has done.[19] In her study of convicted rapists, she categorized research participants as either admitters or deniers. Admitters viewed their behaviour as rape, but used excuses to explain their behaviour in a socially acceptable way. They did not portray themselves as rapists. In contrast, although deniers defined their behaviour as wrong, they denied that it was rape. Sexual violence was justified given the deviant nature of their victims or simply did not occur at all given their very narrow conceptualization of rape.

In a similar fashion, 15 participants who admitted to abusing a girlfriend (25 per cent of the abusers) used excuses to explain why their behaviour was abusive, and why they were not woman abusers. Common themes used by the admitters when excusing abuse were the following (each theme is accompanied by a brief account by some participants in the screening interviews):

1. I'm emotionally disturbed: I black out, have an anger problem, I'm depressed.

    "Supposedly I choked her. I can't remember. She said something and I grabbed her neck. It happened last summer and I didn't hurt her. I've only hurt a girl mentally. I dump them."

2. I was drunk/high at the time.

    "I beat the shit out of girls when I get pissed. I don't remember. It doesn't hurt them anyway."

3. I'm really a nice guy. I beat up guys who rape and beat women.

    "It's the usual joking around, bitch slaps.... We always are joking around. I only shake them, push them (girlfriends). I could never leave a bruise. I could never hurt them.... Once when I was 9, I pulled a knife on this girl and her friends. I told them 'Don't move or you're going to die.' She kicked me in the balls and I got my friend's sister to beat her up, the stupid bitch.

Denying the abuse was a much more common way for the abusers to talk about their behaviour. Forty-five of the sixty abusers (75 per cent) denied abusing a girlfriend and justified their behaviour by constructing narrow definitions of abuse and deflecting blame onto their girlfriends, who were perceived as "legitimate" victims. Common themes used by the deniers when justifying abuse were the following:

1. It's not abuse – she loves sado-masochistic sex.

    "My ex liked me to scratch, bite, and fuck her really hard for a really long time – eight hours. I don't like causing her pain, but she liked it."

2. It's okay because she's a bitch/a slut/high/drunk.

    "At a party two years ago, we fucked her. We knew that she was a slut. She wanted to get fucked by the four of us. She had fucked the three others already, and wanted it real bad from me. What a bitch."

3. She meant yes when she said no.

    "I grab them all the time at parties. They don't care. That's the way they are. You use little tricks, not force, to have sex. Just start it. They're shy. Then you know they want it. Most girls always want it. They're always jumpin' you.... I'd beat a friend (male) if he hit a girl. It's stupid. You just don't. They're lucky they are bitches."

4. It's not abuse – I never hit her.

    "I've never used any kind of physical force on her. She's the boss. I use drugs and alcohol to have sex. You get them drunk or stoned and sex is easy.... Women like being roughed up when they have sex. I've fucked girls hard all night – they wanted it.... It's the women's job."

Conclusion

Girlfriend abuse appears to be socially constructed, although social class of origin plays only a minimal role regarding the participants' experiences at home, their beliefs, or their behaviour with their peers. Large differences are found in the comparison of the abusive behaviour and familial/gender ideologies of marginal and non-marginal youth. Despite the fact that social class make-up was approximately equal in both groups, abusers made up almost all of the marginal group and only less than one-third of the non-marginal group who were, mostly, living at home with their parent(s) and either in school or working. Excuses, justifications, and denial permit these youth to explain their abuses in a socially acceptable way.

The data and concepts derived from these 90 screening interviews provide an overall picture of the life and attitudes of marginal male youth and a context for the in-depth interviews which follow.

Notes

1. For example, see Ptacek, 1988.
2. From Clement, 1990, "capitalists/executives are defined as those who employ on a regular basis three or more people or who command the means of production concerning the number of persons employed, the products made, their amount, methods of production, budget or distribution, with binding decision-making authority either themselves or as voting members of a group. These executives must also be located within the top, upper, or middle management levels. This means, in addition to claiming actual decision-making, executives also have to be a formal part of the management hierarchy.

   The new middle class is composed of employees who either supervise other employees directly in terms of their pace of work, promotion of subordinates, preventing their gaining raises, causing them to be fired or suspended and issuing of formal warnings, or who have been delegated lower level managerial policy-making responsibilities which are not binding (as they are for executives). In other words, they must be sanctioning supervisors or have some policy-setting authority.

   The old middle class includes the self-employed with two or fewer employees.

   The working class has an absence of command over the means of production, labour power of others or their own means of realizing their labour." (Clement, 1990, p. 468)

   Questions 5-9 in Appendix A are modified versions of some used by Clement, 1990.

3. Typically these jobs included fast food preparation, janitorial work and housekeeping, grounds keeping, snow plowing and back-hoe operation, hairdressing, department store sales clerks, and home daycare.

4. In other words, when the physical/sexual/emotional abusers are combined with the physical/emotional abusers, the total number of physically abusive youth is 51, or 56 per cent (34%+22%=56%). Questions 39 g-0 in Appendices A and B are taken from Straus and Gelles' CTS.

5. In other words, when the physical/sexual/emotional abusers are combined with the sexual/emotional abusers, the total number of sexually abusive youth is 40 or 44 per cent (34%+10%=44%).

6. Smith, 1990a. Questions 32-34 in Appendix A are modified versions of Smith's scales.

7. Burt's (1980) Acceptance of Interpersonal Violence Scale was also used to measure participants' approval of using violence to have sex (Appendix A, 36). However, it was later decided not to use the data generated from this scale due to difficulties integrating scores from this scale with the Patriarchal Beliefs and Violence Against Girlfriends Scales.

8. This question was first used by Scully, 1990, and is 35 in Appendix A.

9. Connell, 1991a.

10. See Messerschmidt, 1993.

11. DeKeseredy, 1988.

12. Smith, 1990a. Question 32 in Appendix A is a modified version of Smith's scale.

13. DeKeseredy and Kelly, 1993b. Questions 12-31 in Appendix B are modified versions of DeKeseredy and Kelly's questions.

14. Screening interview participants were asked to state how many of their male friends (all, most, a few, none) had told them to abuse their girlfriends. This is referred to as "peer group support to abuse" in Table 2.6.

15. See Chambliss, 1973; Heward, 1988; Messerschmidt, 1993.

16. This is referred to as "family support to abuse" in Table 2.6.

17. Mathews, 1993.

18. See Kanin, 1967.

19. Scully, 1990.

three

At Home: Learning Familial and Gender Ideologies

The In-Depth Interviews

ALL of the 30 in-depth interview participants reported physically and/or sexually and emotionally abusive behaviour. Twelve of them were in a current relationship with a girlfriend. None was in counselling for abusive behaviour at the time, nor had they ever participated in such counselling.

I encountered numerous difficulties attempting to find those participants who were not living at home. However, through word of mouth at YSB's Drop-In Centres, a youth shelter, and the Boys and Girls Club, I was able to eventually reconnect with them. An additional point of difficulty arose when I had to reject 10 young men because they refused to consent to my contacting their current or ex-girlfriends. The in-depth interviews were conducted at three main locations: the Boys and Girls Club, the youth shelter, and YSB program sites (drop-ins, residences, employment office, young offender's unit). As in the screening interviews, I decided against audiotaping due to the sensitive nature of the research topic and requests by the participants. Each interview took an average of three hours to complete.

All 30 youth were defined as economically and socially marginal, based upon the following criteria. They all had poor relations with their families and received little or no financial support from them. Twenty-four were beaten by fathers and witnessed beatings of their mothers by fathers. Sixteen were living away from home: nine lived in a rooming house, shelter or on the street; five lived in a young offender or group home; two lived in a rented house or apartment. The 14 youth who lived at home told me that they spent very little time there; parental control was minimal. Almost all participants were from working-class neighbourhoods or government subsidized low-income housing communities. The mean school grade completed was 8.3, with a range of grades from 6-10. Many of these youth had dropped out of school; the others reported that, although they were still registered in school, they were either failing or frequently absent. The average age was 15.6 years, with a range of 14-17 years.

Children and youth who live in poverty face a number of risks related to physical and mental health, development, and education not normally associated with middle- and upper-income children and youth. These young people who have limited access to economic resources are much more likely to experience significant health and developmental problems, early school dropout, employability barriers, intervention by child welfare and youth justice systems, and homelessness.[1] Most of the marginal male youth who participated in this study were struggling with many of these issues.

There were significant intra-group differences in the in-depth interview sample. Twenty-five of these youth were heterosexual, one was bisexual, three had serious questions about their sexual orientation, and one was gay. Six were ethno-racial minorities. Seventeen were gang members, and almost all reported engaging in criminal activity and substance use on most days. Although all 30 of these young men were girlfriend abusers, they varied somewhat in the extent and forms of abuse inflicted and their reasons for being abusive. As well, some reported participation in collective beatings of gays, ethno-racial minorities, and males they considered to be woman abusers.

In-Depth Interview Questions and Data Analysis

The method used for analyzing the in-depth interview data, consisting of transcripts regarding how these abusive male youth described their behaviour, is based on the techniques of ethnographic data analysis.[2] The large volume of data provides rich accounts describing these young abusers' perspectives on their behaviour and gives the participants the opportunity to explore the meaning of their behaviour. The analysis examines how they made sense of their abusive behaviour and situates their behaviour in a broader social context.

The dialogue in the in-depth interviews was free-flowing. I began by reviewing the completed 1993 interview and asked the participants the questions contained in Appendix B. Although I attempted to maintain the sequence of these questions, this was not possible in many cases. In all interviews, however, the last five questions were asked at the end of the interview. These focused on defining the participants' behaviour as abusive and challenging them to accept responsibility for it.

Data consist of detailed, handwritten records I made during and immediately following each interview. The narratives were therefore recorded as close to verbatim as possible, using the young men's own words and expressions, graphic and disturbing as these sometimes were. This work took between one and one-half to two hours after the three-hour interview. At most, I was able to conduct two interviews per day. These data were analyzed in order to organize the narratives into meaningful patterns around the conceptual categories tested in the 90 screening interviews (familial patriarchal ideology, masculine identity, male peer group/gang affiliation).

Although I attempted "to document the world from the point of view of the people studied,"[3] the accounts during the in-depth interviews could not be taken simply at face value. I expected there to be inconsistencies. Given my clinical experience working with abusive male youth, the existing literature on adult male abusers,[4] and the screening interviews, it was expected that the participants would rationalize, legitimize, and minimize their behaviour. To make sense of their accounts, two issues were considered: researcher-participant relationship, and the "truth-status" of the participants' accounts.[5]

The relationship between me and the participants included issues related to my personal motivation and position, my value orientation, and the transfer from "facilitate the narrative" interviewer role to confrontative counsellor role following the collection of the interview data. The in-depth interviews conducted were quasi-clinical in nature.[6] To the best of my knowledge, this type of method has not been attempted before on a similar sample. I could not deny the fact that I was an experienced social worker, nor that the subject matter contained serious ethical dilemmas.

Accordingly, I felt that I had an ethical and moral obligation to step outside of the traditional sociological interviewer role. In order to ensure the safety of the participants' girlfriends, I understood that I had no choice but to challenge the participants to take responsibility for their abusive behaviour. Given my clinical experience, I anticipated that some participants might become angry or threatening when confronted. In fact, this only occurred in two interviews. In one situation, Mike, a burly 17-year-old street youth who had tattoos covering his arms, hands, and neck, told me "So you're saying I beat and rape women?... Fuck you! I don't need this shit!" He then abruptly got up and left, slamming the door. This was the only interview in which I feared for my personal safety. In the other case, Curt, also a 17-year-old street youth, told me "Fuck you!" and left abruptly when I confronted him about his behaviour. In one other case, Colin, a 16-year-old staying at a shelter, told me "I don't need this shit from you" and got up in silence, shuffling his feet at the door and not making eye contact with me for what seemed like an eternity. He took my business card and left the room. In this situation, I did not fear for my safety, although I was uncomfortable. I did not know what to expect from him next in this situation.

Related to the counselling role I assumed at the end of each in-depth interview was the fact that ten of these participants broke down and cried when describing the hopelessness and despair they felt about their sexual orientation and/or economic futures. They related these feelings to their perceived masculine deficits. Although all were not asked whether they had attempted suicide, I questioned these ten youth because they appeared to be so depressed at this point. Nine told me that they had attempted suicide previously, and I assessed three of them to be at risk for attempting suicide at that point. All three were provided with crisis counselling by YSB workers immediately following the interview. Only three of the 30 participants followed up on counselling referrals regarding their abusive behaviour. In contrast, eight of the 12 current or ex-girlfriends of the participants I contacted pursued counselling with a YSB worker regarding their victimization (18 of the participants did not have a girlfriend or an ex-girlfriend I was able to contact at the time of the in-depth interviews).

The second issue considered when analyzing the data involved "truth status."[7] Twenty-nine of the accounts have similar patterns, replete with internal inconsistencies, since the participants used "socially approved vocabularies"[8] in which they justified their abusive behaviours. These young men consistently told me that my interpretation of their behaviour was wrong. They had a persona to maintain, and their accounts were characterized by elements of boasting, bragging, and machismo. Despite the fact that I challenged and probed their understanding of their behaviour, there was a high degree of consistency in their narratives. These youth may not have been articulate enough to verbalize the inconsistencies in their accounts, but the fact that many of them broke down and cried led me to believe that they recognized the incongruities. It doesn't really matter if elements of these accounts are untruthful, because the focus of this project is on the perceptions of the participants: how they understood themselves and others. Their accounts are the data. These youth, like any other group of people, lived in socially constructed worlds. The measures used are valid and reliable given their modification (to address shortcomings) and the clear definition of abuse employed. Based on my clinical experience with this population, the literature on abusive males, and the similarities in the accounts, the data should be representative of similar samples.

Developing Familial and Gender Ideologies in the Home

Adherence to familial and gender ideologies is central to the analysis of the abusive behaviour of the young men in this study. By focussing on these ideologies the relationship between poverty and abuse can be qualified. If it can be shown that males who rigidly adhere to a patriarchal-authoritarian model of family and gender are most likely to use direct force to keep women in line, then this hypothesis should apply to all males, regardless of their social class position. Differences among these youth (sexual orientation, ethno-racial origin, type of father-figure, social class of origin, etc.) account for variations in the extent to which these young men embraced these ideologies. Adherence to these attitudes and beliefs was not uniform, and some of these adolescents developed these ideological assumptions through different processes.

Although the participants' development of patriarchal ideas about family and gender was not identical, there were common themes:

1. The sexual division of labour is "natural." Women are "natural" child rearers and homemakers, and men are "natural" breadwinners.

2. Rigid gender roles. In general, females should be obedient to, respectful of, and dependent upon males. Female intimates should be sexually accessible, loyal, and faithful to their male partners. Males should be physically tough and muscular, aggressive, independent, successful, and in control.

3. Sexual objectification and homophobia. Females are sexual objects, to be conquered by males. Heterosexuality is "natural" and "moral," and all other sexual orientations are immoral and therefore punishable.

4. Law and order. Abusive behaviour is justifiable and an appropriate way for the biological father to resolve conflict and maintain traditional sex roles with his children and wife. Physical violence is used for keeping the "good bitch" in line.

5. "Fucking and fighting." In the absence of a good job and material possessions, it's down to the basics for males.

A systematic search for patterns, explanations, and meanings in the data provides the insights into the central research questions of this study. These questions are: how do these males make sense of their participation in their abusive behaviour? What insights can be derived from using the key concepts that will help us analyze the participants' behaviour in a broader social context? By examining each of the five assumptions detailed above, we will reach some answers.

Socialization into Familial and Gender Ideologies

1. The sexual division of labour is "natural"

A number of themes emerged when I asked the participants about the kinds of beliefs and values their parent(s) had about male and female roles, and if they thought that their parents' beliefs had influenced them. Twenty-seven of the participants described rigid, patriarchal gender roles of their mothers and father-figures in their families. "Father-figures" includes the natural fathers, step-fathers, and mothers' boyfriends. "Biological father" denotes the natural father, whereas "social father" denotes step-fathers and/or other male partners of the mother who were not related by blood to the participants.

These young men reported that their mothers did all of the cooking, cleaning, and childcare. They defined their father-figures as breadwinners and "bringing home the bacon,"[9] despite the fact that most of these men were either unemployed or never had worked, and many were dependent upon their partner's Family Benefits (social assistance) cheque or upon their own government cheque. These men, including both biological and social fathers, were characterized as being the boss and in control of virtually all aspects of family life. It is interesting to note that participants were much more likely to accord legitimacy to the physical violence of biological, not social, fathers. However, both biological and social fathers were viewed as being the "natural" heads of families. Of these same 27, 24 told me that they witnessed their father-figure(s) repeatedly beat and degrade their mothers, and that they themselves had been chronically abused.

Not surprisingly, the majority of the participants appeared to have internalized the patriarchal value set modelled at home at a very young age. When asked what they thought about the following familial patriarchal beliefs (FPB), 21 told me that they agreed with one or more of these statements:

1. A male has the right to decide whether or not his wife/girlfriend should go out in the evening with her friends.

2. A male has the right to decide whether or not his wife/girlfriend should work outside the home.

3. Sometimes it is important for a male to show his wife/girlfriend that he is the head of the house.

4. A male has the right to have sex with his wife/girlfriend when he wants, even though she may not want to.

It must be stressed that adherence to one or more of these beliefs is likely quite common in the general population, and in most of these instances there is no associated abusive behaviour. However, the situations of the participants in this study were very different. It would appear that four main factors differentiated the abusers who did not adhere to patriarchal beliefs (9 youth) from all other abusers in the sample (21 youth): family type; sexual orientation and racial origin; support for physical violence against girlfriends; and severity of physical violence.

Table 3.1 compares the FPB participants with the Non-FPB participants.

		FPB PARTICIPANTS (N = 21)	NON-FPB PARTICIPANTS (N = 9)
	Ethno Racial Minorities	29% (6)	0% (0)
	Gay/Bisexual/Questioning	10% (2)	22% (2)
	Harmonious Family	5% (1)	56% (5)
	Family Support to Abuse	52% (11)	22% (2)
	Abuser Type	67% p/s/e (14)	67% p/s/e (6)
		11 sev.	1 sev.
		8 f.i.;	4 f.i.;
		14% p/e;	23% p/e;
		19% s/e	0% s/e
	Biological Father at Home	76% (16)	78% (7)
	Living at Home	43% (9)	56% (5)
	Gang Member	38% (8)	100% (9)
	Abusive Male Peers and Support	100% (21)	78% (7)
	Attitudes Supporting Physical Abuse	43% (9)	22% (2)

*Table 3.1
Familial
Patriarchal
Believers (FPB)
and
Non-Familial
Patriarchal
Believers
(Non-FPB)*

*p = physical
s = sexual
e = emotional
sev. = severe
f.i. = forced
intercourse*

Over three-quarters of both the FPB and Non-FPB groups (16 versus 7 youth) lived with biological fathers during their childhood. Roughly one-half of both these same groups of youth were living at home at the time of the interviews (10 versus 5 participants), and over eleven times as many Non-FPB youth compared to FPB youth reported coming from harmonious families (56 per cent versus 5 per cent). More than double the number of FPB compared to Non-FPB youth received family support to abuse females (48 per cent versus 22 per cent). Second, over twice as many Non-FPB compared to FPB youth were not heterosexual (22 per cent versus 10 per cent), and almost one-third of the FPB youth were ethno-racial minorities. None of the Non-FPB youth were ethno-racial minorities.

Almost double the number of FPB compared to Non-FPB youth supported the use of physical violence by boyfriends with girlfriends (43 per cent versus 22 per cent), unless the girl hit first. Finally, only 11 per cent (1 youth) of the Non-FPB group reported having committed severe acts of violence (1 physical/sexual/emotional abuser who also forced intercourse), whereas almost one-half (4 youth) reported having forced intercourse on girlfriends (all were physical/sexual/emotional abusers). The remaining two who did not adhere to patriarchal beliefs were physical/emotional abusers. However, almost one-half of the FPB group had used severe violence on girlfriends (13 youth, including 10 physical/sexual/emotional abusers and 1 physical/emotional abuser), and 38 per cent of this same group admitted to having forced sexual intercourse on girlfriends (8 youth, including 7 physical/sexual/emotional abusers, and 1 sexual/emotional abuser).

In other words, those girlfriend abusers who did not report adhering to patriarchal beliefs were quite different than those who did adhere to these beliefs. These nine young men presumably learned to abuse through a different process than the others in the sample.

In this account, Phil, a 14-year-old living at home, demonstrated that he had already internalized the patriarchal value set of his family.

> MT: ... So who does the cooking and cleaning at home?
> Phil (snorting) Who else? The old lady of course. It's only
> right that way.

MT: Oh?

Phil: Yeah. If a guy does that shit, he'll only get nagged any-way. I mean, the guy brings home the money, pays the bills, the food, and puts clothes on her back.

MT: But your Dad doesn't work.

Phil: So. He's the head of the house. He makes all the deci-sions …

MT: So you and your older brother think this way too?

Phil: Of course. That's why they have holes – to fuck. Bare-foot and pregnant. That's the way it should be.

Clearly, Phil made sense of his world through an ideological lens characterized by rigid definitions of family and gender. He indi-cated that the sexual division of labour was "natural" and moral, because "that's the way it should be." Despite the fact that his bio-logical father was unemployed (after having run a successful con-struction company for many years, he was forced on disability just after Phil's birth due to heart problems), Phil insisted that his father was the head of his family and made all the important decisions. Ethnicity may have played a role in his strong adherence to patriar-chal beliefs. Phil reported that he was Italian and that, in his culture, men were supposed to dominate and be more important than women. He received strong support from his older brother and fel-low gang members to abuse females. Phil's strong adherence to patriarchal beliefs and his report that he kept a gun under his bed[10] was probably directly related to his anxieties about his sexual orien-tation: at one point in the interview, he became quite upset over the fact that, at times, he was sexually attracted to other males.

Steve, a 15-year-old youth who lived at home with his biological parents, also did not indicate an awareness of the apparent incon-gruity of identifying his father as the "boss" despite his dependence on his wife's welfare cheque and lack of employment. Steve uncriti-cally internalized the rigid gender order modelled at home, telling me "It's only right." This account also suggests a process through which patriarchal attitudes and beliefs may be "grounded" in young children: through modelling by caregivers.

Steve: … My Dad makes the decisions, if that's what you mean. He's the boss of the house. It's only right. I'm gonna

bring in the money, so I'll make the decisions and put
down the rules. So it's only fair that the man decides
what to do — he brings home the dollars. It'll be the
same with me. The woman should stay at home and
look after the kids. That's what my Mom does and it
works. Because it works, it's important that everyone
understands that my Dad's in charge.

MT: So what happens if your Mom doesn't like it?

Steve: She does. I mean sometimes my Dad has to set her
straight to remind her who's boss. But it all works out.
That's the way it should be, and that's the way I'm gonna
run my house.

MT: But your Dad hasn't really worked much — and the welfare cheque goes to your mother.

Steve: So. It's still his money. And even if he hasn't worked
much, he's been looking for work. And like I said, he
usually has worked one or two weeks every year. My
Mom has never worked.

MT: You told me she looks after kids at home. Doesn't she
get paid for that?

Steve: Yeah. But it's not really work. It's only woman's work. It
doesn't really count. I mean compared to my Dad's
work, it's nothing (long silence) …

As in Phil's family, ethno-racial origin may have played a role in
the rigid gender division of labour in Steve's family. Steve identified
as being Lebanese and brought up his religion (Muslim) a number of
times in the interview. His dialogue in the interview suggested that
his family's religious practices provided the moral underpinnings for
his beliefs about the "natural" sexual division of labour.

Feminist theories on woman abuse are helpful in explaining the
relationship between familial and gender ideologies. Steve's family,
like many of the other participants' families, can be analyzed on two
levels: as a social and economic institution, organized primarily by
the division of labour between the husband and wife, and as an ideology, in which the family was presented by the participants as
stereotypically nuclear and heterosexual. As researchers in this area
have argued,[11] the institution and the ideology are inextricably
linked. With the sexual division of labour perceived as being

"natural," the families of the participants likely played a central role in the ideological construction and acquisition of their masculinities.

2. The "ideal man"

All participants were asked to describe the characteristics of the "ideal man." Twenty-eight described him as physically tough and strong; a possessor of material possessions and a good job; a bread-winner; heterosexual and having sex often; and in control of women and his life. All but two of these young men described rigid gender roles as the ideal. In general, they said, females should be obedient to, respectful of, and dependent upon males. "Ideal" girlfriends were portrayed as being sexually accessible, loyal, and faithful to their male partners. The two participants who differed were Paul and Sylvain. Paul was gay, and Sylvain was questioning his sexual orientation. (Their masculine identities will be discussed in the next chapter.) Both of these young men had clearly chosen a path out of tradi-tional masculine identity.

Don, a 15-year-old residing in an open custody young offender facility, described the "ideal" man to me.

> Don: Well, he can't hit girls, and he's gotta be nice to girls. And he doesn't pick fights with anyone. He only fights if he's picked on – and then he's gotta punch the other guy out. And sexually, it's gotta be equal – they gotta treat each other the same.
> And a job, with lots of money. It's good to have a job so you don't have to steal.
> MT: I see.
> Don: And a good car, and a place to live – you know, an apart-ment or a house. And good health – no AIDS.
> MT: What do you mean by good health?
> Don: Strong – well built. A guy's gotta be able to defend him-self – to protect himself and his friends from being picked on.
> MT: Picked on by who?
> Don: Other guys. Like I said, a guy can't ever hit a girl. That's the worst thing a guy could ever do.

Later in the interview, Don told me that he was like this "ideal man," with the exception of not having material possessions, money, and a job. In this context, Don's account is replete with conflicting statements. He was skinny and short, weighing no more than 90 pounds. He had been charged with uttering death threats against his mother and sister, and told me that he had threatened other girls with knives. He also told me of sexual behaviour categorized as forced intercourse. Despite this, Don told me twice in this short conversation that the "ideal man" can't hit girls, and that sexual relationships must be equal. He also told me that this man has got to be tough and muscular. These inconsistencies were highlighted when Don talked about the ideal man needing to protect himself from being "picked on." There is a theme of defensiveness throughout this account.

Interestingly, Don's mother worked throughout his childhood in low-paying service sector jobs. Although he reported that his biological father always worked, Don had had no contact with him since the age of four. This is an example of how some participants learned their ideological assumptions related to family and gender through different processes. In part, Don learned his beliefs and attitudes from observing the dynamics between his mother, her boyfriends, and his step-father. None of his mother's boyfriends nor his step-father had ever worked, depending instead upon his mother for financial support. Don indicated that the father-figures in his life were not comparable to the "ideal man," primarily because they had never worked.

It may be that Don perceived his biological father to be more of a "real" man, either because he really did work, or perhaps because he liked to think that his father worked. Many of the participants who had little or no contact with their biological fathers idealized these men and thought of them as the legitimate heads of their families. By contrast, many of the youth who lived with their abusive biological fathers reported having mixed feelings about them. The only participants who both lived with their biological fathers and clearly indicated that they liked their fathers were those who reported that their families were harmonious. This is an indicator of the different processes through which these young men developed their ideological assumptions, and also an indicator of what Jack Katz has described as two planes of reality in the lives of young male criminals: an ideal plane, and a second plane of reality characterized by the hopelessness and drudgery of daily subsistence.[12] It is possible that one of the coping mechanisms of participants who had minimal contact with their biological fathers was to escape into an idealized dream world.

Don's interview also illustrates another common theme found in many accounts: women are not supposed to have a higher status than their male partners. Don reported that his mother worked for almost all of his childhood. Despite having had no contact with his biological father, he was convinced that his Dad was also working, but in better jobs than his mother. In Don's mind, therefore, it made no difference that his social fathers were not working and his mother was employed, but his biological father had to have more status than his mother.

Also, Don's mother, like most of the participants' mothers, was beaten by male partners who rarely worked. Many of the father-figures of the participants were either unemployed, had never worked, or had only sporadically worked. Resource theory helps to explain the beatings of these women by these men: the greater the degree of power and control men are able to display, the lesser the risk that they will use violence to control their female partners. When certain men perceive that their superiority is being eroded, they are most likely to use violence and the threat of violence to regain their sense of authority. Prolonged unemployment, low-income or low-status jobs can result in elevated rates of stress and conflict in the home and challenge the breadwinner's authority in the family.[13]

Colin, a 16-year-old Francophone street youth, spoke about how the "ideal man" provides for his family, and is clearly the boss at home.

> Colin: Well, he's gotta have a family, a wife and kids. That's real important. Especially if he's got no job. Now a good job or even any kind of job, is real important. Now if a man's got no job, he would still have his family. He should respect his parents and listen to them. And his wife and kids should do the same. They would have to respect him and listen to him (silence). A house and a car are also important. It's kind of like showing you're a man, I

guess. They're proof that a guy's successful. I mean, if a guy's got a nice house and a fast car, people know he's got a good job and cares for his family. That's real important. And I guess a man's gotta be tough. He's gotta take care of himself and look out for his family. If a man can't do that, he's nothin'. As long as a man's got a wife and kids who respect him, do as he says, and he's tough enough to stand up for himself, he can get by without the rest.

Living on the street, Colin had no job, money, material possessions, or "nice house." Yet he still equated these things with masculine ideals, stating: "It's kind of like showing you're a man ... that a guy's successful." Life has been tough for Colin. He has never had the material wealth he associated with the ideal man.

Unlike Don, Colin did not relate his biological father with the "ideal man." He reported that his father worked only a couple of months each year and was dependent on his mother's welfare cheque and unemployment insurance to survive. Moreover Colin's mother had no respect at all for his father. She apparently divorced him and kept the family home.

Colin's last statement in this account reveals a struggle with his definition of what it means to be male. A man can "get by without the rest" (being the material provider) if he is physically tough and can control his family. In Colin's view, gaining the respect of one's wife and children is based upon getting them to obey. As will be discussed later, Colin had difficulty accepting the fact that his mother had more resources than his father following the divorce. Resource theory is useful in explaining Colin's position. Contextualized in his parent's situation, he reported confusion between the traditional and more egalitarian roles and values. His anger related to this clash in values may be helpful in explaining his abusive behaviour towards his girlfriends.

John, a 16-year-old who grew up with an alcoholic, biological father who had significant periods of unemployment, again emphasized the importance of being the material provider. In John's opinion, it was still possible to be a man if you were out of work, as long as you were heterosexual and didn't lose a fight. This is an example of how many of these adolescents constructed power hierarchies when defining their situations to me.

> John: Look at my Dad – poor son of a bitch. I'd love to tell
> him where to go, but he's defenceless. A guy's got sweet
> fuck all without a job and money.... And it's real impor-
> tant that he stand up for himself to other guys. He's gotta
> fight back. A guy can't lose a fight. To get the shit kicked
> outta you, that's almost as bad as being queer (silence) …
> I mean, if you're outta work, you can always defend
> yourself. If you're working and you can't stand up for
> yourself, you're nothing. You're not much of a man.

Growing up with a father who experienced bouts of unemployment seemed to have influenced John's ideas about the "ideal man."
Although he told me that he hated his father because of how he
beat his mother and himself, he seemed to neutralize this by saying
his father was defenceless; he had no job or money. However, John
noted that a defenceless (jobless) man can, as a last resort, defend
himself with his fists.

These accounts illustrate some of the masculine and familial
ideals held by the participants and the similarity in symbols used
when talking about these ideals. These data are similar to the masculine ideals identified in theory and research on middle- and
upper-class youth, and most closely reflect those masculine values
identified in the literature to be associated with working-class and
marginalized male youth, whose access to the labour market is
severely limited or non-existent.[14] This body of work identifies
material success, employment, being a provider, and being able to
take care of yourself as fairly common images for boys and the way
they are socialized.

The views of the ideal man (physical toughness and strength,
material possessions, breadwinner, heterosexual and frequent sex, in
control of life and women) for 28 of the participants were interwoven with their familial ideals (the sexual division of labour is "natural"; abusive behaviour is justifiable and an appropriate way for
biological fathers to resolve conflict and maintain traditional sex
roles within the family). In many cases, these ideological assumptions are inseparable; for example, being heterosexual and using
physical force can compensate a man for not having a job. "Ideal"

masculine identity is directly linked to familial patriarchal ideology. Not only were familial and gender assumptions developed in these families, they also influenced gender development.

3. Sexual objectification of females and homophobia

Almost all of the participants discussed females as sexual objects, to be conquered by males. With two exceptions, heterosexuality was presented as "natural" and moral, and gays and males with feminine characteristics were described as being immoral and therefore deserving of physical punishment. Sex/gender roles and socialization theories are useful in exploring how so many of the participants developed these ideological assumptions of family and gender and how so many of these youth perceived their abusiveness against girl-friends, gays, and ethno-racial minorities as acceptable. By contrast, the abuse of other individuals (such as straight, white males) was not perceived as acceptable.

Further, these theories are helpful in exploring how it is that a significant number of the participants did not experience abuse in their families, yet still abused their girlfriends. Variation in socializa-tion accounts for these differences. For many of these youth, the main agents of male socialization (including family, media, military, sports, and peer group) played a significant role in their portrayal of women as being less powerful and inferior to men. However, the role played by each of these agents differed, given the unique situa-tions of each participant. For those youth who did not learn their abusive behaviour through modelling in their families, these theories point to the elevated importance of extra-familial agents of social-ization in the social construction of their gender and familial ideolo-gies.

This next account by Steve is indicative of the sexual objectifica-tion and homophobia which defined most of the data.

MT: So why don't you hang out with girls?
Steve: They're pussies. I'm no faggot. We look at them and pick them up. But hang out with them? I don't think so. They're not my friends. They're just not. A guy's friends with guys only. Females, you know you can't trust them. What good are pussies for? Fucking. That's about it.

They'll try to fuck you if you don't fuck them first.

MT: When you say females will fuck you – is that the same as guys fucking them?

Steve: (laughing) Of course not. When guys fuck, it's "wham bam thank you ma'am" (gyrating pelvis, holding arms out, simulating sexual intercourse). When a bitch fucks a guy, that's making him look stupid. It has nothin' to do with sex (laughing). You don't think this is funny (silence). I guess not. Well, someday maybe you will (silence) ... It's not just fucking in bed. When a girl goes with a guy, she's his. She can't do that shit. It's like an agreement with her boyfriend. If she can't live up to her end of the deal, she's got what's coming to her.

Steve also made many misogynist statements. In his eyes, women cannot be trusted, let alone be a friend. Instead, they are inanimate sexual objects: "pussies." Parallel to his portrayal of his mother as being a piece of property belonging to his father, Steve told me "When a girl goes with a guy, she's his." Likewise, just as Steve devalued his mother's childrearing ("It's only woman's work. It doesn't really count. It's nothing"), the only role he saw fit for girls was "fucking."

Steve agreed with two of the patriarchal beliefs: "a male has the right to decide whether or not his wife/girlfriend should work outside the home" and "sometimes it is important for a male to show his wife/girlfriend that he is the head of the house." However, he also reported agreeing with a statement supporting egalitarian values: "a male and his wife/girlfriend should have equal say in deciding how to spend the family income." Steve was one of the few participants who was in school (grade 9) and was not involved in criminal behaviour. He also played a lot of sports with his male peers. Although he reported that he was not a gang member, he said that his male peers had instructed him to physically, sexually, and emotionally abuse girls. As well, he said that he had a close male cousin who had instructed him to emotionally abuse his girlfriends.

Steve's account illustrates the different processes through which some of these adolescents learned their abusive behaviour and the differing degrees to which they embraced these ideologies. Steve reported that his family life was harmonious and became angry and confrontational when I probed for any issues related to child abuse or wife assault. It could have been that he was defending his family and that I misread his body language, or there could have been violence in his family that he did not wish to talk about. In any case, Steve was one of the most violent of all the participants. He was a physical/sexual/emotional abuser, who had used severe violence against a girl who was trying to break off their relationship. How did he learn these behaviours if there was no violence at home? Some of the different processes which came into play involved his extremely rigid definition of his own masculinity and the dynamics of his peer group. (These issues will be fully explored in Chapters 4 and 5.)

4. Keeping the "good bitch" in line

Table 3.2 compares the 11 participants with attitudes supporting physical abuse (ASPA) with the 19 Non-ASPA participants.

Not only did many of these youth adhere to familial patriarchal beliefs, just over one-third of the participants (11 youth) reported

	ASPA PARTICIPANTS (N = 11)	NON–ASPA PARTICIPANTS (N = 19)
Ethno Racial Minorities	36% (4)	11% (2)
Gay/Bisexual/Questioning	18% (2)	11% (2)
Harmonious Family	9% (1)	26% (5)
Family Support to Abuse	64% (7)	32% (6)
Abuser Type	82% p/s/e (9)	58% p/s/e (11)
	8 sev.	4 sev.
	6 f.i.;	6 f.i.;
	9% p/e;	26% p/e;
	9% s/e	16% s/e
Biological Father at Home	73% (8)	74% (14)
Living at Home	55% (6)	42% (8)
Gang Member	45% (5)	63% (12)
Abusive Male Peers and Support	91% (10)	63% (12)
Familial Patriarchal Beliefs	73% (8)	68% (13)

Table 3.2 Participants with Attitudes Supporting Physical Abuse (ASPA) compared to Participants without Attitudes Supporting Physical Abuse (Non-ASPA)

p = physical
s = sexual
e = emotional
f.i. = forced intercourse
sev. = severe

supporting the use of violence against a girlfriend by a boyfriend if she failed to meet the expectations of what many called the "good bitch." These expectations are comparable to those described by Smith.[15] When asked what they thought of the following statements, 11 of the 30 participants told me that they agreed with a male slapping his girlfriend in one or more of these situations:

1. She won't do what he tells her to do.

2. She insults him when they are home alone.

3. She insults him in public.

4. She comes home drunk.

5. She is sobbing hysterically.

6. She won't have sex with him.

7. He learns that she is dating another male.

The main factors accounting for the large differences between this group and the remaining 19 youth in the general sample are: the male peer group; adherence to familial patriarchal beliefs; experiencing abuse at home and having family support to abuse; and ethno-racial origin. These are comparable to those factors which account for the differentiation between those youth who reported adhering to familial patriarchal beliefs and the rest of the sample.

Ninety-one per cent of the ASPA participants (ten youth) had both abusive male peers and had received encouragement from these male peers to abuse their girlfriends, whereas only 63 per cent of the 8 Non-ASPA participants had similar experiences with peers. Slightly more ASPA compared to Non-ASPA youth adhered to at least one familial patriarchal belief (78 per cent versus 68 per cent). Slightly more ASPA compared to Non-ASPA youth lived at home at the time of the interview (55 per cent versus 37 per cent), and almost three times as many Non-ASPA compared to ASPA youth reported coming from a harmonious family (26 per cent versus 9 per cent). More ASPA youth compared to Non-ASPA youth reported having family support to abuse females (55 per cent versus 37 per cent), and there was virtually no difference in the numbers of these youth who reported living with their biological fathers during their childhood (73 per cent versus 74 per cent). Almost twice as many ASPA youth were heterosexual (90 per cent versus 55 per cent), and over three times as many were ethno-racial minorities (36 per cent versus 11 per cent). More Non-ASPA youth were gang members (63 per cent versus 45 per cent), and many more ASPA youth reported having abusive peers and peers who had told them to abuse females (91 per cent versus 63 per cent).

The following accounts are illustrative of the interconnectedness of the participants' familial and gender ideologies, which are related to the use of physical force to keep the "good bitch" in line.

> MT: So what happens if the guy's girlfriend or wife doesn't think that's the way things should be?
>
> Phil: Of course he's gotta keep her in line. Like if she disses me in front of my friends, that would be embarrassing. I'd punch her out. If she's fucking around on me or beats on me, I'd punch her out. If she won't fuck when I'm ready, I'd just go fuck someone else.

Phil made sense of the beatings by his biological father of his mother by seeing these assaults as justified: "of course he's gotta keep her in line." Clearly, he also supported the use of violence against women who failed to conform to the roles ascribed to them in this patriarchal world. Phil told me that his Dad was the head of the house and made all the decisions because he "brings home the money, pays the bills, the food and puts clothes on her back." It made no difference to Phil that his father had been on a disability pension for as long as he could remember. After all, "it's only right that way." As described earlier, Phil said that in Italian culture, his viewpoint about women was acceptable, even encouraged. He also had serious questions about his sexual orientation. These factors may have served to amplify his beliefs about women. He reported engaging in severe violence and forced intercourse with his girl-friends.

In the following account, Colin, the 16-year-old Francophone street youth whose parents had divorced, described his need to fight back against "all this equal rights bullshit." Characterizing his mother as a "bitch" and a "fool," he told me that she "fucked him (his father) bad" after the separation, because she kept the house.

> Colin: My Dad's in a shithole apartment. My Mom kept the house when they split (laughing, sarcastic voice).
>
> MT: So you didn't agree with that?
>
> Colin: Fuck no. My Dad earned the bacon. He brought home the money. He shoulda got the house. She's nothin' without him. It's not fair. A man makes the decisions at home. He's the head of the joint. The woman should stay at home. It's the woman's job. Men don't do dishes. They don't do nothin' inside. He's doing the real work. He's got the pay cheque. Fuck her if she just wants to go out with her friends and shit. He shouldn't let her.
>
> MT: So why did your parents split? Were there any arguments or fights?
>
> Colin: It was constant arguing, my Dad with my Mom. But it was always mutual put downs. He never assaulted her or nothin'. Once he threw an axe at me. I was 10. I guess he was pretty violent with me. But that bitch never shoulda kicked him out. He's got no bitch now. She's a fool. On welfare and all. I mean he provided for her (silence).
>
> MT: You sound pissed off at your Mom.
>
> Colin: Big time. She fucked him bad.
>
> MT: So was there any violence between them?
>
> Colin: No, never. My Mom and Dad always told me not to hit girls. Girls are weaker and they can't defend themselves. It's different for guys. It's sad to hit girls. But they want all this equal rights bullshit. And we can't lay a hand on them. They've got all the fuckin' rights they need. It's time to give some back.

Colin's anger and hatred of women were rooted in his understanding of his home life. There are many inconsistencies in his account, none of which he appeared to recognize. He first denied that his father assaulted his mother, yet described beatings to me later on in the interview. He was able to neutralize the fact that

"Once he (Dad) threw an axe at me. I was 10." The reason for this may be found in his statement "My Mom and Dad always told me not to hit girls." Although his father told him this, Colin witnessed him (Dad) beating his mother. Further, Colin totally devalued everything about his mother, referring to her as "that bitch." He appeared to believe that his mother deserved to be beaten. He indicated that she, along with all women in general, had stolen the rights of men. Colin's struggle with this issue is apparent when he told me: "It's sad to hit girls. But they want all this equal rights bullshit. And we can't lay a hand on them. They've got all the fuckin' rights they need."

This account is representative of the other narratives, in that Colin denied that he abused his girlfriends and justified his behaviour by blaming women for stepping outside of their traditional roles. As was discussed earlier, resource theory is helpful here in explaining how abusive behaviour can result when males perceive that their status and authority is being eroded by the women's rights movement. According to Colin's patriarchal-authoritarian lens, biological fathers should "naturally" have authority over their wives, who "naturally" should be dependent upon their husbands and be the homemakers. His parents' divorce had resulted in a clash between these traditional and more egalitarian roles and values. Colin's response is to put the "good bitches" back in line through the use of physical force. As well, it is apparent that as some researchers have previously noted, the male gender identity and familial ideology are inextricably intertwined.[16]

In this final account, Dillon, a 14-year-old living in an open custody young offender facility, expressed many disturbingly misogynist beliefs. It soon became apparent to me that his value system was rooted in his understanding of the cause of his father having rarely worked: his mother worked as a secretary! Dillon's account is rich with conflicting statements, none of which he seemed able to recognize.

> MT: Do you like girls?
> Dillon: (silence) No. Not really. (silence) I hate those bitches. Fucking cunts.
> MT: Why?
> Dillon: They're all the same, you know.

MT: Really.

Dillon: Yeah. Always trying to show you up – be better than you. I hate it when a girl does that to me. It's as if they're telling the whole world, "Look at that idiot. He can't even get a job. He can't even get it up." They're always trying to make us look bad. So fuck em. I'll get them before they get me. Now take my mother. She's a nice woman and all, but she makes more money than my Dad. He's sitting at home on the pog (UI) or welfare and she's out having a ball working.

MT: As a secretary.

Dillon: Exactly. She's out doing whatever the fuck she wants while he's at home too embarrassed to go out. She doesn't mean it but it's like she's pussy-whipping him.

MT: Oh?

Dillon: Yeah. It's like she was fucking around on him. Well she is, in a way. She's doing what he's supposed to be doing. It's like she's walking around with some other guy's dick in her, and everyone's laughing at my Dad. That bothers me.

MT: So you're angry at your Mom because she works full time and makes more money than your Dad?

Dillon: Yeah.

MT: Is she screwing around on him?

Dillon: Not with another guy. But she's screwing with his job.

MT: His job?

Dillon: Yeah. He's the one who should be working.

MT: She's a secretary. You mean your Dad should be a secretary?

Dillon: Fuck no. He's not a pinko-queer. But she's working so he can't …

MT: I'm still trying to figure out how come you hate women so much. Is it just your mother?

Dillon: Fuck no. That's part of it. But she's no different than any other bitch out there. Those cunts have all taken this equal rights bullshit too far. It's hard enough for a man to get a job now, let alone when all the bitches want to work too. It was never like that. When girls used to stay at home to do the cooking and shit, they never took a man's job away. Now those little cunts think they've got balls. They think they can take all our jobs and at the same time they tell us "Don't lay a hand on me. I'll have you up on assault charges" or they'll cry "rape." Who the fuck do those little cunts think they are? It's not fair. That's why I hate those little bitches. Equal rights has sweet fuck all to do with it. They just want us guys to look like a piece of shit.

Although Dillon denied that his hatred of women originated from his hatred of his mother, his account suggests this to be the case. Earlier, Dillon had described a brutal patriarchal home, in which his father often beat his mother. He seemed to be able to justify these beatings because he saw his mother as having stepped outside of her natural and acceptable role; it was his biological father's "job" to "beat" her back. In fact, although Dillon initially denied that his father beat him, he inadvertently mentioned the name of his Children's Aid Society (CAS) worker after the interview. I later found out that Dillon was a CAS ward because of his father's beatings.

Dillon was talking about his mother when he told me: "But she's no different than any other bitch out there ... When girls used to stay at home to do the cooking and shit, they never took a man's job away." He used sexual imagery when he talked about how his mother had humiliated his father by working as a secretary: "... it's like she's pussy-whipping him ... It's like she's walking around with some other guy's dick in her and everyone's laughing at my Dad." To Dillon, it would appear that a job was a penis. Only men can work outside the home. Women like his mother "think they've got balls" when they work. Because she was not at home, Dillon indicated that his mother was unfaithful. He made sense of his father's unemployment by blaming his mother for taking his job. In his patriarchal world, fathers are supposed to be the breadwinners and the "pussy-whippers." By working, Dillon suggested that his mother not only had taken his father's job (despite stating that his father can't be a secretary because "he's not a pinko-queer"), but had rendered him (his father) sexually impotent. The benefits of resource theory in explaining Dillon's abusiveness are evident.

Despite being only 14 years old, Dillon's internalization of his parents' patriarchal value set and abusive behaviour is striking. He justified his violent, chaotic family life by these rigid familial and gender beliefs. Seen in this light, everything made sense to Dillon: his father's joblessness, his mother working outside the home, the child abuse, the wife-beating. Within this context, Dillon's girlfriend abuse makes perfect sense as well. After all, girls "just want us guys to look like a piece of shit." The way in which he presented his abusive childhood is illustrative of the other accounts. Familial and gender beliefs played a crucial role in justifying abusive experiences. Further, it would be surprising if many of these young men did not adhere to such consistent assumptions of familial and gender ideologies. They were acting according to values modelled by their families.

5. "Fucking and fighting"

Despite the fact that I did not mention unemployment when asking the participants about the qualities of the ideal man, all but two (Paul and Sylvain) identified a minimum set of qualities necessary for a jobless "ideal man." The fact that the majority of the participants came from a home where many of the father-figures were unemployed or never had worked may have influenced their definition of these masculine ideals. However, there is variance here. Many fathers never or rarely worked, and therefore cannot be categorized as "unemployed"; instead, they were the dependent poor. Also, one can't compare the 28 youth who had never worked with those unemployed father-figures who did work for significant periods of time. These issues point to the different processes through which some of these youth learned their abusive behaviour, and the varying degrees to which they embraced familial and gender ideologies. As will be discussed in the next chapter, Paul and Sylvain were the only two young men in this study who were working. They were also the only two participants who had "negative" masculine identities. These factors contributed to their variation from the rest of the sample.

After probing about the qualities of the "ideal man," I asked the participants the following questions about their own masculine identity:

1.   What does it mean to you to be male?

2.   Do you think this has anything to do with the way you get along with females, gays, and other guys?

When asked these questions, 29 of the 30 participants told me that they were like the "ideal man" they previously had described to me, with one exception: they had neither material possessions nor a job and questioned their chances of being a breadwinner. These youth described themselves as powerful fighters, "fuckers," gang members, and protectors of women. They explicitly told me that they were not "faggots," "bitches," "pussies," "wimps," "woman-beaters," or "rapists." Again, social learning and sex/gender role and socialization theories are useful in the analysis of the participants' accounts on this issue. Adolescence is a critical period of time in which youth construct their identities and belief systems. Young females and males are flooded with cultural images of the heterosexual romantic ideal. Many of these images, transmitted through the key agents of socialization, contribute to the social construction of traditional male and female roles in dating relationships. Adoption of these roles can lead to power imbalances, which in turn can result in the use of abusive behaviour to maintain inequality.[17]

The theme of rejecting femininity is present in many of these interviews. Nancy Chodorow has written extensively on this topic, and her insights are useful here.[18] The participants, like many other boys in the general population, probably had strong attachments to their mothers early on in their lives. With maturation into adolescence, most boys begin a process of detaching themselves from their mothers, and many develop strong bonds with their fathers and male peers. Eight of the participants grew up in homes where there was a succession of different social fathers and had little, if any, contact with their biological fathers. Just about all of these boys reported despising these social fathers due to their violence and the fact that they did not regard them as being their legitimate fathers. Of the remaining 22 young men, many had either left home in early adolescence, or, if they were living at home, spent very little time there.

In the general population, a significant amount of time is spent in same-sex peer groups, particularly at school. In the absence of consistent father-figures, the peer group for some of the participants took on a heightened role as a primary reference point in which to develop masculine identities and to continue the natural separation from their mother's identities.

Gender role theorists have identified a number of patterns in school-based peer groups that may lead to abusive behaviour. Of particular relevance here are the patterns of being aggressive, debasement and sexual objectification of females and humiliation of gays, and a commitment to peer group conformity.[19] Although many of the participants were not in school at the time of the in-depth interviews, almost all had strong attachments to either male peer groups or gangs. Many of these friendships were formed in the primary schools which all participants attended. For many, there was an absence of healthy bonding with a caring, positive, adult role model consistently throughout their childhood. This relationship is arguably the most important factor in determining whether or not a pre-adolescent will make a successful transition into the teenage years and adulthood.[20] In the absence of this, many of these youth were forced to look elsewhere to navigate their identities.

Brian, a 14-year-old skinhead gang member, told me that he had recently returned home after living on the streets for a couple of years. He described the power hierarchy in his world. He associated his masculine identity with beating up the less powerful.

> Brian: If I can't work it'll be hard to get people to respect me. It's like a kind of status. But I know as long as people know not to fuck with me – well, I'll always have that. As long as I've got my balls, I'll be all right (laughing). A guy's nothing without that. No, let's say I wasn't a fighter or I was a faggot, or I was a nigger. Now that would be bad. They ain't got nothing – no respect, no power. It's all about power really. I mean, I get what I want because people know if I don't get it, I'll kick the shit outta them.
>
> MT: So, do girls respect you?
>
> Brian: Fuck, yeah.
>
> MT: Are they afraid of you?
>
> Brian: Afraid? No. They know I'll protect them and kick the shit outta any guy who tries to fuck them. Girls like that … I know. I can smell a faggot a mile away. They all talk the same, dress the same, act the same. A faggot's a woman with a cock. He acts like a woman, but he's got a cock instead of a pussy. So what does he do? He rams it up another guy's ass-hole. Figure that one out. That's why I never bend down (laughing) …

As we saw above, Jack Katz has previously identified a power hierarchy in the world of violent, marginal young criminals. From a social-psychological viewpoint, he suggests that male youth with few resources find excitement and adventure in violent crime, simultaneously finding an outlet to express their anger and rage. Brian, like the male youth identified by Katz, controlled the less-powerful through physical and sexual violence. Girls, gays, and racial minorities occupied the bottom rungs of his power hierarchy. He told me "it's all about power … I get what I want because people know if I don't get it, I'll kick the shit outta them." Twenty-nine of the 30 participants identified a similar power hierarchy in their accounts. It is interesting that one-third of the participants actually occupied the very same bottom rungs of this power hierarchy that they reported to be enforcing: five were either gay, bisexual, or had serious questions about their sexual orientation, and six were ethno-racial minorities (one participant fit both categories).

Phil told me that all of his friends were pimps. In the absence of material possessions, masculinity is basic: strength and guns.

MT: So, are you anything like all those things you said you liked about a guy?

Phil: Of course. Everything but the house, car, and bucks. But my friends have a car, and I get lots of money – not from a job (laughing). It's enough to get them to fuck and listen to you. Money is real important. I can take care of myself. Besides, I'm no faggot.

MT: So?

Phil: We fuckin' roll faggots for a laugh. Sometimes they have money – sometimes a jacket. Goddam queers. They're not men. Bitches. No, they're worse than bitches. They haven't got any balls, you know? What the fuck do they have balls for – to ram each other up the ass? What a laugh when we find one.

MT: So you're violent with gays?

Phil: Fuckin' right. So I'm no faggot. And at least I've got my strength. Nobody can take that away from a guy – even if he's got nothing else. He's still strong and can pound the crap outta anyone. A guy can never lose that. Strength and guns. If you can't beat 'em, shoot 'em.

MT: So, if you have a gun you're strong?

Phil: Yeah. No one will ever fuck with you. You get respect.

When Phil told me that "at least I've got my strength. Nobody can take that away from a guy," he meant that he had nothing left to lose. Indicating that his economic future was in jeopardy, he neutralized this issue by presenting himself as powerful and invincible. Guns, fists, and a penis compensated him for a lack of material possessions. In this, Phil highlights a common theme found in all but one of the interviews: a belief that no matter what else happens, a guy will always have his physical strength, guns, and "balls." This finding, along with the importance that Phil and the other participants placed upon frequent sexual activity, confirms the results of previous research in the area of marginal male youth and masculinity.[21]

However, Phil is also one of those very same individuals he professes to dominate so totally: he is an ethnic minority, and he has serious questions about his own sexual orientation. At one point in the interview, he admitted to having been sexually attracted to other males. Phil was likely coping with his own self-loathing by beating up anyone resembling himself.

Brian told me about how beating up people made him feel powerful. He described for me the key features of being male.

Brian: … Fight. Especially with niggers, faggots, and other guys. But faggots and niggers don't have balls so they're not really guys. Black balls and no balls (laughing). Yeah. We're pretty violent. We'll fight over just about anything.

MT: So what do you get out of fighting? How does it make you feel?

Brian: It's just me. I mean, when you kick the shit outta someone, you know you're respected. He won't touch you again and neither will his friends. People know real quick who can fight and who can't.

MT: So, do people know you can fight?

Brian: Oh yeah. They know. They look up to me. My friends know that I'll always help them to get someone. It's a feeling of knowing nobody's ever gonna fuck with you. Yeah. It makes me feel good to know nobody's ever gonna push me around. I guess I can get pretty much whatever I want because people respect me.

Similar to the themes identified in virtually all of the other participants' accounts, Brian told me how "kicking the shit outta someone" made him feel powerful and respected. When he told me that "it's a feeling of knowing nobody's ever gonna fuck with you," he highlighted a pattern of defensive posturing found in all but one interview. Despite describing themselves as being powerful and invincible when beating up the less-powerful, the participants made numerous statements regarding the necessity of defending themselves. This pattern has been previously identified in the literature.[22] Brian, like most of the other participants, did not recognize a conflict between feeling that he constantly had to defend himself and "knowing nobody's ever gonna fuck with you." However, there may be a number of reasons for this. The other adolescents in this study, like Brian, may in fact have been aware of these issues, yet lacked the verbal skills to express them. Perhaps these conflicts were simply too painful to deal with.

Along with the other theoretical explanations for male violence discussed in this chapter, lifestyle/routine activities theories are also applicable. The lifestyles of almost all of the participants were similar, in that they were for the most part marginal to the mainstream youth population. Most were not in school. One-half did not live at home and therefore were not under the supervision of an adult caregiver. Almost all had begun the process of separation from their families many years prior to this study, and all had developed other primary reference points: gangs and/or male peer groups. These groups are settings where violence is most likely to occur in the youth population. Finally, many of these youth were engaging in significant substance use and abuse. (These routine activities will be explored in greater detail in Chapter 5.)

Childhood Experiences of Being Beaten and Witnessing Mothers Being Beaten

Data on the participants' experiences of abuse in their own homes reveals the interwoven nature of the ideological assumptions of family and gender in these young men. Three themes emerge: 1. making sense of the abuse; 2. family support; and 3. protecting mothers and paying back social fathers. Each of these includes a discussion on the ideological assumptions of family and gender.

The following questions were asked about the participants' families:

1. What do you think about your family?

2. How do you feel about the way they treat you?

3. Was/is there any abuse between your parents? If yes, what type? How often?

4. Did/do you experience any abuse from your parents?

5. How have your parents influenced you?

Twenty-four participants reported incidents throughout their childhood in which they experienced beatings and severe emotional abuse by father-figures and in which they witnessed the beatings and severe emotional abuse of their mothers by father-figures. Of this group, 13 reported having one or more social fathers in their home and no or minimal contact with their biological fathers during their childhood. The remaining 11 reported that their biological father was in their home for most or all of their childhood. Of this group, two had been adopted at a very young age and had remained with their adoptive parents for the duration of their childhood.[23]

The remaining six participants reported that they came from harmonious families, in which there were no reported beatings or severe emotional abuse. Of this group, four reported that they had grown up with their biological parents, and the remaining two reported that they had been adopted at an early age and had remained with their adoptive parents during their childhood. Therefore, all individuals in this group of six youth grew up with a consistent set of parents in a "nuclear" family. One participant was unwilling to talk about issues of child abuse and wife assault. Three persons in this group of six were ethno-racial minorities, and all were heterosexual. Three were classified as coming from middle-class families of origin, one from a working-class family, and two came from dependent poor families. Two of these six youth claimed to be gang members.

Eleven of the group of 24 participants who reported experiencing beatings and severe emotional abuse at home were living at home at the time of the interviews; four of the group of six who reported coming from harmonious families were living at home. In both groups of families (harmonious and abusive) roughly one-third of father figures rarely or never worked (dependent poor families), while the remaining fathers consistently worked. There was no difference in employment status between social and biological fathers. Roughly one-third of both these types of fathers rarely or never worked (were dependent poor).

The criteria used to classify the participants' reports of these incidents into the categories of beatings and severe emotional abuse are based upon the definitions discussed in the Introduction. Beatings included incidents wherein the participants or their mothers were repeatedly kicked, punched, hit with objects, choked, strapped, burned, thrown down stairs or through walls by father-figures. Some injuries requiring medical attention were reported as a result of these beatings, and the police and/or child welfare authorities were reported to be involved as well. Severe emotional abuse included repeated threats of physical violence or death; being screamed at, belittled and humiliated on a daily basis; and/or the destruction of possessions by father-figures. Only a small minority of the participants understood the behaviour in these incidents to be abusive and wrong (see below).

Apart from witnessing the severe abuse of mothers and being severely abused themselves, the primary factors which contribute to the differences between youth coming from harmonious (HF) versus abusive families (AF) include the following:

1. Ethno-racial origin. Fifty percent of the HF youth (3 participants) were ethno-racial minorities compared to only 14 per cent of the AF youth (3 participants).

2. Family type. All of the HF youth (6 participants) had grown up with their biological parents (including 2 youth who had been adopted during infancy who considered their adoptive parents to be their "natural" parents) and 67 per cent (4 participants) were living at home at the time of the interviews. None of the HF youth had received family support to abuse. Only 33 per cent of the AF youth (8 youth) grew up with their biologi-

cal fathers, and 46 per cent (11 youth) were living at home at the time of the interviews.[24] Fifty percent of the AF youth had received family support to abuse from father-figures.

3. Sexual orientation. All of the HF youth were heterosexual, compared to 79 per cent (19 participants) of the AF youth.

4. Abuser type. The AF youth were much more likely to have used serious violence compared to the HF youth. Whereas 46 per cent of the AF youth (11 participants) had used severe violence on girlfriends, only 17 per cent of the HF youth (1 participant) had used severe violence. Further, 42 per cent of the AF youth (10 participants) had forced sexual intercourse on girlfriends compared to 33 per cent of the HF youth (2 participants).

5. Gang membership. The AF youth were almost twice as likely to be gang members compared to the HF youth. Whereas 63 per cent of the AF youth (15 participants) reported being gang members, only 33 per cent of the HF youth (2 participants) said that they were gang members.

There were no large differences between these two groups concerning abusive male peers and peer support to abuse, and adherence to both familial patriarchal beliefs and attitudes supporting physical girlfriend abuse.

1. Making sense of the abuse

A number of common themes emerge from the participants' accounts of witnessing their mothers being beaten and emotionally abused and being beaten and emotionally abused themselves by father-figures. First, despite their reports of horrific abuse by their biological fathers, step-fathers, and mothers' boyfriends, only five of these males indicated that this behaviour was abusive and wrong. The majority of the participants were likely affected by the abuse (as displayed by depression, suicide attempts and psychological problems), but they told me that they were treated "okay" or "fine" by their families. This inability to articulate the impact of their victimization by severe child abuse supports previous findings in this area.[25]

This relates to the second and fourth ideological assumptions of family and gender: rigid gender roles and "law and order." Almost all participants reported that their experiences of abuse at home had not hurt them and later in the interview told me that the "ideal" man is always in control of his emotions ("big boys don't cry"). Further, the participants who grew up with their biological father in the home were most likely to report that "law and order" was justifiable in keeping their mothers and themselves "in line."

In the following account, Peter, a 16-year-old street youth, spoke about his feelings of rejection and hurt. The fact that Peter was adopted at an early age by an aunt and uncle, whom he thought to be caring and loving, probably influenced his ability to tell me about his personal pain.

> Peter: I was adopted by my aunt and uncle when I was two. My Dad broke my jaw when I was a baby. I've never seen my real parents since.
> MT: That's rough (silence). How does it make you feel – to know that your natural parents hurt you so badly that you had to get another mom and dad?
> Peter: Hurt, I guess. I mean they rejected me – almost killed me. I mean, my aunt and uncle took me in and raised me. They're good people. But it still doesn't change the fact that my real mom and dad hurt me so badly – would have killed me, I bet – that I was taken away. I guess I have felt unwanted (silence).

Peter was one of the small number of participants who reported that his parents (adoptive, in this case) did not adhere to traditional gender roles, did not engage in abusive behaviour, and did not approve of using violence against females. Peter himself denied adhering to any patriarchal beliefs, although he approved of using violence against girlfriends. Nevertheless, he physically, sexually, and emotionally abused his girlfriends. The process through which he developed his attitudes and behaviour related to his treatment of females therefore differed significantly than that of the majority of participants. As will be discussed later, it was evident that Peter's gang was instrumental in providing him with encouragement and a rationale for engaging in girlfriend abuse.

By contrast, in the next account Nick, a 17-year-old Francophone street youth and gang member, told me that his father tried to kill him when he disclosed that he might be gay. Following this brutal assault at the age of 11 or 12 years, Nick's father and uncle gave him money every week to use prostitutes to "fix" his sexual attraction to males. Although Nick was taken into the care of the local child welfare authority following the assault and then adopted by his grandparents, his father continued to exert psychological control over Nick through the provision of money for buying services of prostitutes.

> Nick: Well, I've never told anybody this. I don't know why the fuck I'm gonna tell you but here goes. I can remember way back wondering what the fuck? I'd get hard-ons for guys and girls. Like I was some kind of pervert. And I'd shoot a load when I was sleeping – but sometimes I'd be dreaming about a guy.
>
> MT: Shoot a load?
>
> Nick: A wet dream.
>
> MT: Oh yeah. Sorry. I've got a thick head.
>
> Nick: So I thought what the fuck. I was about 11 or 12. I thought I was going crazy. So I asked my fucking Dad. He was some pissed. He kicked the living shit outta me. He threw me through some drywall. He was screaming at me "No son of mine's gonna be a fuckin' queer! No son of mine's gonna be a fuckin' queer!" Then he put his hands around my throat and held me up against the wall and screamed in my face "Don't you ever, ever tell anyone what you just said to me. From now on, it's my rules. You're gonna get fucked every night by a cunt even if it costs me a million dollars." And that's when I started using 'hos [whores] ...

At this point in the interview, Nick's eyes glazed over, and he disengaged from the interview for approximately three minutes. In the abuse literature, this is referred to as disassociation, a common coping mechanism used by abuse survivors.[26] It allows a person to temporarily exit from reality and the emotional pain associated with trauma.

The specific assumptions of familial and gender ideologies evident in Nick's account include those related to rigid gender roles, sexual objectification and homophobia, and "law and order." As is clear in his statement when he said, "I think I've got it under control now" (see below), Nick suggested he was to blame for the abuse because of his sexual attraction to males. At no point in the interview did he tell me that his biological father's actions were wrong. Instead, he indicated that his father's violence was a legitimate attempt to cure him of his homosexual desires; he rationalized why his father introduced him to and supported his use of prostitutes. In fact, Nick told me that most fathers do this with their sons around the age of 12 years. When he said to me "and that's when I started using 'hos,'" it was as if this was a choice he made of his own free will. He did not relate it to almost having been killed by his father.

> Nick: That's why I had to go live with my grandparents. So did my brother and sister. DPJ (child welfare) took us away for a while and then we were adopted by my grandparents.
>
> MT: Because of the violence?
>
> Nick: Yeah.
>
> MT: You know I'll have to call the DPJ just to make sure your Dad isn't abusing any kids.
>
> Nick: I don't give a fuck. Just don't tell him it had anything to do with me. He'd kill me. I'm serious.
>
> MT: So your Dad would still wire you money even after you got adopted?
>
> Nick: Yeah. We still got to see him.
>
> MT: I see. So have you ever had sex with a guy?
>
> Nick: Fuck no. I'm too scared. All I can think of is my Dad's hands around my throat. I'll never do that. He'd kill me.
>
> MT: Do you want to sleep with another guy?
>
> Nick: Kind of. But it's not worth it. I think I've got it under control now.
>
> MT: What?
>
> Nick: As long as I'm fucking 'hos – those little cunts – pretty often, and I'm fighting a lot, I don't really think of being attracted to another guy.

Prior to this, Nick had told me that his father and uncle were members of a notorious motorcycle gang. He described routinely seeing women led around the house on spiked dog chains by male family members and said that his uncle was in jail for murdering a woman. As well, Nick described his sexual relations with prostitutes: "I fuck them really hard. When I fuck them too hard, they scream. I like it when they scream. I never force them, I always pay ... You can't hurt a prostitute." This is an example of how the participants, like Nick, were engaging in behaviour that in most contexts would be seen as criminal. However, they did not see their behaviour as such.

Nick neutralized the conflicts in his life. For example, he was brutally abused and likewise witnessed woman abuse by his father at home, yet justified his own sexual violence against prostitutes. Nick did not present his sexual relationships with prostitutes as involving women; instead, he told me that prostitutes were "little cunts": inanimate sexual objects. Nick routinely beat up gays on the street with his gang, yet had homosexual desires. Finally, despite almost being killed and his ongoing fear of being killed by his father due to his sexual orientation, Nick suggested this was his own problem: "I think I've got it under control now."

Striking differences are apparent in the participant's articulation of their mother's beatings and severe emotional abuse. Like Nick, the majority of the participants who witnessed their biological fathers abuse their mothers (11 out of 12) reported these assaults as justifiable and caused by their mother. By contrast, the majority (10 out of 12) of these youth who saw their mothers being abused by social fathers (step-fathers, boyfriends) presented these assaults as wrong. The only youth who reported that his biological father's abusiveness was unjustified was Paul, who made a conscious choice to be gay so as not to repeat the cycle of abuse in his family. Paul was one of the few participants who did not report adhering to any patriarchal beliefs nor support the use of physical violence against girlfriends. He was told by his father to never abuse women. The only two youth who agreed with their social father's abusiveness had received specific instructions from these men to abuse females. Both were gang members and had also received explicit instructions from their male peers to abuse their girlfriends.

Social learning, sex/gender roles, and socialization theories are useful in explaining the ways in which the participants made sense of their experiences of abuse in their homes. Evidence of the specific assumptions of familial and gender ideologies was found in almost all of the participants' accounts. As discussed in detail in the previous section, almost all of these youth reported that the traditional sexual division of labour and the adherence to rigid gender roles in their homes were "natural." They came from homes in which the sexual objectification of women and homophobia were commonplace. Finally, they all felt that the abusive behaviour of their biological fathers was justifiable and an appropriate way to resolve conflict and ensure the appropriate behaviour of other family members.

For most of these youth, the existence of these various ideological assumptions resulted in a consistent way of seeing their world, a world in which their childhood experiences of abuse made sense within the context of rigid gender roles and related behaviours.

2. Family support to abuse

Significant differences emerged during the participants' accounts of their early childhood. Thirteen were routinely instructed by father-figures who were abusing their mothers and themselves to physi-cally, sexually, and/or emotionally abuse women (eight social, five biological father figures). Six were routinely told not to abuse women by abusive father-figures (four social, two biological), and one participant who reported coming from a harmonious family said that his parents told him not to abuse women. Two participants experienced both sets of instructions from different social fathers.

In the following account, Nolan, a 17-year-old Aboriginal and satanic cult member who resided at home, told me about how every single male family member (biological father, step-father, grandfa-ther, uncle) had been abusive towards female family members and/or himself. He was severely abused as a child and explained how this had left him feeling "worthless – like a piece of shit." Nolan had attempted suicide a number of times, routinely cut his forearms with knives, and said that his psychiatrist had diagnosed him as being manic-depressive. His ability to talk about the impact of this abuse was probably related to his history of psychiatric involvement.

Nolan: Yeah. My real Dad beat my Mom. And I've been told that he ritually abused me.

MT: Really. What happened?

Nolan: I guess he burned and strapped me a lot. I was too young to remember.

MT: So who told you that you were ritually abused?

Nolan: My Mom and shrinks. I've had a few of them. My Step-Dad's not much better. He's been really violent. He threatens to kick the shit outta me. Once he slapped my Mom. She kicked him in the nuts. He's told me lots of times that if a girl hits you or touches you where you don't want to be touched, punch her out. I guess you could say the men in my family don't treat women very well. My uncle's told me that if you do things for a girl, she's got to fuck you. My grandfather and my real Dad put women down all the time. They call them "Hey bitch, you goddam whore" all the time. I know my grandfather sexually assaulted two of my cousins.

MT: That's no picnic. It must be rough.

Nolan: Yeah.

MT: How do you think that has affected you?

Nolan: Well, I think I'm worthless – like a piece of shit. I guess it's been all the put-downs and physical violence. It gets to you after a while. I've seen psychiatrists at the hospital. I'm on medication. They say I'm a manic-depressive.

MT: What does that mean to you?

Nolan: That I'm pretty fucked up.

Nolan did not say there was anything wrong with his step-father telling him repeatedly "if a girl hits you or touches you where you don't want to be touched, punch her out," or his uncle telling him that "if you do things for a girl, she's got to fuck you." Later on he said, "My uncle always says to me 'She's gotta fuck you. She's gotta. You're doing stuff for her so she's gotta fuck you.' He doesn't think there's any choice" (laughing). I asked Nolan: "Is your uncle right?" He replied: "I dunno (serious). Maybe (long silence). I guess he is."

Nolan reported that he could understand how being severely abused himself "got to him after a while," how it has caused him to have such serious psychological problems that he has attempted to take his own life a number of times. However, he did not identify his own abusive behaviour against his girlfriend as causing her similar suffering. Nolan stated that "the men in my family don't treat women very well." Throughout the interview, however, he distanced himself from these male relatives. It is interesting that, on the one hand, Nolan neutralized his own abusiveness, but, on the other, he could identify the abusive behaviour of the other men in his family. As well, Nolan did not question being told to abuse women by male family members. Ironically, the uncle who instructed him to sexually abuse women was the same uncle whose two daughters were sexually assaulted by Nolan's grandfather (his uncle's father).

Again, social learning, sex/gender role, and socialization theories are helpful in explaining the behaviour of the participants. As will be discussed in the next chapter, the process of gender identity for these youth is of critical importance. Like most boys, many of the participants' behaviours were founded upon a rejection of femininity, which was most probably heightened with their realization that many men have more power and higher status than women. It was natural for these youth to search for associations and relationships which could provide them with the elevated status of the cultural depiction of the "ideal" man.

In this next account, Paul, the gay 17-year-old, explained to me how his violent father would tell him, after beating his mother, "don't hit women." This account is representative of the differences related to gender and familial ideologies within the sample. Paul told me that his father's abusiveness was wrong, and that at a young age he decided that the only way not to be like his father was to be gay.

Paul: ... And I hustled for two months right after I left home – that would have been over a year ago.

MT: You hustled?

Paul: Yeah. On Mackenzie. You know. I was turning tricks for bucks. I had no money. I guess I should tell you I'm gay... I was still in the closet then. My Dad's an alcoholic. Everyone had to listen to him. He was the boss and he solved everything by violence. If he didn't like dinner, he beat my Mom. He put my Mom's head through dry walls, hit her chest with a hammer. When he broke her wrist, I called 911. Every day, it was "You're stupid. You can't cook, clean. You'll never do anything." He'd say to me "I'll kill you. I dare you to try to hit me. It will get even worse." Then he would tell me "Don't hit women" (silence). They found out I was gay a while ago. Ever since then, they've been bugging me about sleeping with women.

MT: I can see why you got out of there when you did. It must have been rough.

Paul: Yeah (silence). The guys I know are all queens (drag queens). I hang out with lots of women…. Well, I see my Mom occasionally. No one else. They all fucked me too bad. I mean, a guy can only get hurt so much and then he moves on…. I don't think it's any coincidence that I discovered I was gay so young, and that I did this with my Dad being so verbally and physically violent. What a role model. And being adopted on top of that! I think I rejected all that typical male bullshit at an early age because of him. I mean I've never fought guys, never played sports, and obviously I haven't been keeping track of all the broads I've recently laid (laughing) … At first it was hard. I was suicidal for a while. And hustling on Mackenzie was weird. I mean I hadn't come out to anyone but I knew I was gay. I had no money and no place to stay. And I had had no emotional attachment to anyone.

When Paul stated "I mean, a guy can only get hurt so much and then he moves on," he employed a common, everyday expression ("move on") to describe his own radical lifestyle change. He suggested that, by rejecting his father's heterosexuality, he could break the cycle of violence. In fact, Paul not only turned to a gay lifestyle, he only associated with drag queens (most of whom prostituted as women), gays, and straight women. Paul was the only participant who reported his biological father's wife abuse as wrong. As for being told by his Dad "don't hit women," Paul never did. Instead, he sexually and emotionally abused two girlfriends while he was still "in the closet" regarding his sexual orientation. Pretending that he was heterosexual, Paul told me that he abused his girlfriends "for social approval." He did not identify his own abusiveness as in any way related to his father's behaviour, perhaps because he decided that he was gay. His father, of course, was not gay. However, when Paul abused his girlfriends, he was pretending to be heterosexual. Paul did not verbalize the inconsistency in this situation.

As stated earlier, Paul was one of the few participants who did not adhere to patriarchal beliefs nor support the use of violence against girlfriends. When I questioned him about this, he said that adherence to these beliefs would make him too much like his father, that being gay provided him with the opportunity to develop a different set of beliefs about how people should relate to each other.

John, a 16-year-old living at home with his mother, used humour to avoid talking about the suffering he and his mother endured because of his biological father's violence. He made sense of his father's abusiveness by rationalizing it; he explained how his father was an alcoholic and unemployed. John emphasized the fact that his father had the "right" to work and be the breadwinner of his family. He believed in the "natural" sexual division of labour and rigid gender roles and reported that his father's abusive behaviour was somewhat justifiable because he was not working and was an alcoholic.

John laughed when telling me how his father always told him "never hit a girl, no matter what." Although he indicated an understanding of the irony of his father's words, John did not relate his own abusive behaviour with girlfriends as being wrong or in any way similar to the behaviour of his father. This is likely related to the powerful imagery of the biological patriarch. Although John laughs at his father's instructions not to abuse females, he is unable to follow through on this. He told me at the end of the account "I've never hit a girl. I'm not like my Dad."

> John: ...Yeah. He's an alcoholic though. He's in AA now. He used to beat the shit outta me and my Mom. I was too young to remember. I know he tried to choke me once (laughing). He didn't succeed. When he's drunk, I don't know what he's capable of. I know he beat my Mom real bad. And he threatened her – he said he was gonna kill her all the time. Funny thing is, he always tells me "Never hit a girl, no matter what." What a laugh. Him telling me that. He's one to talk, he is. Tried to kill both of us and all. He's unemployed now though. I don't have the balls to tell him where to go. Maybe I will when he starts working. But I know it's different for guys and girls. It's bad if you hit a girl. Girls are weaker, I'd never hit a girl. Never. But now if she started beating on me first, I think I'd probably hit her back – just to protect myself and all.

MT: It sounds like your home was pretty rough.

John: Yeah. I guess so.

MT: Do you think you have been affected by any of that?

John: Yeah. Of course. I mean I've learned the hard way why a guy can't hit a girl. I'll never do that. I saw how much it hurt my Mom.

MT: And you too.

John: Yeah (silence, eyes tearing) I've never hit a girl. I'm not like my Dad ...

3. Protecting mothers and paying back social fathers

A final common theme which emerged during the participants' accounts of their early childhood was protecting mothers and paying back boyfriends and step-fathers for the beatings. Six of the 12 participants who witnessed their mothers being abused by social father-figures told me that they used violence to protect their mothers from the abuse. None of the 12 who witnessed their biological fathers abuse their mothers told me that they attempted to stop their father's abusiveness. This is not surprising, given that 11 of these same 12 seemed to justify their biological father's wife abuse. Similarly, 10 of the 12 participants who witnessed their mothers being abused by social father-figures (including the 6 who used violence to protect their mother) told me that they beat up stranger-"rapists" and woman-beaters in their community as part of regular gang activities. By contrast, only 3 of the 12 participants who witnessed their biological fathers abuse their mothers reported engaging in similar activities. (Chapter 4 will discuss this in greater detail.)

These data illustrate the intertwined nature of the participants' ideological assumptions of family and gender. Wife-beating by biological fathers was viewed as a way in which these men punished their spouses for their failure to adhere to the strict gendered division of labour and for confronting patriarchal power. Challenges by mothers about biological fathers' dominance in the family were perceived by participants as threatening to their fathers' self-identity and his power and control over the traditional division of labour in the family; any challenges by mothers to the rigid gender roles in the home were a direct affront to the masculinity of the biological father and thus deserved a violent response. Many of these same participants explained their behaviour with their girlfriends in a similar fashion.

Don, the 15-year-old residing in an open custody young offender facility, justified being charged with threatening to kill his mother and sister. He told me that "they stole my liquor at home. They're both alcoholics." He matter-of-factly spoke of his violent, chaotic home life.

> MT: So what is it like at home? Were there ever any fights or arguments?
>
> Don: I don't have much to do with them. I got charged with uttering threats against my sister and my Mom. I told them I was gonna kill them. They stole my liquor at home. They're both alcoholics. My Mom's ex-boyfriend, I punched him in the head. He tried to break her leg and I chased him out with a baseball bat. He beat on me and my sister all the time. I told him "if you hit her, I'll kill you." And my Step-Dad, I'll punch him out if he touches my sister. He always calls them "bitch." Once my sister knocked me out. She hit me over the head with a billy club. I punched her back when I woke up.

Don described using violence to protect himself, his mother and sister at home. He did not view his social fathers as possessing the "natural" right to use physical discipline on other family members, including himself. There was an element of bravado in his account of using violence against his social fathers. This is illustrative of the other accounts wherein participants reported protecting mothers and paying back social fathers for abuse. These young men constructed a form of masculinity which contrasted the image of them being helpless victims of abuse in their homes. All of the young men who reported using violence in these situations described the "ideal man" as someone who was physically tough and muscular and someone who would use violence to protect his family.

However, Don legitimated his own threats against his mother and sister. The abusiveness at home was so routine that, after being knocked out by his sister with a billy club, it was perfectly normal to have "punched her back when I woke up." Although this passage speaks to the interwoven nature of familial and gender ideologies, it is also illustrative of how lifestyle/routine activities and social learning theories are applicable to the explanation of abusive behaviour. Many of the lifestyles of these youth were directly related to abuse perpetration and victimization. The majority of these young men had learned to behave violently in reaction to stress and conflict in their homes. Legitimacy was awarded to using violence as a coping mechanism in their families. Males for the most part were viewed as rightfully holding a position of power over other family members. Finally, visible rewards for violent behaviour were evident to participants in many of their families. These young men told me that their fathers got what they wanted by means of their violence. Typically, this included winning a fight or argument with another family member, getting someone to do what they should "naturally" be doing, and demonstrating that they were the "boss."

William, a 15-year-old gang member, told me how he paid one of his mother's boyfriends back for abusing both her and himself. Despite having his head put through a wall by his mother's boyfriend, he told me that his family treated him "okay, I guess."

> MT: ... Okay. What do you think about your family? I mean, how do they treat you?
> William: Okay, I guess.... I think some of them hit her. I dunno. I remember they called her "you fucking bitch" all the time. This one ass-hole used to say to me "I'm hitting you because I can't hit her." He threatened to put my head through a wall – and he did it. I slashed the fucker's tires and cracked his head with a crowbar. Me and my buddies are tracking some of them down. We gotta pay them back ...Yeah. They used to say "if any bitch fools with you, smack her."

Like many of the other participants, William seemed to make sense of the abuse at home by distancing himself from his mother's boyfriend: "I slashed the fucker's tires and cracked his head with a crowbar." Although he prided himself on "paying them back," he didn't verbalize any inconsistency when he told me "Yeah. They used to say 'If any bitch fools with you, smack her.'" He told me later on in the interview that it was okay for a guy to hit his girlfriend "if she hits him first, fucks around, you know, turned into a slut or got into porno." It is interesting that while William indicated that his mother's boyfriend's assaults were wrong and worthy of revenge, he agreed with their (his mother's boyfriends) instructions to use physical force against other women should they violate certain feminine codes of behaviour. This apparent inconsistency in William's account is illustrative of the other narratives. These young men were confused and at times terrified by the violence in their lives. At the same time, however, they were struggling to piece together their lives and make sense of their often chaotic experiences.

As well, there was a tendency for those participants who had minimal or no contact with their biological fathers to idealize these men and place them upon a pedestal. It could be that this had little to do with their familial and gender ideologies, but instead was an indicator of their attempts to escape from a chaotic life into an ideal dream world. Katz's work on the sensory and creative aspects of the actions of young criminals is applicable here.[27]

Conclusion

The findings of this study suggest confirmation of many reports regarding the serious consequences of witnessing wife assault and being victimized by child abuse.[28] Most participants did not indicate that they had been adversely affected by this abuse or even defined their victimization as abusive; however, they experienced many of the indicators of abuse described in the literature. These include criminal behaviour, suicide attempts, depressive symptomatology and emotional problems, psychological distress, and abuse perpetration against family members, peers, strangers, and girlfriends.

How can we make sense of the participant's description of their mother's and their own victimization by their father-figures? It is common for boys to lack the language necessary to describe their pain and suffering associated with being victimized.[29] Talking about being victimized and the associated feelings are not considered to be masculine (see Chapter 4). As well, the adherence to common assumptions of traditional familial and gender ideologies by many of the participants likely significantly influenced the way in which they legitimized and rationalized a terrifying childhood.

However, this was not a homogeneous sample. Eight of the 30 youth became abusers despite the fact that their abusive father-figures routinely told them not to abuse women. Nine reported not adhering to familial patriarchal beliefs, and 19 said that they did not support using physical violence against girlfriends in any situations. Seven of the participants became abusers, although they did not adhere to familial patriarchal beliefs nor attitudes supporting the abuse of girlfriends. Two abused girlfriends yet resisted their father's violence by becoming gay or seriously questioning their sexual orientation. One-third of the sample were either ethno-racial or sexual minorities. Although the experiences of these participants may seem insignificant, they reveal important differences among this small sample. How did they become abusers? The differences help explain the variations in the extent to which these male youth adhered to some of the specific assumptions of familial and gender ideologies

The presence of biological and social fathers had a differential impact on the participants in relation to their development of ideological assumptions about family, gender, and sexual orientation. The participants with no biological fathers in the home had no respect for social fathers as "natural" patriarchs. They likely developed their patriarchal ideas about family and gender through a different process than did youth who lived with their biological fathers. Race, ethnicity, and sexual orientation differentially impacted upon the development of attitudes and beliefs about family and gender.

The participant's familial and gender beliefs provided a common lens through which they interpreted their own and their mother's victimization. The biological fathers had a natural and moral authority to enforce a strictly gendered behavioural code. The beatings and emotional abuse by these men were reported as justifiable, normal, and acceptable. Viewed through this lens, conflicting instructions by these same fathers to either abuse or not abuse women did not appear to be incongruent to some participants. In contrast, the majority of participants who were victimized and witnessed their mother's victimization by social fathers (step-fathers, boyfriends) indicated that these assaults were wrong. They did not portray these males as being the legitimate heads of their families. Instead, they reported their biological fathers to be the only legitimate rulers of the house (even if they had no contact with them), and accordingly, the only legitimate abusers. Social fathers had no legitimacy as violent patriarchs. As a result, one-half of these same participants fought back against their social fathers' abusiveness. In contrast, none of the participants who witnessed or were victimized by their biological father's abusiveness retaliated against him with violence. These issues relate to the first, second, and fourth ideological assumptions about family and gender: the sexual division of labour is "natural," rigid gender roles, and "law and order."

At this point it is useful to compare intra-group differences related to the participants' beliefs. Table 3.3 compares the eight participants who reported having ASPA and FPB (the Believers) with the seven youth who reported that they did not adhere to any of these beliefs (the Non-Believers).

Of the total sample, 21 youth adhered to at least one patriarchal attitude, 11 supported the use of physical violence against girlfriends, and 7 youth did not adhere to patriarchal beliefs nor support the use of physical violence against girlfriends. Eight had at least one patriarchal belief and also supported violence against girlfriends. Two participants agreed with at least one attitude supporting physical girlfriend abuse, yet did not adhere to patriarchal beliefs, and 10 participants adhered only to familial patriarchal beliefs.

The mean age of the Believers and Non-Believers was 16 years. Six of the Believers were physical/sexual/emotional abusers (all had used severe violence and two had forced intercourse), one was a physical/emotional abuser, and one was a sexual/emotional abuser. Four of the Non-Believers were physical/sexual/emotional abusers (two had forced intercourse), and three were physical/emotional abusers (one had used severe violence). No large social class differences in the families of origin were apparent. Four of the Believers and two of the Non-Believers were ethno-racial minorities. One of the Believers and five of the Non-Believers came from a harmonious family. Four of the Believers received family support to abuse, and all belonged to abusive peer groups whose members encouraged them to abuse girlfriends. None of the Non-Believers received family support to abuse, and although all received encouragement to abuse girlfriends from male peers, only five belonged to peer groups in which members were abusive. Six of the Believers grew up with biological fathers; all of the Non-Believers grew up with their biological fathers. One of the Believers was not heterosexual, and two of the Non-Believers were not heterosexual.

Table 3.3
Believers and
Non-Believers

	BELIEVERS (N = 8)	NON-BELIEVERS (N = 7)
Ethno-Racial Minorities	50% (4)	29% (2)
Gay/Bisexual/Questioning	13% (1)	29% (2)
Harmonious Family	13% (1)	71% (5)
Family Support to Abuse	50% (4)	0% (0)
Abuser Type	75% p/s/e (6)	57% p/s/e (4)
	6 sev.	0 sev.
	2 f.i.;	2 f.i.;
	13% p/e;	43% p/e;
	13% s/e	0% s/e
Biological Father at Home	75% (6)	100% (7)
Living at Home	100% (8)	29% (2)
Gang Member	50% (4)	43% (3)
Abus. Male Peers and Support	100% (8)	71% (5)
ASPA/FPB	100% (8)	0% (0)

p = physical
s = sexual
e = emotional
sev. = severe
f.i. = forced
intercourse

Therefore, the Believers were much more likely than the Non-Believers to have engaged in all three forms of girlfriend abuse, to have used severe violence, to have come from an abusive family, and to have received family support to abuse girlfriends. The comparison of these two groups suggests that patriarchal and pro-abuse beliefs are linked to the more serious forms of abuse, and that directions from father-figures to abuse (along with living in an abusive familial context) are related to adherence to these beliefs and abusive behaviour. Although slightly more Believers than Non-Believers were ethno-racial minorities, one cannot generalize from this small difference that abusive behaviour may be more concentrated among certain ethno-racial groups. Indeed, in the screening sample, almost twice as many ethno-racial minorities were non-abusers compared to abusers (23 per cent and 12 per cent respectively). However, this is not to say that the particular experiences of these minority youth (in the in-depth sample) were not important in the development of their rigid familial and gender ideologies; indeed, they were.

These findings verify and expand upon the concept of social

learning and the assumption that being abused as a child and witnessing wife assault can lead to the formation of pro-abuse beliefs and perpetration of girlfriend abuse.[30] Unlike these researchers, however, I am suggesting that the formation of these beliefs in boys, (which may be associated with attitudes supporting violence against women) may also be rooted in witnessing and experiencing severe and prolonged abuse from a male caregiver. The development of this rigid familial and gender belief system in these boys was an effective mechanism to cope with childhoods characterized by male-perpetrated abuse. The participants acquired their patriarchal and pro-abuse beliefs at such an early age for a number of reasons: they modelled the patriarchal and/or abusive behaviour of their father-figures; for those who experienced abuse, these beliefs helped them understand the traumatic abuse at home; and some received explicit instructions from male family members to abuse women if they stepped outside of their expected roles.

The findings in this section suggest support for the hypothesis of feminist researchers that perceived threat to patriarchal power is a key motive for woman abuse by adult men. In addition, support is found for the feminist assumption that patriarchal husbands may beat their wives. However, in contrast to previous studies, my data on these abusive father-figures comes from the sons, not the wives, of these men. Half of the participants were from homes where the father-figure never or rarely worked. Instead, these men depended upon the participant's mother's welfare cheque or their own government cheque for an income. These men had no economic power base to legitimize their patriarchal power, yet the participants nevertheless indicated that they were the breadwinners and the heads of their families. The participants did not suggest there was any inconsistency with a jobless breadwinner ruling their family.

Intergenerational transmission theory cannot explain why only some of the participants reported perpetrating abuse at home, and all of them were abusive in extra-familial contexts. Also, six participants who were abusive reported coming from harmonious families. Why? Scant attention has been paid by researchers to how children acquire rigid familial and gender value sets. It has been assumed that patriarchal practices are developed in peer groups in high school or university settings, in which young boys devalue and objectify girls and behave with a sense of superiority.[31] The data in my study suggest that most of the participants initially acquired their familial and gender belief systems in their families at a very young age.

Despite the fact that none of the participants identified the apparent incongruity of their "jobless breadwinner" fathers, this striking image in their childhood challenged their masculine identities. Almost all of the participants expressed feelings of hopelessness about their economic futures, and directly related this to their own masculine fears and anxieties. This direct intersection between the ideological assumptions about family and gender of these young men will be further explored in the next chapter.

Notes

1. For example, see Offord, Boyle, and Racine, 1990; Wharf, 1993; DeMontigny, 1995; Swift, 1995; Danzig, 1996; Gonzales-Ramos, 1996; Wallace, Wallace, and Andrews, 1997.

2. See Glaser and Straus, 1967.

3. Hammersley, 1992, p.165.

4. For example, see Scully, 1990.

5. Ptacek (1988) conducted in-depth interviews with a small sample (18) of adult woman abusers who were in a group treatment program for male batterers. He looked at similar issues when analyzing the accounts of his participants. See also Silverman, 1993.

6. Ptacek, 1988. Quasi-clinical refers to the role I undertook at the end of each interview to challenge these youth to take responsibility for their abusive behaviour. I also counselled some of these youth regarding suicide.

7. Silverman, 1993.

8. Scott and Lyman, 1968, pp. 46, 52.

9. In many families these beliefs and values could also be described as "traditional," and involve no abusive behaviour.

10. This fact was later confirmed when I reported it to his probation officer, along with Phil's report that his gang was involved with violent pimping activities.

11. For example, see Barrett and MacIntosh, 1982.

12. Katz, 1988.

13. For example, see Bersani and Chen, 1988, or Finkelhor, 1983.

14. See Chambliss, 1973; Greenberg, 1977; Tolson, 1977; Kessler et al., 1985; Schwendinger and Schwendinger, 1985; Heward, 1988; Connell, 1989, 1991; Messner, 1989; Messerschmidt, 1986, 1993; Willis, 1977; Cernkovich and Giordano, 1992.

15. See Smith, 1990a.

16. For example, see Messerschmidt, 1993.

17. For example, see Mercer, 1988.

18. Chodorow, 1974, 1979.

19. For a review, see Thorne-Finch, 1992, pp. 81-87.

20. Totten, 1997.

21. See Schwendinger and Schwendinger, 1983, 1985; Messerschmidt, 1986, 1993; Connell, 1991a; Hill and Santiago, 1992; Willis, 1977; Campbell, 1984; Fishman, 1988.

22. See Schwendinger and Schwendinger, 1985; Messerschmidt, 1986, 1993; Chambliss, 1973; Willis, 1977.

23. These two sets of adoptive parents were categorized as biological parents for the following reasons: the participants had been adopted during their infancy; they had never met their biological parents, nor did they know much about them; and they considered their adoptive parents as their "natural" parents.

24. Ten of the participants who were living at home at the time of this project told me that despite being under the same roof as other family members, they had little to do with them.

25. See Kivel, 1992.

26. For example, see Bass and Davis, 1988.

27. Katz, 1988.

28. For example, see Wolfe et al., 1985; Deykin, 1985; Jaffe et al., 1986a, 1986b; Aber et al., 1989; Allen and Tarnowski, 1989; Jaffe and Reitzel, 1990; Mangold and Koski, 1990; Jaffe et al., 1990; Fantuzzo et al., 1991; Holden and Ritchie, 1991; Kaufman, 1991; Wind and Silvern, 1992; Johnson, 1996; O'Keefe, 1998.

29. For example, see Kivel, 1992.

30. Bandura, 1973; Smith and Williams, 1992; O'Keefe, 1998.

31. See Kanin, 1967; DeKeseredy, 1998; Willis, 1977; McRobbie, 1980; Spender, 1982; McLaren, 1986.

four

On the Street:
Developing Familial and Gender Ideologies

THIS chapter explores the common experience of the participants of developing familial and gender ideologies outside of their homes, and analyzes the methods by which they coped with challenges to their masculine identities. We will examine the participants' fears and anxieties about their own masculine identities, the common ways in which they negotiated these identities, and why they abandoned their biological families for a sense of belonging, status, and acceptance in male peer groups/gangs, which they defined as their "new" families.

In the previous chapter, we saw that participants' familial and gender beliefs provided them with a common lens through which to understand their childhood. They acquired this belief system at an early age for a number of reasons: they modelled the patriarchal and/or abusive behaviour of their caregivers; for 24 of these youth, these beliefs helped them understand the traumatic abuse at home; and some received explicit instructions from male family members to abuse women if they stepped outside of their expected roles. Participants indicated that their biological fathers were the legitimate rulers of their home and justified the abuse of mothers who did not obey house rules. The participants who witnessed their mothers being abused by social fathers considered these assaults to be unjustified, since these men could not be the "natural" heads of their families. However, regardless of whether they indicated their mother's victimization to be right or wrong, over two-thirds of the participants internalized patriarchal beliefs and over one-third internalized attitudes supporting the use of violence against girlfriends who violated these beliefs.

Differences in the participants regarding their ethno-racial origin, sexual orientation, male peer associations, and family type can account for differential adherence to these familial and gender ideologies. The belief systems of some of the sub-groups within the sample of 30 young abusers were probably developed through different processes. Further, the majority of the participants seemed to neutralize the impact of their own beatings and emotional abuse by father-figures. Their apparent rationalization of their own victimization makes sense when we consider that most of these adolescents identified their father-figures as being the natural rulers of their families who had to be obeyed at all costs. However, half of the participants came from homes where the father-figure never or rarely worked. Although these men had no economic base to legitimize their patriarchal power, the participants nevertheless identified them to be the breadwinners and the heads of their families.

Despite the fact that none of the participants verbalized the apparent incongruity in the situations of their "jobless breadwinner" fathers, this does not necessarily mean that they were not aware of this. It may have been too painful to admit. I suggest here that this striking image in their childhood contributed to a struggle in their masculine identities. Almost all of the participants expressed feelings of hopelessness about their economic futures and directly related this to their own masculine fears and anxieties.

Challenges to Masculine Identity

When asked about whether or not they could achieve the material wealth, good jobs, and breadwinner status they described when telling me about the "ideal man," two participants reported that they would; the accounts of the remaining 28 youth were characterized by despair and hopelessness. They said that they would have no job or a "shit job," would be dependent upon crime or welfare for money, and would have few material possessions. Interestingly, however, they were adamant that they would still have to be the "bread-winner." Although I did not ask all participants about whether they had attempted suicide or not, I questioned nine youth regarding this issue because they appeared to be so depressed at this point in the interview.

The two participants who responded differently on this issue regarding their future expectations were Paul, the gay 17-year-old who reported escaping from his adoptive father's abusiveness by choosing a path out of heterosexuality, and Steve, the Lebanese youth in grade 9 who came from a harmonious family. Both told me that their economic futures were positive, and neither expressed feelings of despair or hopelessness about their future expectations. Both expected to gain adequately paying jobs. How could it be that these two youth were so very different than the rest of the sample on this issue?

For Paul, the answer would appear to be simple. He was one of the few youth in this study who was working at the time of the interviews. He had grown up in a middle-class adoptive family; his father was a manager in a high profile police force. Paul saw his father work almost every working day. Paul's aspirations about his own working life appear to be directly related to having had a care-giver model positive behaviour in this area. It is not surprising that he reported wanting to have nothing to do with policing, his father's line of work. After all, he told me that the primary reason he was gay was to be as distant from his father (whom he said was hetero-sexual) as possible. It is interesting, however, that Paul seems to have embraced his father's work ethic.

For Steve, this issue is more complex. Steve was adamant with me that his biological father was the boss of his family because he "worked," and his mother did not "work." However, Steve's father in reality only "worked" at most two weeks of the year, whereas his mother "worked" every day with her home daycare business. Never-theless, Steve steadfastly maintained that because his father was the "breadwinner," he was the head of the family. Steve was also one of the participants whose familial and gender ideologies were most closely intertwined. He indicated that unemployment and any other deviance from traditional gender and familial roles would pose a direct threat to his own masculinity. Perhaps it was the case that because of the interconnectedness of these ideologies for him, it would have been unbearable for him to even envisage a future wherein his economic prospects were marginal. Steve was also one of the few participants who did not report engaging in criminal activities. He did not regard economic gains from crime as being "manly."

Jim, a 15-year-old "skateboarder" in a young offender facility, matter-of-factly told me that he was not ever going to achieve the economic standards of a middle-class lifestyle and was therefore choosing a future of crime for material gain.

> Jim: I've got nothing, I mean as a guy. If you take away the
> fucking, girls, and fighting I've got sweet fuck all. I wasn't
> born with a silver spoon in my mouth. There's fuck all I
> can do about that. So now it really pisses me when I see
> some rich mother-fucker my age driving around in a fast
> car with lots of gold. 'Cause I know that'll never be me.
> I'll never have any of that shit from a real job – like a
> lawyer or a doctor. If I get a job it'll be picking up
> garbage or flipping burgers. Well, excuse me. I think I'll
> steal cars and deal. But guys like me I figure we're real
> men compared to those rich son of a bitches. We gotta
> fight and live on the edge to get our cash. Them, those
> faggots go off to some pukey university and come out
> millionaires. Not me. Where I come from, you drop
> outta school early and drop into crime earlier. We don't
> need any of that 9-to-5 kiss-ass bullshit. You gotta have
> more balls to make it rich my way. Those rich faggots
> get it all handed to them on a fucking silver platter.
> They're pussies. They probably get rammed up the ass
> every night by their boss.
>
> MT: Rammed up the ass by their boss?
>
> Jim: Yeah. You gotta be a fuckin' faggot – kissing some guy's
> ass – to get a job like that.

Jim was one of a core group of participants who reported that they would achieve the material wealth and elevated status of the "ideal" man through criminal activities. Unlike Paul and Steve, who expected to attain this status from traditional employment, Jim indicated that he would take a different pathway than middle- and upper-income men, who have easy access to education and high-paying jobs. Jim was a physical/sexual/emotional abuser, who had used severe violence on an ex-girlfriend. He had fired a gun over her head because she had allegedly stolen his hat. He had grown up with a succession of social fathers in his home and had received explicit instructions from these father-figures to abuse females. He reported that his male peers were abusive and had instructed him to abuse his girlfriends. He adhered to one patriarchal belief ("a male has the right to decide whether or not his wife/girlfriend should go out in the evening with her friends") and said that he would not support the use of physical abuse against girlfriends. He reported being involved in substance abuse and criminal activity on most days with his fellow gang members.

Jim, like many of the other young men in this study who reported that they had minimal chances of gaining good jobs, seemed to neutralize the fact that he believed he had "nothing ... as a guy" without the "fucking, girls, and fighting." He negated everything masculine about middle- and upper-class life: if you were rich, according to Jim, you couldn't be a man. Despite his bravado, his feelings of inadequacy and frustration regarding his lack of economic opportunity are apparent. The insights of Richard Sennett, Jonathan Cobb and Lillian Rubin are applicable here, as well as David Matza's concepts of negation and neutralization.[1] Jim, like 27 of the other young men in this study, clearly recognized that he had no economic future in the traditional sense. Accordingly, he negated anything masculine about employment, material possessions, and wealth.

Notwithstanding this neutralization and negation of male privilege attained through wealth and high status jobs, almost all told me that they would nevertheless have to achieve male superiority through the only other means available to them: "fucking and fighting." This is another example of how closely linked were their familial and gender beliefs. Their male gender was inseparable from being the "breadwinner": almost all told me that they had to support their wives and children in the future. Failure to do so would be considered to be disastrous for their manhood. These young men indicated that in the absence of a good job, breadwinner status could still be attained through heterosexuality, physical toughness, and the protection of families from harm.

Dave, a 16-year-old Ojibway street youth, also reported that he had no economic future. He told me that "It's like I was born a guy but no one gave me the stuff I need to be successful."

> Dave: But it's like I've got nothing left – I mean, to me – as a guy, I've got no good job – no money, house, car and shit. I'm a fucking Indian. So I've got my balls for fucking and being blowed whenever I want. And I've got my fists. I've got fuck all else. It's like I was born a guy but no one gave me the stuff I need to be successful. I was fucked as soon as I was born. So I'm fucked as a guy. I've got my prick, my fists, and a girlfriend to tell what to do. Fuck all else. I'm no fucking man unless I've got those things. The only thing going my way as a guy is that I'm not queer. Can you imagine a queer unemployed Indian? You might as well kill yourself. You'd be a nothing. Zero. Cut off your cock and flush it.

In addition to the "hidden injuries of class,"[2] Dave was also deeply affected by racism. He articulated that he had no future, and felt worthless, that his "prick," "fists," and "girlfriends to tell what to do" were the only remaining defences of his masculinity. Dave had been adopted into a white, middle-class harmonious family during infancy. He was part of the group of youth making up one-third of the sample who occupied the very bottom rungs of the power hierarchy they reported to despise so much. Most probably an indicator of his own self-hatred, Dave relished in describing how he beat up gays, ethno-racial minorities, and girlfriends. Later in the interview (see below, p. 136) he used the powerful imagery of putting on hockey equipment to shield himself from the outside world, possibly a parallel to his own "deculturation" in his adoptive family. Although he did not talk about this issue in any great detail, it was as if he presented himself as "naked" when discussing his masculinity. Stripped of his culture in his white adoptive family, he compared his aboriginal culture with being a gay. A theme of powerlessness echoes throughout his account, powerlessness rooted in his adoption, race, and life on the street. He presented himself as being an "object" throughout his young life, subject to an external locus of control.

Twenty-five of the participants told me they were heterosexual, one said that he was bisexual, one told me that he was gay, and three indicated that they had serious questions about their sexual orientation. With the exception of the gay participant, all of these young males told me about having to prove their heterosexuality continually to their male peers, and many expressed anxieties about their sexuality. Many of these youth defined themselves through their heterosexuality and their apparently insatiable appetite for frequent sexual activity. Almost all spoke of their penises as key attributes of their personas, and many of them reported beating up anyone with effeminate features. It was as if a male with any hint of femininity posed a direct threat to their masculinity. This again is an example of how closely interrelated were the ideological assumptions of family and gender. In particular, the two ideological assumptions of relevance here are sexual objectification and homophobia, and "fucking and fighting."

Bob, an Afro-American 16-year-old, who was a ward of the CAS, broke down when telling me about his sexual anxieties.

Bob: (Sobbing) I guess I am trying to prove myself to my friends. I mean, would you like to be called a faggot and a pussy all the time? I gotta show them that I can fuck, and fuck a lot. I'm no queer.

MT: So if you were queer, what would that mean?

Bob: What's the point to life if you're a faggot? You would be nothing.

MT: So to be a guy, it's like you have to fuck lots of girls.

Bob: Yeah. To prove that you're not a faggot.

MT: And the money, cars?

Bob: You mean are they as important as fucking?

MT: Yeah, I guess so.

Bob: Well, it's not so bad if you've got a girlfriend. I mean, you can handle not having too much money and shit.

The emphasis which Bob and the other participants placed upon frequent sexual activity confirms previous findings in the research on this topic, which suggest that marginal male youth present heterosexual intercourse to be a fundamental behaviour through which manhood and heterosexuality are proven.[3] Bob, like the other participants, spoke about the tremendous pressure he was under to demonstrate to his friends that he was not gay or female. When he asked me "Would you like to be called a faggot and a pussy all the time?," he revealed not only this constant harassment by his male peers, but also his own fears about his sexuality. Although he told me a number of times that he was not gay, he sobbed throughout this conversation. Bob, like the other participants, seemed to be obsessed with proving that he was "no faggot." Further, he compared the importance of having material possessions to "fucking" when he talked about his own masculine identity. By having a girlfriend, he was proving to his friends that he was not gay. Clearly, he saw this as being more important than having money and cars. Later, Bob said that having money and cars "is the guy thing to do," and that he would be embarrassed if his girlfriend "showed him up" by having money. However, he then qualified this statement, telling me "But if you're fucking, it wouldn't be so bad." "Faggots" occupied the bottom rung on Bob's hierarchy of the powerless.

Originally from a middle-class family, Bob had spent the majority of his teenage years bouncing from one group home to another. He was never placed in a culturally sensitive setting. He indicated that the reason why he came into the care of the CAS was related to his mother's inability to protect him from beatings by her boyfriends. All his peers were abusive and had instructed him to abuse his girlfriends, although he had never received family support to abuse. As well, he indicated that he adhered to one patriarchal belief ("a male has the right to decide if his wife/girlfriend should work outside the home"), and would not support a male using physical violence against his girlfriend. His primary routine activities consisted of using substances, engaging in criminal behaviour, and going to school.

Bob was among the most severe of all the abusers in this study. A physical/sexual/emotional abuser, he reported acts categorized as severe violence and forced intercourse. In fact, staff at the group home in which he was staying informed me after the interview that he was a prime suspect in a violent sexual assault on a female which had occurred the evening before (Bob did not tell me about this incident). It may be the case that the processes through which Bob learned his abusive behaviour differed significantly from those of the other participants. For example, he did not embrace a patriarchal-authoritarian ideology to the same degree as the others. He had been victimized by racial violence and had spent the majority of his adolescence in male CAS group homes. He also had serious questions about his sexual orientation. These experiences could be part of the different process through which he learned to abuse. Compared to the majority of the sample, Bob had relatively little "structural space"[4] in which to define, develop, and negotiate his masculinity. Being black, a ward of the CAS, questioning his sexuality, and economically and socially marginal, Bob had very few resources at hand with which to construct his masculinity.

The haunting imagery evident in this account by Bob again points to the interconnectedness of the participants' ideological assumptions of family and gender. In the context of social and economic marginalization, a man can only prove his manhood in the presence of what he is not: a "bitch" (girlfriend) or a "faggot." In Bob's opinion, as in the eyes of most of the other participants, the presence of material possessions was not enough to demonstrate masculinity. Instead, masculinity appears to be a much more precarious, malleable trait, needing to be negotiated and created daily and defined by the social situations in which they found themselves. For example, within the context of male peers, perceived threat to masculinity was at its highest. This may explain the great emphasis they placed on gay-bashing.

As well, the potential relevance of resource theory in explaining the abusive behaviour of these youth is again highlighted in this account by Bob. He explained to me that, if his girlfriend had more money than he did, this would be considered as an implicit put-down. However, he immediately informed me that this inequality could be balanced by "fucking." It is possible that what he meant in this conversation was that perceived inequality in status could be evened out by male control of sexual relations.

Sylvain was a 17-year-old Francophone who recently moved into a rooming house after living on the street for a couple of years. Like Bob, he also had serious questions about his sexuality. However, Sylvain appeared to legitimate these questions by relating them to his father's violence.

Sylvain: Yeah. I guess so. I mean, I guess I can tell you. I went through a period of time – a couple of years – I was I guess 13 or 14. I didn't know if I was queer or straight – like normal. And I think it was because my Dad was so violent – and he is obviously not a queer. It was like I thought – stupid, isn't it – that if I was gay, I wouldn't be like him. And that lasted for a while. I've never told any one (crying, long silence). Now I know I'm not gay.

MT: It would still be okay if you were.

Sylvain: Well, I'm not. But it's like I had to get rid of everything my father stood for to not be violent. So I guess I have rejected some of that stuff but also kept some of it. It's weird. I kind of feel that I am floating in space – neither in or out. Maybe it would have been easier if I would have been gay.

Crying throughout this conversation was evidence that Sylvain found speaking about this issue extremely painful. There were many inconsistencies in his account. Although he desperately wanted to "get rid of everything my father stood for," he was abusing his girl-friend. How could Sylvain see such similar behaviour as so different? Part of the answer to this question is found in his questions about his own sexuality. He stated that "If I was gay, I wouldn't be like him." Although Sylvain told me a number of times that he was not gay, he also described feeling "that I am floating in space – neither in or out." Further on in this conversation, still speaking about his sexuality, Sylvain told me "It's kind of like I'm caught between these two worlds."

Sylvain's imagery of floating between two worlds in outer space represents his struggle with his own sexual orientation. It is also indicative of the presence of two planes of reality in the lives of some young male criminals.[5] In Sylvain's case, the key defining feature was sexual orientation. In his mundane, everyday plane, he was a straight male confronted with the cycle of beatings in his own family and in his dating relationships. On the other, he was a gay male who had consciously chosen to take a direct pathway out of his father's violence.

Eight of the participants told me that they routinely beat up gays. When I asked why they did this, they spoke about how important it was to prove that they were not gay and to defend themselves against homosexuals. Brian, 14 years of age, spoke defensively about beating up "faggots." It is clear from this conversation that he felt threatened by gays.

> Brian: We roll 'em all the time. Not for their fuckin' jackets but just because they're fags. You gotta watch out for them. Bend over and they'll ram their cock up your ass. It's fucking disgusting. We always keep an eye out for fuckin' fags. You never know when they'll try to ram you.

This pattern of defensive posturing when talking about gays is common in most of the accounts. Like Brian, these participants indicated that they faced a daily risk of being raped by gays, and that the only way to protect themselves from this constant threat was to beat up anyone they thought was gay. Their fear of being raped by a homosexual was likely unfounded. None reported having been sexually assaulted by a gay, nor did any of them report having been physically assaulted or harassed by gays. In fact, with the exception of the one gay participant, they reported no contact with gays apart from perpetrating frequent beatings upon them. Gay-bashing and heterosexual relations with girlfriends were useful ways to negotiate masculinity for many of these young men.

John, a 17-year-old gang member, was candid about why he "beats on faggots," and "gets into a different pussy every night."

> John: ... If you want the truth I think a lot of it's about a guy being paranoid that his friends will think he's a faggot. So if you beat on faggots and get into a different pussy every night, no fucker in their right mind would ever think you were a queer. I've never had a faggot for a friend. The only faggots I've ever known are the ones we've pounded. Even when I was really young – like around 8 or 9 – I can remember beating guys me and my friends knew were faggots.

John clearly thought that by beating up gays and having sex with a different girl every night he was proving his heterosexuality. However, John's and Brian's cases are not representative of the complete sample. All participants did not equally embrace rigid ideological assumptions of family and gender. Twenty-two of these young men did not report participating in gay-bashing. It is useful to compare these two groups of youth with the goal of exploring the different processes through which these participants became abusers. Table 4.1 describes the main differences between the gay-bashers and the non-bashers.

	BASHERS (N = 8)	NON-BASHERS (N = 22)
Ethno-Racial Minorities	13% (1)	23% (5)
Gay/Bisexual/Questioning	38% (3)	9% (2)
Harmonious Family	0% (0)	27% (6)
Family Support to Abuse	63% (5)	36% (8)
Abuser Type	63% p/s/e	63% p/s/e
	25% p/e	22% p/e.
	13% s/e	14% s/e
	50% sev	36% sev
	25% f.i.	45% f.i.
Biological Father at Home	75% (6)	91% (20)
Living at Home	63% (5)	45% (10)
Gang Member	88% (7)	45% (10)
Abus. Male Peers and Support	88% (7)	82% (18)
ASPA/FPB	50% (4)	23% (5)

p = physical
s = sexual
e = emotional
sev. = severe
f.i. = forced
intercourse

As Table 4.1 indicates, there are some major differences between the gay-bashers and the non-bashers. None of the bashers reported coming from harmonious families. Bashers were over four times as likely than non-bashers to be gay, bisexual, or have serious questions about their sexual orientation. They were almost twice as likely to have received instructions from father-figures to abuse females and to be gang members; they were over two times as likely to both adhere to familial patriarchal beliefs and support the use of physical violence by boyfriends against girlfriends. One-half of the bashers and just over one-third of the non-bashers reported having engaged in severe violence against girlfriends, but the non-bashers were much more likely than the bashers to have engaged in forced intercourse with their girlfriends (45 per cent compared to 25 per cent). Finally, non-bashers were almost twice as likely to be ethno-racial minorities than bashers.

These differences point to a variation in the processes through which these young men learned their violent behaviour. The bashers engaged in more severe forms of physical violence due to their rigid familial and gender ideologies. Facilitated by support from social fathers and gang members to abuse females, they were more likely than the non-bashers to have adhered to some of the specific assumptions of these ideologies, including rigid gender roles, sexual objectification and homophobia, law and order, and "fucking and fighting." Albert Cohen's concept of reaction formation is applicable here.[6] One of the few ways in which the three non-heterosexual bashers had at their disposal to prove their masculinity was through the collective beating of gays. They also feared for their safety if their peers found out that they were not heterosexual. Would these young men have felt so compelled to prove their masculinity in such a public way if they believed they had viable economic futures?

Protest and Compensation: Constructing Manhood by Abusing Others

Twenty-eight of the participants compensated for, and protested against, their lack of economic future and sexual fears by engaging in a common set of behaviours with their girlfriends. They also were defending against their own insecurities.

The concept of abuse was based upon what the participants told me about their sexual experiences and methods of resolving conflict with their girlfriends. Their reported behaviour was classified into the categories of physical, sexual, and emotional abuse based upon the illegality of most of these behaviours and the definitions of abuse offered in the literature (see the Introduction). All 30 participants reported behaviour with their girlfriends that was emotionally abusive. None was exclusively emotionally abusive. Instead, 20 participants were emotionally, physically, and sexually abusive; four were emotionally and sexually abusive; and six were emotionally and physically abusive.

Twenty-six participants reported behaviour with girlfriends

which was physically abusive. These males had physically assaulted their girlfriends on at least one occasion since age 13. Of this number, 14 engaged in minor forms of physical abuse (throwing something at her, pushing, grabbing, shoving, slapping) and 12 used one or more acts of severe violence (punching, kicking, beating, choking, using a knife or a gun). In only one case was there only one act of minor violence. Instead, participants reported patterns of physical abuse that were ongoing and paired with other types of abuse.

Twenty-four participants reported behaviour with girlfriends which was sexually abusive. These males had sexually assaulted their girlfriends on at least one occasion since the age of 13. Twelve participants reported acts of unwanted sexual contact, and 12 reported acts of forced intercourse. In all cases the sexual abuse was paired with other types of abuse. All of the participants who reported acts of forced intercourse also reported having perpetrated many acts of forced sexual contact.

The patterns of abusive behaviour in my study expand upon those findings in the existing literature on woman abuse, which suggests that abusers tend to individually perpetrate one or two forms of abuse in a given assault, rarely exhibit all three forms of abusive behaviour in the same incident, rarely commit collective acts of abuse, and rarely assault other individuals as well as their female intimates.[7] Clearly, my findings do not support these ideas. Twenty of the 30 participants in my study engaged in all three forms of girlfriend abuse during many of the assaults they committed and engaged in collective and individual acts of abuse. As well, the majority of these young men reported having beaten gays, males they perceived to be woman abusers, and ethno-racial minorities.

In contrast to this categorization of abuse, none of the participants defined their behaviour as abusive. Their definition of abuse was limited to violent "rapes" and physical beatings by male strangers on females unrelated to them. They felt that their behaviour was normal. In addition, there are important intra-group differences in this small sample related to the severity of physical and sexual abuse. Comparisons between the groups of severe and minor physical abusers (Table 4.2) and between those sexual abusers who forced intercourse and those who forced sexual contact (Table 4.3) sheds some light on the different processes involved in the learning of abusive behaviour.

	SEVERE PHYSICAL ABUSERS (N = 12)	MINOR PHYSICAL ABUSERS (N = 14)	
Ethno-Racial Minorities	25% (3)	14% (2)	Table 4.2
Gay/Bisexual/Questioning	8% (1)	14% (2)	Severe and
Harmonious Family	8% (1)	29% (4)	Minor Physical
Family Support to Abuse	67% (8)	21% (3)	Abusers
Abuser Type	92% p/s/e	35% p/s/e	p = physical
	8% p/e	36% p/e.	s = sexual
	0% s/e	29% s/e	e = emotional
	50% f.i.	43% f.i.	f.i. = forced intercourse
			sev. = severe
Biological Father at Home	42% (5)	86% (12)	
Living at Home	50% (6)	43% (6)	
Gang Member	58% (7)	57% (8)	
Abus. Male Peers and Support	83% (10)	79% (11)	
ASPA/FPB	50% (6)	7% (1)	

	FORCED INTERCOURSE (N = 12)	FORCED SEXUAL CONTACT (N = 12)	
Ethno-Racial Minorities	25% (3)	17% (2)	Table 4.3
Gay/Bisexual/Questioning	17% (2)	17% (2)	Sexual Abusers
Harmonious Family	17% (2)	25% (3)	by Severity
Family Support to Abuse	50% (6)	42% (5)	
Abuser Type	92% p/s/e	75% p/s/e	
	8% s/e	25% s/e	
	50% sev.	50% sev.	
Biological Dad at Home	58% (7)	83% (10)	
Living at Home	58% (7)	42% (5)	
Gang Member	58% (7)	58% (7)	
Abus. Male Peers and Support	83% (10)	67% (8)	
ASPA/FPB	50% (6)	25% (3)	

Tables 4.2 and 4.3 suggest that the participants who reported exhibiting the most serious forms of physical and sexual abuse underwent different processes through which they learned their abusive behaviour. In the comparison of severe and minor physical abusers, there are two large differences: family type and support to abuse, and adherence to familial patriarchal beliefs and attitudes supporting physical girlfriend abuse. Severe physical abusers were over three times as likely as minor physical abusers to have received familial support to abuse girlfriends, over twice as likely to have grown up with social father(s), and were over three times less likely to have come from a harmonious family. These severe physical abusers were seven times more likely than the minor abusers to adhere to familial patriarchal beliefs and attitudes supporting physical girlfriend abuse. There were minimal differences related to ethno-racial origin, sexual orientation, abuser type, living arrangement, gang membership, and having abusive male peers and peers who provided support to abuse girlfriends.

In the comparison of sexual abusers by severity, there is only one area of large difference: adherence to both familial patriarchal beliefs and attitudes supporting physical girlfriend abuse. The group who reported having forced sexual intercourse was twice as likely as the group who reported having forced sexual contact to adhere to these beliefs and attitudes. Those who had forced intercourse were slightly more likely than the participants who had forced sexual contact to be ethno-racial minorities, to have experienced abuse in their families and received family support to abuse, to have grown up with social fathers, to be living at home, to have abusive male peers and peer support to abuse, and to have used minor physical violence. There were equal numbers of gay/bisexual/questioning youth and gang members in both groups of sexual abusers.

Given the fact that the two groups of physical abusers suggest more differentiation on the variable of abuse severity than the two groups of sexual abusers, it is useful to compare the 22 youth who used severe violence and/or forced intercourse (SV/FI) with the 8 youth who used minor violence and/or forced sexual contact (MV/FSC). Table 4.4 describes the differences between these two groups.

There are three large areas of difference here: abuser types, sexual orientation, and family types. The most striking difference is in

	SV/FI (N = 22)	MV/FSC (N = 8)	
Ethno Racial Minorities	18% (4)	24% (2)	Table 4.4 Use of Severe Violence and/or Forced Inter-
Gay/Bisexual/Questioning	9% (2)	38% (3)	course (SV/FI) Compared to
Harmonious Family	13% (3)	38% (3)	Use of Minor
Family Support to Abuse	41% (9)	38% (3)	Violence and/or Forced Sexual Contact
Abuser Type	82% p/s/e	24% p/s/e	(MV/FSC)
	13% p/e	38% p/e	p = physical
	5% s/e	38% s/e	s = sexual e = emotional
Biological Father at Home	68% (15)	88% (7)	f.i. = forced
Living at Home	45% (10)	50% (4)	intercourse
Gang Member	50% (11)	75% (6)	sev. = severe
Abus. Male Peers and Support	83% (18)	67% (5)	
ASPA/FPB	73% (16)	100% (8)	

abuser type, where SV/FI youth were over three times more likely to have used all three forms of abuse compared to the MV/FSC youth. Consequently, the MV/FSC youth were over seven times as likely to use sexual and emotional abuse, and almost three times as likely to use physical and emotional abuse. In addition, the MV/FSC participants were over four times as likely to be gay, bisexual, or questioning their sexual orientation. Finally, the MV/FSC youth were almost three times as likely than the SV/FI youth to come from a harmonious family.

Two unexpected findings here relate to gang membership and attitudes/beliefs. Although the differences are not large, the MV/FSC participants were more likely to be gang members and also more likely to adhere to familial patriarchal beliefs and have attitudes supporting physical girlfriend abuse. Finally, the SV/FI youth were slightly more likely than the MV/FSC youth to have received support from father-figures to abuse and to have abusive male peers and peer support to abuse. The MV/FSC youth were slightly more likely to be ethno-racial minorities, live with biological fathers, and live at home.

Overall, when Tables 4.2 to 4.4 are taken into consideration, the following observations can be made: the most variation in the processes related to learning abusive behaviour is associated with severe and minor physical abusers. Family type, gang membership, and familial patriarchal beliefs and attitudes help to explain the variation in these processes. With the sexual abusers, the largest variation regarding severity of abuse is related to familial patriarchal beliefs and attitudes. Abuse type, family type, and sexual orientation account for the variation in the processes when the most severe sexual abusers are compared to the least severe.

Dave, the 16-year-old Ojibway street youth, told me about how treating his girlfriend in an abusive way was a means of covering up his own insecurity. He "owned" his girlfriend's sexual body parts. He denied being abusive.

> Dave: Yeah. I would say I'm supposed to be superior. But you know this male superiority thing is a pretty hard thing to do if you're a fucking unemployed Indian on welfare. Am I superior? I don't think so. Am I gonna let her know it? I don't think so. So what do I do? I guess you could say it's like putting on hockey equipment. Then nobody can see how scared shitless you are. It's like I have the hockey pads I put on everyday before I see her and I never can let her see beneath my pads. She'd laugh at the real me. Scared shitless and feeling totally worthless. It's weird how treating a girl like that makes you feel better. It's the same as not ever being pussy-whipped. It's like it doesn't matter if you never speak to your girlfriend or think she's a fat pig. As long as no one fucks her when I'm going with her, that's what's important … My girlfriend's pussy is mine as long as we're together. Fuck, if I can't even have that I'm nothing of a man – zero. Like I said, I've got sweet fuck-all else.
>
> MT: What about her mouth?
>
> Dave: What?
>
> MT: Her mouth. You told me it's mostly blow jobs she gives you.
>
> Dave: Well, her mouth is her pussy. It's all the same. It's all fucking to me – wherever I stick my cock – whether it's

in her mouth or her cunt or up her ass. It doesn't matter. The main thing is that she doesn't fuck any other guy while we're going together (silence).

As has been argued previously, two planes of reality are evident in Dave's life. In his mundane, everyday existence, he was a "fucking unemployed Indian on welfare … scared shitless and totally worthless." He was acutely aware of the reality of his future, a future of homelessness, dependency, and racism. At the same time, he stated that as a male, he was "supposed to be superior" to females. He indicated that being an Ojibway without a job or material possessions made it difficult to assert his dominance over his girlfriend. He may have compensated for the absence of these traditional male entitlements by sexually, emotionally, and physically abusing his girlfriend. His use of the imagery of putting on hockey equipment when dominating his girlfriend was indicative of a second, ideal plane of reality in his life. In this ideal world, Dave was momentarily at the top of the power hierarchy. He felt confidently masculine and did not speak about his lack of access to material possessions or a job. On this plane of reality, his life was exciting and seductive. By using hockey images, Dave demonstrated that he had created this ideal plane. When he was forcing intercourse on his girlfriend, his feelings of inadequacy and worthlessness were transformed into feelings of power. Dave told me: "It's weird how treating a girl like that makes you feel better."

Like Dave, most of the participants used fairly homogeneous symbols in their accounts, indicating the existence of two different but interrelated value sets or planes of reality. They spoke of a mundane, everyday reality, characterized by boredom and an occupation with survival on the streets and the drudgery of daily life. They talked about feeling powerless, worthless, and humiliated. They related these feelings to being abused as children, a lack of access to material possessions and a job, and fears about their sexuality. In contrast, they also created symbols and images of an ideal plane of reality, characterized by a rigidly gendered power hierarchy, abuse of girlfriends and violence against gays and racial minorities. These males told me that they felt superior, righteously moral, confidently masculine, and in complete control at these times.

How can we make sense of the apparent existence of these two

planes of reality? Many participants engaged in behaviour characteristic of their ideal plane of reality as a way of protesting against and
compensating for the unattainable ideals and masculine anxieties
which defined their mundane, everyday reality. They were also
covering up their fears and insecurities. In so doing, they were
developing the familial and gender ideologies that they had acquired
early in their childhood.

Dave justified being abusive. How was it possible for him to neutralize the fact that his frequent oral and anal sexual abuse of his girlfriend may have caused her pain or suffering? He believed that he
owned his girlfriend, that any of her orifices in which he had
inserted his penis were his.

> MT: You said sticking your cock up her ass. Do you do that?
> Dave: (silence, looking at floor, shuffling feet) Yeah. I've done it
> (silence). Sometimes I'll get her to blow me after we've
> ass-fucked (silence). Sometimes I like that ... Yeah. If
> she's gonna get me to ass-fuck her, it's the least she can
> do, blow me clean. It's her shit so she can blow me clean.
> So I know she wants it up the ass or we wouldn't do it.
> But eating her own shit? I dunno. But she's responsible
> for it. There's no way I'm gonna get her shit on my dick
> and stop there. It works both ways this equal rights shit. I
> do something for her and she's gotta do something for
> me. So yeah. I like it. It makes me feel good.

Dave reported that his girlfriend enjoyed anal intercourse and
that "If she's gonna get me to ass-fuck her, it's the least she can do,
blow me clean ... So I know she wants it up the ass or we wouldn't
do it ..." This activity is significant for the way in which Dave constructed his social world. It is possible that Dave's girlfriend con-
sented to anal and oral sex and found these acts to be sexually stimulating; however, there is no way to prove this. Dave, along with
almost all the other male youth, sexually objectified his girlfriend.
This supports previous findings in the literature on marginal male
youth's sexual objectification of women.[8] Dave justified his actions
as moral and righteous, seen through the rigid familial and gender
lens through which he viewed the world. Clearly, for him, it was his
girlfriend's duty to perform fellatio on him after anal sex. He was

able to deny any wrongdoing on his part by placing the blame on his girlfriend for her excrement on his penis. Analyzed from within his viewpoint, his behaviour makes sense.

Dave's attitudes and beliefs are representative of those held by many of the other participants. Their accounts suggest that these beliefs, in interaction with their masculine identities, had to be constantly reinforced and confirmed. Their beliefs and identities were not firm, but were instead malleable.

A central inconsistency in the accounts of all the participants lies in the fact that they told me that they were not abusive, despite describing to me behaviour that can be categorized only as abusive. Further, the majority told me that they protected defenceless women in their community by hunting down suspected violent "rapists" and woman-beaters. The next chapter explores the circumstances under which these similar situations were defined as being so very different.

Some researchers have suggested that juvenile delinquents employ techniques of neutralization which allow them to carry on with their lives while engaging in deviant behaviour.[9] This concept is helpful and is supported by much of the data from this study. Seen through their familial and gender ideologies, these males did not identify their behaviour as being wrong. Instead, they portrayed their values and actions to be morally right and superior to those societal values in their mundane, everyday reality. Their accounts are characterized by the use of a vocabulary of adjustment, in which their socially unacceptable behaviour was denied through the sophisticated use of justifications, the denial of wrongdoing.[10] Denial characterizes the accounts of all but one of the participants in this study; these 29 young men reported their behaviour as non-abusive and justifiable for two reasons:

1. Any injury suffered or pain inflicted on their girlfriends was denied. They were able to neutralize any suffering caused by their beatings, forced sexual intercourse, and threats of violence.

2. The failure of their girlfriends to fulfil the obligations of what many participants referred to as the "good bitch." These males symbolized their behaviour as righteous and in defence of a

higher moral order. They described their girlfriends as failing to abide by the rules of this idealized, abstract plane of reality.[11]

Therefore, the participants did not make excuses to deny responsibility for their actions. This contrasts with the existing clinical literature on abuse. For example, in Ptacek's sample of abusive adult men enrolled in a group treatment program, the majority of participants reported their behaviour as abusive but excused it (denied responsibility) because they lost control (due to substance abuse, frustration/aggression, psychiatric problems) or were physically or verbally provoked by their wives. Although a small minority of participants in my sample used similar excuses, they strongly denied any wrongdoing on their part.

Paul, the gay 17-year-old with the "negative" masculine identity, was the only participant who did not use a vocabulary of adjustment in his account. He did not use justifications to deny that he had been sexually and emotionally abusive with an ex-girlfriend. Instead, he admitted that he had behaved in this way to gain approval from his peers (he was not "out" about his sexual orientation at this point in time). Neither did he make excuses to deny responsibility. Instead, he demonstrated a remarkable degree of insight into his actions, linking them to his father's abusiveness and to peer pressure. He accepted full responsibility for his abusiveness, saying that his sexual orientation was in large part a conscious decision to escape from the traditional male identity. He associated his father with the stereotypical patriarchal-authoritarian male, who uses violence to reassert his power and control over his family.

It is interesting that Sylvain, the other "negative" masculine type, also spoke about escaping his father's abusiveness through questioning his sexual orientation. However, Sylvain physically, sexually, and emotionally abused his girlfriend. Interestingly, he did not relate his actions as in any way comparable to his father's beatings. Although he denied that he was gay, he associated his sexual orientation with being very different than the identity of his own father, thereby allowing him to report his behaviour as non-abusive and justifiable.

This next account provides more striking images, illustrating the participants' two planes of reality. Marty, a 16-year-old ex-racist skinhead, told me about the "power high ... a feeling of being king shit" he used to get when beating up racial minorities and gays. His description of the dress and behavioural codes of his gang and how his feelings of being "scared shitless ... a loser" were transformed into a "power high" when perpetrating violence confirm previous research findings in this area.[12]

Marty: At the time, it was a high. A power high. It was a feeling of being king shit – no one could touch you. It was like niggers were to blame for everything and we made them pay for everything. They were the reason we had no money, no jobs, no decent place to live. Being a part of the gang [white supremacist] gave us a sense of belonging. We felt like we were accepted and someone cared for us. They told us we had an important job to do. We felt really important – because we were white – because we were guys. I mean skins don't exactly respect females either. At lot of them pounded on their girlfriends too. It wasn't just blacks. And gays as well. People think skins just hate blacks. It's not true. They hate gays, women – you name it. I think I was part of it because it made me feel good as a guy – respected. I had status. It was like I was a member of some very important club – doing really important work. Kicking the living shit out of anything that wasn't like me. It gave me an image – as a guy I mean. With the docs [Doc Martens, a style of boot], a shaved head, the bomber jacket, the white laces – people automatically know you're part of the gang. They're scared of you even though they know nothing about you. It's sad, really. Most of the guys into it were losers – stupid, no money, no place to stay, addicts. It's like we didn't want anyone to see that side of us – a guy who really has no balls pretending he's got the biggest prick in the world. It's all about fear and status. I was scared shitless inside – I felt like shit, a loser. But as soon as people knew I was a skin, that all changed. I had power. Respect. People were scared of me and didn't know all the shitty stuff inside of me that I was hiding.

Steve, the 15-year-old Lebanese youth in grade 9, said that his behaviour was caused by girls who pissed him off, made him look stupid, and didn't know their place in society. Girls all "liked" to be hit, but he was not abusive. It is likely that the process through which Steve became abusive was much different than the majority of the other youth in the sample. As mentioned previously (p. 75), Steve contextualized his patriarchal-authoritarian views in his religion and his male peer group. He spent much of his time at home with other male family members (for the most part in religious activities), from which female family members were excluded. He was one of the few participants who reported that male family members other than father-figures consistently instructed him to abuse girls. It may be that there was something in the dynamic of these same-sex religious activities, in combination with his abusive peer group, which elevated the risk for Steve to abuse.

> Steve: One time at school I slammed her against a locker. I choked her until she was red. She was making me look stupid with lies and shit. I got sent to the pickle room. I was talked to by the psychiatrist. I almost got suspended. The principal is an ass-hole. Last year I shoved a girl into a snow bank. There was a big block of ice in it. I rammed her in. I wanted to hurt her … Yeah. I've got nothing to hide. Who'd believed it? Locked in a fucking pickle room for just giving my ex what she wanted. I told you that she's weird. She always was wanting me to hit her. It was nothin'. I never even laid a hand on her (long silence).
>
> MT: You told me before that you choked her until she was red against a locker.
>
> Steve: Yeah. But I never hurt her. She turns red when she knows she's wrong – kind of like being embarrassed. (Blushing) I wouldn'ta done anything if she hadn't made me look so stupid. What she said was all lies. She made me look like a goof in front of my friends. If she would'a only listened to me, I never would'a gotten in shit. It was all her fuckin' fault.
>
> MT: So do you like girls?
>
> Steve: No, not really … I think most of them are stupid bitches. I'll call them bitch, slut, whore all the time. They're always trying to show me up – make me look stupid, like

a goof. What am I supposed to do – sit there and look stupid? No, I can't do that …

Steve's account is riddled with inconsistencies. At one moment, he said that he choked his ex-girlfriend "until she was red" and talked about how his school dealt with the matter. A few seconds later, he claimed that his ex-girlfriend wanted him to do it and that in fact he "never even laid a hand on her." Under what circumstances could Steve present his violence to be non-abusive? His account was characterized by the use of a vocabulary of adjustment, in which he denied his socially unacceptable behaviours through a complex use of justifications. He knew the assault on his ex-girlfriend was socially unacceptable because he got caught by the school administration. However, he denied the wrongdoing of the attack by justifying his actions. He told me that she "was making me look stupid with lies and shit" and wouldn't listen to him, and that "the principal is an ass-hole." He denied that his ex-girlfriend suffered any injuries as a result of the choking, attributing the redness of her face to having been embarrassed. The inconsistencies and complex usage of justifications in the accounts of all participants suggest that these youth did indeed have some insight into their behaviour. These young men put on an act for themselves and their peers to cover up their insecurities.

As Steve's account continued, it was clear that he, like Dave, created a second, ideal plane of reality, in which he didn't have to face girls who were "always trying to show me up – make me look stupid, like a goof." In this alternate plane, Steve told me that everybody knew their place, and he felt respected as a guy

Steve: It's all about knowing your place in society. Some girls do, but most girls don't know what they're supposed to do. It really pisses me off when I see a girl who pretends that she doesn't have to be in her place. I feel like I have to teach her a lesson. How the fuck are girls ever gonna know that their job is to take care of shit at home – cooking, cleaning, the kids – if we don't tell them? I mean, it's me who's supposed to be making the big bucks to support my family. Where the fuck do girls get off thinking that they can do it too?… I've never agreed with hitting a girl and I never will. I think I treat girls really well. In fact, I think I'm doing them a favour. They're gonna find out sooner or later that they can't fuck around with a guy.... I mean, can you imagine if guys didn't do that – I mean, making sure that women do what they're supposed to be doing instead of fucking around? What a fucked-up world it would be. No, guys need to remind girls that they should be doing what they're supposed to be doing. I mean, all this equal rights bullshit! Women have all the equality they need. The bottom line is that men are more important – we do the necessary things – working, bringing the bacon home, protecting our families – and if a woman's not going to respect that, then fuck her. A guy's gotta take that responsibility and tell 'er not to fuck around.

MT: So how does it make you feel, when you're treating a girl like that?

Steve: It's the only way. So I feel good. It feels right. It's like I've got my place in the world, and I know women do too. I guess you could say that it makes me feel respected as a guy.

Steve considered it to be a direct affront to his own masculinity that girls did not keep within their traditional gender role. He told me that these actions made him "less of a man." This is another example of how the participants' ideological assumptions about family and gender were inextricably intertwined. Parallel to what Katz has argued, Steve was describing a moral, righteous plane of reality. Unlike Katz's thesis, however, the foundation of Steve's superior moral plane was gender: "the bottom line is that men are more important." Steve, like many of the others, symbolized his abusive behaviour as righteous and in defence of this higher moral order. In his mundane, everyday reality, girls "don't know their place"; they had too many rights. Masculine identity was directly challenged because the position of men as material providers was threatened.

Earlier, Steve had mentioned that his father had never worked. Instead, as Steve bitterly recounted, he had to depend upon his wife's welfare cheque and under-the-table babysitting earnings. In Steve's ideal plane of reality, his anxieties about not being a material provider were compensated for. Girls were taught by boys "that their job is to take care of the shit at home," so that Steve could be "making the big bucks to support my family." Girlfriend abuse was therefore justified. In Steve's ideal plane of reality, all of his masculine fears and anxieties dissipated. He told me that in this rigid gender order, "I feel good. It feels right. I guess you could say that it makes me feel respected as a guy."

Like Steve, almost all the other participants shared a common set of symbols, ideals, and values when telling me about the role of males and females in society. When discussing their mundane, everyday reality, these males made frequent reference to the rights of females, the power women now hold, and the need to put them back in their place. In contrast, when they spoke of their ideal plane of reality, girlfriends were required to be obedient, respectful, loyal, dependent, accessible sexually at all times, and faithful. In this brutally abusive, patriarchal gender hierarchy their girlfriends were "taught" the rules of this superior set of moral values, and they were disciplined for stepping outside of this righteous code of conduct. The other participants, like Steve, did not present their behaviour with their girlfriends as abusive. Instead, they justified their actions because of the failure of their girlfriends to fulfil the obligations of what the participants referred to as the "good bitch."

This final account highlights the ways in which 28 of the participants compensated for, protested against, and covered up their perceived masculine deficits. Peter, a 16-year-old street youth, told me that he liked to be in control sexually. I asked him how that made him feel

Peter: So it's like I control the sex – the fucking – and it makes the other stuff seem better. I mean, there's nothin' I can do about not being able to pay her back physically – hitting her. I won't even try.[13] So it's like I've gotta prove it sexually – I mean, that I'm good – that I can fuck with the best of them ...

MT: So when you're fucking a girl really hard – rough, you called it – what's going through your head – what are you thinking?

Peter: It's like being high. It's a total rush. Not just getting your rocks off. It's more than that. It's like you're in control;

you're on top of the world. No one can fuck with you.

MT: Do you think you'll ever be a doctor?[14]

Peter: (Silence) No.

MT: Will you ever have lots of cash?

Peter: Probably not.

MT: A house, car?

Peter: (Shaking his head, beginning to cry) I guess it's not in the books for me. Who am I fooling? Maybe deep down I do think about that. It's like I'm being weighed on the scale. I mean, how I think of me as a guy. I know I won't have that shit you just asked me about, so what do I have? It's like I have to exaggerate the stuff I have – so I can live with myself as a guy, I mean. Being a guy isn't all it's made out to be … I don't trust no one and I know there's nobody who really cares about me. I guess I'm pretty lonely and scared shitless about who I am – what other people think of me as a guy (crying).

Robert W. Connell suggests that there are at least three distinct forms of masculinity evident in male youth on the margins of the labour market.[15] Some males practise individual and collective behaviours along a path out of traditional masculine identity. Transvestites, gays, and bisexuals typify those males practising a "negative" or "transformist" masculinity. Although there were five youth in this study who were not heterosexual (1 gay, 1 bisexual, and 3 youth who were questioning their sexual orientation), only two of these youth could be categorized as having "negative/transformist" masculinities: Paul (who was gay) and Sylvain (who was questioning his sexual orientation).

Both Paul and Sylvain told me that they had chosen a sexual orientation different than that of their fathers' in order to distance themselves from these abusive caregivers. There were large differences between these two young men and the other 28 youth in this study. Neither Paul nor Sylvain reported adhering to familial patriarchal beliefs or had attitudes supporting physical girlfriend abuse. Neither had engaged in severe violence or forced sexual intercourse with girlfriends. Neither belonged to gangs, and both were working part-time during the study. Both grew up with fathers they considered to be "natural" (Paul was adopted during his infancy; Sylvain was raised by his biological parents), and neither were living at home at the time of the study. Both despised their fathers because of their abusive behaviour, and neither fought back against their fathers' beatings. Both were told by their fathers to never hit women. Both defined the "ideal man" as someone who was not abusive, independent, and someone who did not need lots of money and material possessions to gain status. However, Sylvain also reported that he would always need to be tough and physically protect himself. He was one of the eight participants who reported having bashed gays.

Connell defines the second form of masculinity of marginal males as "complicit": those males who participate in the subordination of females and gays without resorting to physical and sexual violence. Although all of the youth in the in-depth interviews were emotional abusers, none of their masculinities were categorized as "complicit" due to their usage of physical and/or sexual violence to dominate those they perceived to be less powerful. Finally, of the three forms of masculinity identified by Connell, his concept of "protest" masculinity is most closely associated with the behaviour of 28 participants. These youth played out their marginalization in a hypermasculine fashion. Reacting to their economic powerlessness, they acted out the traditional, aggressive male role, enforcing the social relations of patriarchy in a violent way. They presented a public, objective display of masculine power over gays, females, and other males. The participants were both protesting against the unattainable imperatives of the masculine ideal and using the only means that they had to defend themselves. Abusive and violent behaviour compensated for whatever could not be realized. The male attributes of toughness, competitiveness, and dominance were pursued to varying degrees in their lives.

Abandoning Natural Families for Peer Groups/Gangs

Twenty-four of the 30 participants reported incidents throughout their childhood in which they experienced beatings and severe emotional abuse by father-figures. They also reported incidents throughout their childhood in which they witnessed beatings and severe emotional abuse of their mothers by father-figures. Of this same group, 14 told me that their caregiver(s) used substances (drugs and/or alcohol) and /or engaged in criminal activities on most days. These 24 participants reported having minimal contact with their families of origin; only six participants, all of whom were living at home at the time of the interview, told me that they had conflict-free, harmonious relationships with their families.[16] As discussed in the previous chapter, there are large differences between this group who reported coming from harmonious families, and the remaining group who reported experiencing father-perpetrated abuse at home.

Accordingly, the family of origin did not exist as a viable place for them. It is not surprising, therefore, that these youth had little or no contact with their families. Seventeen of these participants told me that they belonged to gangs, and the remaining 13 reported belonging to male peer groups. All participants told me that they spent at least 4-5 hours each day with their male peer groups/gangs. The 17 gang members named 11 different gangs to which they belonged.[17] They said that the activities of their gangs were focused upon collective violence with varying degrees of criminal motivation. Using Mathews' continuum, the key defining feature distinguishing gangs from groups was the participants' involvement in serious criminal activity.[18] The gangs had varying degrees of organization for criminal objectives.

Only two of these gangs can be classified as "hard core criminal" using Mathews's definition. One of these was the Skinheads. Around the time of the study in Ottawa-Carleton, the Skinheads demonstrated a high degree of organization for criminal objectives, including aggravated and common assaults on racial minorities, sexual minorities, and women. The participants who told me that they were Skinheads also reported frequently engaging in other criminal activities, including auto theft, robbery, break and enter, drug-dealing, and pimping. The second hard core gang in which some participants reported membership also had a similarly high crime profile in this area at the time of the study. Members of this gang told me that they frequently engaged in collective crimes including aggravated and common assaults, pimping, gun trafficking, auto theft, robbery, and break and enter. Although all of the 13 participants who belonged to male peer groups engaged in collective violence, criminal activity was not their motive.

Twenty-four participants spoke of their groups/gangs as refuges from their abusive and chaotic childhood. For these youth, their peer groups/gangs had replaced their natural families. With no familial reference point from which to gain acceptance and a sense of belonging, the importance of the peer group escalated for these youth. In order to survive, they gained acceptance into gangs where criminal activity for material gain was commonplace. When talking about their gangs, most of these participants used distorted images of happy nuclear families: these groups/gangs provided them with feelings of acceptance, status, and identity. Their language of family did not fit the violent street behaviour of their fellow gang members. Therefore, contrary to DeKeseredy and Schwartz's assumption, the peer groups/gangs of the research participants were much more than resource pools that encouraged and legitimized girlfriend abuse.[19] They were described by these youth as the families they never had.

In addition, two of the youth who reported coming from harmonious families also said that they were gang members. These two young men spoke of their gangs in a similar fashion as did the 24 who experienced abuse at home, except that they did not define any conflicts at home as abusive. Instead, they told me that they simply did not spend much time with their families because they didn't "get along." One of these participants was living at home at the time of this study.

The intersection of familial and gender ideologies was again evident in the participants' description of their peer groups/gangs, which were an important site of ideological influence for them. All of the specific assumptions of familial and gender ideologies were evident in these groups/gangs: the sexual division of labour is "natural," rigid gender roles, sexual objectification and homophobia, "law and order," and "fucking and fighting." These assumptions (as they relate to groups/gangs) will be discussed in detail in the next chapter.

The following brief accounts demonstrate how the participants reported their groups/gangs to have replaced their natural families:

> Carl: Lots of assaults, B and E's, auto theft and shit. And tons of
> drugs. Hash, all the chemicals. We're always high. And
> sometimes we just hang out. What the fuck do you
> want? It's my family. I got nothin' else. It's like I'm
> divorced from those fuckers who said they were my par-
> ents. Now I've got no parents and lots of brothers. It's

great. No ass-hole parents to beat you all the time. So yeah. Gang is family ...

John: What home? I've got nothin'. The old gang was my home. I'm looking for a new one now. I think the new gang will be it ... Yeah. I've got no other family. I mean I do but they're not my family. Too much violence and shit. Too heavy for me. It's a lot better this way. No one to tell you what the fuck to do.

Paul: Well, I see my Mom occasionally. No one else. They all fucked me too bad. I mean, a guy can only get hurt so much and then he moves on.... You could say I've been adopted by a bunch of queens (laughing) ...

Carl, John, and Paul grew up watching their mothers being beaten and emotionally degraded. Likewise, they themselves had been subjected to routine beatings and emotional degradation during their childhood. At the time of the interviews, Carl and John told me that they spent 5-6 hours most days with their gangs. Based upon Mathews's continuum, I classified their gangs as hard-core criminal. Paul told me that he spent most of his time with a group of drag-queens (this was not a gang).

Like the other participants, these three youth indicated that their groups/gangs were their home, their family. Their use of distorted images of happy families when describing the brutal violence of their groups/gangs is striking. That is, they articulated their own victimization by child abuse, but appeared to be able to neutralize their own engagement in collective group/gang violence. None of these youth verbalized an awareness of this apparent inconsistency. Instead, they talked about having an identity, a sense of belonging, and a feeling of acceptance in their groups/gangs.

Conclusion

Up to the point when I began questioning the participants about their economic futures, 28 of these 30 youth told me that they were just like the "ideal man," using a common set of masculine ideals and similar imagery. They were like this ideal man, they told me, with the exception of not having material possessions and a job. They spoke about the bare minimum set of qualities in their identities which characterized their masculinity: powerful, sexual, fighting machines; "King Shit" in a hierarchy of the powerless – a hierarchy made up of girls, gays, and racial minorities. One-third of these youth, however, were members of two of these same oppressed groups (ten youth were gay/bisexual/questioning their sexual orientation and/or ethno-racial minorities) that they reported abusing. When initially speaking about their masculine identities, therefore, none of the participants talked about personal feelings of inadequacy or failure regarding the difficulties they faced in acquiring material wealth and good jobs.

How can we explain such similar self-reports of masculine identities? It is helpful to revisit the common early childhood experiences of the participants. The fact that the majority of the participants came from families where father-figures were not working or never had worked may have been related to their definition of masculine ideals and identities. It is striking that despite not mentioning unemployment this issue dominated their accounts. However, when I began probing around the issue of their lack of economic future, one-half of the participants broke down and cried. It was as if I had opened an emotional floodgate. I questioned nine of these participants regarding any past suicide attempts and present plans to kill themselves because of their apparent hopelessness and despair regarding this issue.

The participants made use of a common set of symbols when talking with me about their future expectations. Twenty-eight clearly stated that due to their lack of economic opportunity, their future would be defined by economic powerlessness in the traditional sense: no job or a "shit job"; little money, forcing a dependence on welfare or crime; and few material possessions. Usually in the same breath, they told me "but I still will have my balls and my fists." Interestingly, these young men associated "fucking and fighting" with being a "breadwinner." This association is indicative of the juxtaposition of the ideological assumptions about family and gender for most of the young men in this study: all but two of the participants indicated that superior female status posed a direct threat to their own masculinity. They told me about how inferior it made them feel when females did not stay within their traditional gender roles. These young men said that the more power females got, the "less of a man" they felt. Many of these youth spoke about the necessity to fight against the women's rights movement, and to put females "back in their place."

Clearly, therefore, almost all participants recognized their lack of an economic future. This finding – that these participants expressed feelings of powerlessness, despair and humiliation regarding their economic futures – expands upon existing work in this area,[20] which is largely focused on an adult population. As the sample in my study ranged in age from 13-17 years, it suggests that the realities of a life based upon no future can be verbalized at an early age by marginal male youth.

Around the same time that we discussed future aspirations, most of the participants told me about their anxieties and fears surrounding their sexuality. Twenty-nine of the participants spoke about their need to have frequent sexual intercourse to prove that they were heterosexual, and employed defensive posturing when I questioned them about their sexual orientation. Eight of these youth told me that they regularly beat up gays to protect themselves from being raped and to demonstrate that they themselves were not gay. Yet, three of these youth who reported beating up sexual minorities were themselves either bisexual, or had serious questions about their sexual orientation. Further, four of the youth who said that they needed to prove that they were heterosexual were either bisexual or were questioning their sexual orientation.

These findings verify and expand upon the existing literature in this area. The fact that a significant number of heterosexual marginal males perpetrate violence against gays has been previously documented, as well as the finding that these youth report frequent sexual activity to be an important component of proving masculinity.[21] However, the finding that bisexual male youth and male youth who are questioning their sexual orientation also engage in gay bashing, and consider heterosexual intercourse to be fundamental activities for proving manhood, is new. These issues suggest that these young men were confused and struggling to make sense of the fear and pain in their lives.

Almost all of the participants described indicators of being socialized into a role of dominance, aggression, and power. However, most knew that they would likely be unable to wield this power outside of peer and family relationships. They knew that their access to the institutional benefits of patriarchy – a house, a car, a good job – had been blocked. Because they realized that they had only minimal access to the traditional resources associated with male dominance and authority, it is apparent that they had only a limited variety of resources at hand to practise their gender.

How did the participants make sense of their situations? The lives of almost all of these young men were characterized by varying degrees of adherence to the traditional male attributes of toughness, competitiveness, and dominance. Building upon the arguments of other researchers in this area, the abuse of girlfriends and other persons perceived to be weaker by these participants compensated for and masked the perceived threat to their masculine identities.[22] The construction of masculinity was an ongoing process for these marginal male youth, and the practice of girlfriend abuse and the abuse of other individuals was an aspect of their identity construction, expression, and reaffirmation. Abusive behaviour was one of the few resources over which the participants had control.

Masculine identity was interwoven with and a product of the familial and gender ideologies of the participants. This common type of masculinity was the product of similar familial and gender beliefs, which were developed in early childhood. Defining their world from this viewpoint, they did not present their abusive behaviour as incongruous. They were engaging in behaviour that in most contexts would be defined as criminal, yet they indicated that their actions were moral and righteous. They were acting according to their values and those of their peers and families. These youth learned how to protect their own self-image and overcome challenges to their masculine identities by picking on the less powerful. Many of the narratives are characterized by a theme of constantly having to defend oneself. The way in which they defined their masculine identities suggests a constant need for reinforcement and self-affirmation. This explains in part the persistence of their abusive behaviour.

However, the in-depth interview sample was by no means homogeneous. One-third of these young men told me that they beat up racial and sexual minorities, despite being minorities themselves. They did not verbalize any inconsistency in these actions. They likely developed their racist, sexist, and homophobic attitudes and beliefs through a different process than did the 20 heterosexual, white participants. These youth did not all embrace the same concept of masculinity. One gay and one bisexual youth demonstrated "negative" masculine types, whereas the remainder of the sample exhibited behaviour characteristic of a "protest" masculine type. The accounts of these young men suggest that their masculine identities were the outcome of at least two complex processes: a) a more passive gender role socialization and b) active negotiation and resistance.

Other intra-group differences included family type (biological versus social fathers; harmonious versus abusive families; instructions from fathers to abuse or not to abuse females); living arrangement (at home versus away from home); male peers (gangs versus groups); having or not having male peers who are abusive and/or provide encouragement to abuse females; abuser type (severe versus minor violence; forced sexual contact versus forced intercourse; usage of emotional and physical and/or sexual forms of abuse); victims of abusive behaviour (girlfriends, sexual minorities, ethno-racial minorities, heterosexual white males, perceived stranger-"rapists" and woman beaters); and adherence to familial patriarchal beliefs and attitudes supporting physical girlfriend abuse.

These differences account for variations in the extent to which they embraced familial and gender ideologies. In turn, this differential adherence is helpful in explaining the variation in the extent of abuse inflicted on girlfriends, sexual minorities, and ethno-racial minorities. The participants' development of these patriarchal ideas about family and gender was not identical; some did not report adhering to any of these beliefs and attitudes, and others developed these assumptions through different processes.

These data suggest that the linkage between poverty and abuse needs qualification by focussing on familial and gender ideologies. Males who rigidly adhere to a patriarchal-authoritarian model of family and gender (as indicated by gay-bashing, and adherence to familial patriarchal beliefs and attitudes supporting physical girl-friend abuse) may be the most likely to use physical and sexual violence to keep females in line and to use physical violence on ethno-racial and sexual minorities. It has been demonstrated in this chapter that these males are most likely to use the most severe types of violence and to use all three forms of abuse against their girl-friends (physical, sexual, and emotional). Those young men who adhered most rigidly to patriarchal-authoritarian beliefs about family and gender were also most likely to have received instructions from father-figures to abuse, have grown up with social fathers, and to have experienced abuse at home. This argument is further supported by data suggesting that sexual minorities in the sample, although more likely to be gay-bashers, were most likely to use less severe physical and sexual abuse against girlfriends (minor violence and forced sexual contact) compared to the heterosexual young men in the study.

In the next chapter, I will argue that the participants' male peer groups/gangs were an important site of ideological influence. These groups/gangs provided the participants with acceptance and identity, yet also threatened masculine identity. These sites provided an opportunity for the entrenchment of abusive behaviour and the development of familial and gender ideologies. A rigid definition of masculinity in almost all participants resulted in significant harm to girlfriends, racial and sexual minorities, and to themselves.

Notes

1. Sennett and Cobb, 1972; Rubin, 1976, 1983; Matza, 1964.
2. Sennett and Cobb, 1972.
3. Willis, 1977; Campbell, 1984; Schwendinger and Schwendinger, 1985; Fishman, 1988.
4. Messerschmidt, 1997.
5. See Katz, 1988.
6. Cohen, 1955.
7. For example, see DeKeseredy and Hinch, 1991; Johnson, 1996; and DeKeseredy, 1998.
8. Willis, 1977; Campbell, 1984; Schwendinger and Schwendinger, 1985; Fishman, 1988; Messerschmidt, 1986, 1993.
9. Sykes and Matza, 1957; and Matza, 1964.
10. Kanin, 1967; Ptacek, 1988.

11. I do not want to leave the reader with the impression that the girlfriends of the participants were all passive victims. Undoubtedly, some females are abusive, and some of these girlfriends probably engaged in abusive behaviour with the participants as well. See Totten (1999) for an overview of the issue of young women's use of violence.

12. Katz, 1988.

13. There was a conflict in Peter's statement here. He later told me that he did hit his girlfriend.

14. I asked Peter this question at this point in time because I had not yet probed his future aspirations, and I was worried that he might have ended the interview without discussing this issue.

15. Connell, 1991. See Chapter 2 for further discussion on this.

16. Of these six participants who reported having harmonious families, one displayed obvious discomfort when I asked him about issues pertaining to wife assault and child abuse. Nevertheless, he denied that there was abuse in his home.

17. With the exception of the well-known hard-core criminal gangs (for example, Skinheads), actual gang names are not presented here to protect participants' anonymity.

18. Mathews, 1993.

19. DeKeseredy and Schwartz, 1991, 1998.

20. See Sennet and Cobb, 1972; Rubin, 1983; and Connell, 1991.

21. Beirne and Messerschmidt, 1995; Comstock, 1991; Weissman, 1992; Harry, 1992.

22. Rubin, 1976; Klein, 1982; Messerschmidt, 1986, 1993; and Connell, 1991.

five

In the Gang:
Consolidating Familial and Gender Ideologies

THE interview participants who most rigidly adhered to a patriarchal-authoritarian model of family and gender were most likely to commit the most severe harm to girlfriends, racial and sexual minorities (gay and bisexual youth, and youth questioning their sexual orientation), and to themselves. Many of them were involved in group/gang activities, which had an impact on girlfriend abuse. In this chapter, we will look at the socialization into the group/gang, including familial patriarchal values and support for abusive behaviour, then explore the common ways in which many of the participants engaged in group/gang assaults on females and on males they referred to as "rapists" and woman beaters. Differences among the sample of 30 youth in these areas highlight important intra-group variations that help us understand how these youth varied in the extent to which they embraced familial and gender ideologies and the forms and severity of their abusive behaviour.

These male peer groups/gangs provided a significant space for the expression and development of their members' familial patriarchal beliefs, masculine values, and related behaviour. They provided acceptance and belonging, yet at the same time they threatened the masculine identity of their individual members.

Socialization into the Group/Gang: Development and Expression of Familial and Gender Ideologies

1. Routine Activities

All participants were asked if and how much time they spent each week with male friends. They were also asked to describe the three things they did with their male friends that took up most of this time spent together. Most replied that they spent 4-5 hours most days with their male friends. Only four of the 30 participants reported having regular contact with family members, despite the fact that 15 of them lived at home.

The most frequent activities reported by the participants were drug and alcohol use (23 cases); criminal activities, such as auto theft, drug dealing, weapons offences, aggravated assaults (23 cases); hanging out at malls, pool halls, on the street (22 cases); and sports (11 cases). Twenty-one participants reported that they engaged in three or more of these activities, and all 30 told me that they engaged in at least one of these routine activities.

The following three brief accounts are representative.

> Brad: I'm with the gang all the time – for at least a couple of days a week ... Lots of partying. I drink probably five days a week. About seven beers a day. And we're the [hard-core criminal gang]: auto theft, assaults, rolling, swarming. Lots of that.

> Brian: When I'm on the streets there's anywhere from 10-15 of us (guys) ...
> MT: And how often are you with them for?
> Brian: Every day, all week ... criminal shit. We drive stolen cars to the States and sell them. And lots of partying. Drinking and chemicals. I started when I was nine. And I'm a Skin. So we're into violence a lot. And we hang out at arcades and malls.

> Phil: I'm with them (guys) every day for six or seven hours.
> MT: So what do you usually do with them?
> Phil: Drinking at bars. Working on cars. And picking up girls and dealing. Criminal shit. We drive around. There's five

or six of us picking up girls and screwing them ...
They're (male friends) all 18, 19, 20. Some of them are
pimps. But I'm not.

These findings correspond with the literature on the routine activities of working-class and marginal male youth.[1] Brad, Brian, and Phil spent a significant portion of their waking hours with their gangs, where activities were characterized by substance abuse, crime, violence, and boredom (hanging out). With few resources, they found excitement and adventure in violent crime, simultaneously finding an outlet to express their anger and rage.[2] Many of the participants created their own excitement and thrills through crime, violence, and substance abuse to contrast the boring, daily drudgery of hanging out.

As described previously, two different but interrelated planes of reality typify the lives of many of the participants. One is the mundane, everyday reality characterized by boredom, a preoccupation with survival on the streets, and the drudgery of daily life. In this mode, the participants talked about feeling powerless, worthless, and humiliated. They related these feelings to having been abused as children, a lack of access to material possessions and a job, and fears about their sexuality. In contrast, the symbols and images of an ideal plane of reality – characterized by a rigidly gendered power hierarchy, abuse against girlfriends, and violence against gays and ethno-racial minorities – allowed these youth to feel superior, righteously moral, confidently masculine, and in complete control.

2. Beliefs Supporting Abusive Behaviour

Twenty-four participants told me that their friends would agree with slapping their girlfriend in at least one of the following situations:

1. she won't do what he tells her.

2. she insults him when they are alone.

3. she insults him in public.

4. she gets drunk during an evening out together.

5. she is sobbing hysterically.

6. she won't have sex with him.

7. he learns that she is dating another man.

The most commonly identified situations were "she won't do what he tells her," "she insults him when they are alone," and "he learns that she is dating another man." All 24 youth said that their friends would slap their girlfriends if they were unfaithful. In Chapter 3 we saw that 11 of the 30 participants personally agreed with at least one of these same attitudes supporting girlfriend abuse.

My data expand upon the work of others in this area. These researchers hypothesize that patriarchal peer group practices are central to university/college dating relationships, and that male students who hold familial patriarchal attitudes and beliefs and who are supported by their male peers are most likely to assault their dating partners.[3] My data support the existence of a patriarchal structure of youth subculture in the context of economic marginalization and the assumption that patriarchal male peer groups supportive of abusive behaviour are most likely formed in or prior to high school.[4]

There are not any large differences between the group of six participants whose male peers would not approve of slapping a girlfriend (MPNS) and the group of 24 whose male peers would approve (MPS). In fact, three of the six MPNS youth later told me that their male peers were physically abusive against their girlfriends, and five told me that these peers had encouraged them to physically abuse their own girlfriends (the one peer who did not instruct this participant to physically abuse told him to sexually abuse instead). It may have been that this question about what male friends might do was not an accurate measure of the peers' actual behaviour, or that some of these six participants did not answer this question honestly, for a variety of reasons. However, as will be discussed below, large differences are apparent when the participants who did not receive male peer support to abuse girlfriends are compared to those youth who did receive this kind of encouragement.

3. Pressure To Have Sex

Twenty-nine participants told me that their male peers regularly pressured them to have sex. The following accounts are representative and reflect the nature of this pressure.

> Phil: ... It's always "C'mon, you faggot. What's the matter, can't get it up? Fuck her. Fuck her. What are you, a fucking queer? A woman? A bitch?"

> Stewart: There's tons of pressure, like "Did you fuck her yet? Did you get banged? What did you do with her, what did you do?" I have a girlfriend – there's no five-knuckle shuffle for me.
> MT: Five-knuckle shuffle?
> Stewart: You know, jerking off.

> Colin: All the time (laughing). They'll say, "Women are only good for fucking. Go fuck her." They'll say, "If you spend money on her, she's gotta fuck you in return."

These data verify previous findings in the literature on male peer groups/gangs and sexual activity and expand upon results with a college/university sample.[5]

4. Informational Support

When asked if their male peers had told them to use physical force or sexual force with their girlfriends in certain situations, all 30 participants told me that this happened regularly. In addition, all told me that their male peers had encouraged them to regularly put their girlfriends down and constantly pressure them for sex (as discussed in the Introduction, these actions were not categorized as abusive behaviour in order to maintain a strict definition of girlfriend abuse). Twenty of these youth reported that their male peers had encouraged them to use physical and sexual force, three said that they had been told to use physical force, and seven reported that they had been encouraged to use sexual force with their girlfriends.

There are some small intra-group differences related to gang membership, family support to abuse, and having abusive peers when the 20 youth who received instructions to both physically and sexually abuse (PASA) are compared to the 10 who received instructions to physically *or* sexually abuse (POSA). Sixty-five per cent of the PASA youth (13 youth) were gang members, whereas only 40 per cent of the POSA youth (4 participants) were gang members. Slightly more PASA youth had received family support to abuse (45 per cent versus 40 per cent) and had abusive peers (85 per cent versus 70 per cent).

The following account is indicative of the nature and variety of instructions given to participants by their male peers regarding the circumstances under which they should abuse their girlfriends.

> Steve: They'll say, "Give her a bitch-slap if she mouths off or hits you first." But it's only if she's your girlfriend. I mean, they joke about it all the time. "If she disses you, smack her. If she gets drunk and makes an idiot of herself, smack her. If she fucks around on you – you know, talks to other guys, give a bitch-slap … Girls are good for two things: cooking and screwing." I go along with it. There's tons of joking about sex. "What base are you at? First? Dump her." If you want your friends to look up to you and like you then treat girls like shit. Like I said, girls are good for cooking and cleaning. They're not my friends.

This member of a violent youth gang told me how his male peers encouraged him to "fake-rape" his girlfriend and film it so that the gang could watch it.

> Stewart: They all can't wait until the next time we hop in bed. They love hearing about that shit. I mean, that's where I get half my ideas.
> MT: Your ideas?
> Stewart: Yeah. The fake-raping shit. My buddies told me about that. And spanking. I mean, we rent S&M pornos sometimes. They show pretty much everything – group sex, leather, chains, violence. But you can always tell that those bitches love it and beg for more. So I guess you could say that my friends are cheering me on.
> MT: Cheering you on?

Stewart: Yeah. Sometimes I think they like it more than I do. They want me to film a fake-rape sometime ...

MT: How does it make you feel, telling your friends about your sex life?

Stewart: (silence) Pretty good I guess. They think I've got balls (silence).

MT: Is that a good feeling for a guy or a not-so-good feeling?

Stewart: Good, I guess. I think they look up to me for that shit.

Steve's and Stewart's accounts are characterized by images of game-playing and sports. Steve told me that his friends "Joke ... all the time" about "bitch-slaps" and "screwing." He used imagery of a baseball game when recounting his friends' encouragement to have intercourse: "What base are you at? First? Dump her." In a similar manner, Stewart told me "my friends are cheering me on ... they want me to film a fake-rape." These images of game-playing and sports support Katz's ideas regarding two planes of reality and the creativity and seduction of youth crime.[6] Stewart justified his actions, suggesting that he believed that "those bitches love it and beg for more." Like most of the other participants, he created a moral and righteous code of behaviour in his second plane of reality. He indicated that his friends thought he's "got balls" and "look up" to him because of his stories of sadomasochistic sex with his girl-friend. This hierarchy of the powerless characterizes most of the other accounts as well. Steve told me that "if you want your friends to look up to you and like you, then treat girls like shit."

On the Hunt: Attachments to Abusive Peers

Twenty-seven participants told me that at least a couple of their male peers had committed physically and/or sexually abusive acts against their girlfriends. All 27 of these young men had witnessed and/or taken part in at least one incident of this type. Seventeen told me that their male peers had used both types of abuse, six reported that their peers had used physical force, and four said that their peers had used sexual force with girlfriends. All participants likewise told me about individual acts of abuse they had committed against their girlfriends.

It is interesting to compare the three young men who told me that none of their male peers had physically or sexually abused girlfriends (although all three had received informational support from male peers to abuse) with the other 27 (all of whom had abusive male peers and also had received informational support from these peers to abuse girlfriends). These three young men were 17 years old, and one was living at home at the time of the study. Two came from working-class families, and one came from a middle-class family. None were ethno-racial minorities, and one was questioning his sexual orientation (the other two were heterosexual). One had a harmonious family, none reported having familial support to abuse, and all grew up with biological fathers.

All three of these youth said that they did not adhere to familial patriarchal beliefs, and only one reported having attitudes supporting the physical abuse of girlfriends. All three reported having male peers that encouraged them to physically or sexually abuse their girlfriends (one was told to physically abuse, one to sexually abuse, and the third was told to do both). The two youth who said that they were gang members (the youth questioning his sexual orientation said that he was not a gang member) reported that they beat up woman abusers with their gangs, although neither reported that they beat up gays (however, the youth questioning his sexual orientation told me that he beat up gays with his male peers). Finally, two of these youth were physical/sexual/emotional abusers. The one youth who was a sexual/emotional abuser had forced intercourse on his girlfriend. None of these three young men had used severe physical violence on girlfriends.

In summary, three primary factors separate these two groups of young men. The three participants with non-abusive male peers were much more likely to not adhere to familial patriarchal beliefs nor attitudes supporting physical girlfriend abuse compared to the others (67 per cent of the former group and 19 per cent of the latter group were "non-believers"). The instructions from father-figures and male friends to abuse girlfriends varied considerably between these two groups. None of the participants with non-abusive male peers had received family support to abuse, whereas 44 per cent of the others had. In addition, the type of instructions to abuse from peers differed between the two groups. Whereas only one youth in the group with non-abusive peers was told to physically and sexually abuse his girlfriend (of the other two young men, one was told to physically abuse, and the other was told to sexually abuse), 70 per cent of the group with abusive peers had received instructions to engage in both forms of abuse. As well, the 27 youth who had abusive male peers were much more likely to have used severe and/or forced sexual intercourse (the most serious forms of girlfriend abuse) compared to the three young men who did not have abusive male peers (78 per cent of the former group and 33 per cent of the latter group had used these most serious forms of girlfriend abuse).

These data point to social learning in a peer group setting as a process wherein many of the participants' ideological assumptions about family and gender were influenced. The two young men who were "non-believers" (in the group of three who did not have abusive peers) did not embrace a patriarchal-authoritarian model of family and gender to the same degree as the other young men in this study (in fact, the youth questioning his sexual orientation had a "negative " masculinity type). As well, severity of abuse is linked to associating with other abusive young men. This suggests the relevancy of lifestyle/routine activities theory in the explanation of girlfriend abuse. These three youth, not having been exposed to the modelling of abusive behaviour by peers, likely developed a more egalitarian model of family and gender through associations with other friends. However, they were abusive nonetheless, although not committing the most serious forms of girlfriend abuse. They still heeded the advice of non-abusive male friends who told them to abuse their girlfriends. These instructions, however, were not as likely to include suggestions to both physically and sexually abuse.

The focus now shifts to the analysis of peer group/gang differences within the sample. Some of the variation in the degree to which these young men embraced familial and gender ideologies, and the forms and seriousness of the abuse they committed, can be explained by their peer group/gang differences. Table 5.1 compares the 17 gang members with the 13 participants who did not report being members of gangs.

Table 5.1 suggests large areas of difference: ethno-racial origin, family support to abuse, and beating up suspected stranger-"rapists" and woman beaters. Peer group members were more than twice as likely to be ethno-racial minorities (31 per cent versus 12 per cent),

	GANG MEMBERS (N = 17)	PEER GROUP MEMBERS (N = 13)
Ethno-Racial Minorities	12% (2)	31% (4)
Gay/Bisexual/Questioning	12% (2)	23% (3)
Harmonious Family	12% (2)	31% (4)
Family Support to Abuse	53% (9)	23% (3)
Abuser Type	65% p/s/e	69% p/s/e
	11% s/e	15% s/e
	24% p/e	15% p/e
	41% sev.	38% sev.
	41% f.i.	38% f.i.
Biological Father at Home	71% (12)	77% (10)
Living at Home	59% (10)	42% (5)
Beats Abusive Strangers	76% (13)	38% (5)
Abusive Male Peers and Support	88% (15)	69% (9)
ASPA/FPB	24% (4)	31% (4)

Table 5.1 Gang and Peer Group Members

p = physical
s = sexual
e = emotional
sev. = severe
f.i. = forced intercourse

and gang members were more than twice as likely to have received direction from father-figures to abuse girlfriends (53 per cent versus 23 per cent) and to report that their gang was on a mission to beat up male strangers whom they believed had "raped" and/or used physical force on a female. In addition, all gang members had "protest" masculine types, whereas two peer group members had "negative" masculine types. In Table 4.1 we saw that of the eight gay-bashers in the sample, seven were gang members, and only one basher was a peer group member. In other words, gang members were almost six times more likely to be gay-bashers than were male peer group members (47 per cent versus 8 per cent).

Other small differences between the gang and peer group members are presented in Table 5.1. Peer group members were slightly more likely to be sexual minorities (23 per cent versus 12 per cent), to have come from harmonious families (31 per cent versus 12 per cent), and to adhere to both familial patriarchal beliefs and to have attitudes supporting physical girlfriend abuse (31 per cent versus 24 per cent). Gang members were slightly more likely to use severe violence, to have used physical force for sexual intercourse (41 per cent versus 38 per cent for both), to have abusive male peers, and to have received encouragement from these male peers to abuse girlfriends (88 per cent versus 69 per cent).

In summary, there are a number of key factors differentiating the gang members from the male peer group members. This variance can account for differences in the extent to which these young men embraced patriarchal-authoritarian familial and gender ideologies and the forms and extent of the abuse inflicted. In particular, these youth did not all embrace the same concept of masculinity. The accounts of both Paul (who was gay) and Sylvain (who was questioning his sexual orientation) suggest that their "negative" masculinity types were the outcome of active negotiation and resistance against continuing their fathers' pattern of violence. The fact that more sexual minorities were found in male peer groups may be related to the elevated risk of being beaten (should sexual orientation be revealed) in gangs as opposed to peer groups. (One of the defining features which distinguishes gangs from peer groups is the presence of habitual, severe violence.)

The fact that over half of the sexual minorities were themselves gay-bashers (two were gang members, and one belonged to a male peer group; all three had "protest" masculinity types) is also indicative of the active negotiation and resistance involved in the participants' expression of their masculinity. Despite the fact that the peer group members were slightly more likely to adhere to both familial patriarchal beliefs and attitudes supporting physical girlfriend abuse, gay-bashing was found almost exclusively among gang members. Arguably, the very public act of collective gay-bashing, along with the finding that twice as many gang members compared to peer group members reported beating up suspected woman abusers, were more refined measures of a patriarchal-authoritarian model of family and gender than the presence of attitudes and beliefs supporting this type of model.

When the data on gay-bashers and "woman abuser" bashers are combined, the result is very interesting: all 17 gang members reported collective gay-bashing and/or woman abuser bashing (four did both forms of bashing; four only gay-bashed; and nine only bashed woman abusers). Only 46 per cent of the male peer group members (six youth) reported gay-bashing or woman abuser bashing (one gay-basher and five woman abuser bashers). Accordingly, gang members were much more likely than male peer group members to use violence in a public way (all reported gay and woman abuser bashings were collective assaults) against individuals they considered to be lower than themselves on the hierarchy of the powerless. (This excludes violence against ethno-racial minorities. Although many participants reported violence against ethno-racial minorities, this question was not consistently asked to all individuals in the sample.)

This very public face of the gang members' collective violence against individuals perceived to be powerless is directly related to their "protest" type of masculinity, which was actively negotiated by these participants within a specific social setting and with the available resources at hand. However, this is not true for Paul and Sylvain, the two youth who had negative masculinity types. While these two young men actively negotiated their identities within specific social settings with the available resources at hand, they also actively resisted the dominant, traditional form of masculinity. Of course, the more passive role played by the main agents of gender role socialization must also have been a significant contributing factor in the construction of the masculinities of all the young men in this study.

The following three accounts reflect the collective nature of the girlfriend abuse committed by all participants.

> Serge: … At a dance, this girl slapped this guy. He punched her back. And my best friend pushed his girlfriend to the floor once … All my friends and me, we all think the same about what girls should and shouldn't do. We all think that girls should do what we want them to. And it pisses us off when they don't. So I've seen some of them when they've hit girls. And all the time we are just joking around, calling them names – slut, cunt, whore, bitch, fat cow – we all do it. So I guess you could say that we all agree to treat girls like we do. We're just all the same.

> Chuck: …We grab their asses, breasts. It's just for fun … When I see a girl with big tits at school, I start play-fighting with her so I can feel her breasts. I always say "I'm sorry. I

slipped."... We'll chase a girl down at school or in the park (motioning behind him, out the window). And then we'll trip her or corner her. Some of us will hold her and we'll grab her nipples hard. It makes them purple. It didn't hurt them though. Because their nipples always got hard ...

MT: So how did that make you feel?

Chuck: It made us feel like King Shit.

MT: King Shit?

Chuck: Nobody fucked with us, because they didn't want it to be their turn next.

Peter: But I guess you could say that we all tease each other about beaver hunting.

MT: Beaver hunting?

Peter: Yeah. Finding pussy. It's like a contest. You gotta fuck your brains out – every night if you can. So I guess you could say that my friends – we all tell each other to go do it – fuck anything on two legs that's got tits. It doesn't matter what hole you ram your cock in.

MT: Oh.

Peter: Yeah – her mouth, her cunt, or up her ass. And we talk about it all the time. It's a joke. But I guess it's like there's pressure to be the best – to fuck girls no matter what they want. Like it's about getting girls to do whatever you want them to do ... My friends look up to me for doing that. It's like kind of status.... We keep score. We've done it for a couple of years. Every different girl you fuck, it's another notch in your tree (silence).

MT: Oh.

Peter: Yeah. And sometimes you get another notch if you've done something else than straight fucking. That's the easiest.

MT: Oh. Like what?

Peter: Well, like cumming in her face. Shooting your load in her face if you know she doesn't like it. Or getting her to blow you after you've straight fucked or done it up her ass.

Serge, Chuck, and Peter used symbols characteristic of children's play, sporting events, and comedy when telling me about their group/gang's treatment of females. Similarly, the other participants described their abusive behaviour with their girlfriends as playful, funny, and game-like, as "joking around"; they often laughed when telling me about these incidents. They described their behaviour (which was classified as abusive) as children's games and sporting contests (for example, "purple nipples" and "beaver hunting"). The participants' usage of this type of language again supports the concept of two planes of reality.

Many of the participants created an exciting, seductive plane of reality to relieve the drudgery and hopelessness of their daily existence. As if on a superior moral plane, many told me about the important role their groups/gangs played in teaching and disciplining their girlfriends regarding rules of conduct. Serge said, "We all think that girls should do what we want them to. And it pisses us off when they don't." These young men's feelings of powerlessness were transcended when they defined themselves to be at the top of the hierarchy. As Chuck remarked, "It made us feel like King Shit ... Nobody fucked with us because they didn't want it to be their turn next."

The collective nature of the physical, sexual, and emotional abuse perpetrated by the participants against their girlfriends is disturbing. Whereas previous research suggests that peer supported girlfriend abuse consists primarily of individual acts of violence against girlfriends,[7] my qualitative data suggest something very different. All of the participants reported many collective as well as individual acts of abuse against their girlfriends, and at least 23 reported beating up gays and/or woman abusers and/or ethno-racial minorities. The most commonly identified types of collective acts of abuse against females were emotional and sexual abuse. All of the participants participated in at least one collective act of emotional or sexual abuse. (Collective act of abuse means that at least two males participated in the act.)

One of the most striking inconsistencies in the accounts appeared when these youth talked about the "rapes" and beatings of women other males apparently committed. The participants at times used symbols characteristic of romantic nobility. As if on a superior moral plane, 18 of the 30 spoke of their groups/gangs being on a mission to rid their community of violent rapists and woman beaters. The accounts of Brad and Don are representative.

Brad: I've used tons of violence against guys who have assaulted their girlfriends. Kicked the living shit out of them. It's just not right (playing with gun on necklace) ... We kick the shit outta guys we know who have raped or beaten girls.

MT: I'm trying to understand how your gang is against rape and beating girls, but some gang members pimp girls. I'm confused.

Brad: They only pimp girls who want to work the streets. There is no forcing going on.

MT: Oh.

Brad: Yeah. 'Ho's are all bitches anyway. They wouldn't be 'hoing if they didn't want to. Pimps are just doing them a favour, protecting them from violent tricks ... What's a 'ho? Shit. That's all.

Don: We beat up guys who hit girls. We were walking down the street and we saw this guy punch a girl in the face. We beat him up ... We're into kicking the shit outta guys who rape and beat girls. We track them down and kick the shit outta them. That's important. That's the worst. A guy cannot hit a girl ...

MT: Why do you think it's important for me – and for other people, I assume – to know that you beat up guys who abuse females?

Don: I dunno. I guess I'm proving something.

MT: Proving what?

Don: That I'm a guy. But now that you put it that way, I'm beating up other guys for exactly what I'm doing. I guess I'm lying about it – covering up my own shit. I mean, if I show other people I'm against abusive guys, they'll think wow – he's cool. They respect me for it. But I'm doing the same shit.

Conclusion

These last accounts illustrate one of the most striking findings of this study: most participants were able to justify their own abusive behaviour, yet at the same time were on a mission to rid their community of perceived "rapists" and woman beaters. How could such similar behaviour be presented so differently by the participants? It is helpful to revisit the early childhood of these 18 participants. We saw in Chapter 3 that 13 participants were routinely instructed by father-figures (who were abusing their mothers and themselves) to physically and/or sexually abuse women. The majority who witnessed their biological fathers abuse their mothers (11 out of 12) justified these assaults, indicating that they were caused by their mother. By contrast, the majority (10 out of 12) of the youth who saw their mothers being abused by social father-figures (step-fathers, boyfriends) said these assaults were wrong. It is not surprising, therefore, that six of the 12 participants who witnessed their mothers being abused by men other than their fathers told me that they used violence to protect their mothers from the abuse. None of the 12 who witnessed their biological fathers abuse their mothers told me that they intervened in these assaults. They did not protect their mothers because of their rigid adherence to a patriarchal-authoritarian model of family and gender: they could justify their father's abusive behaviour. Of the 18 participants who told me that they beat up stranger-"rapists" and woman beaters, 10 witnessed their mothers being abused by social fathers (including the six who used violence to protect their mothers), and five denied that their mothers were abused or refused to discuss this issue. Only three of these participants witnessed their mothers being abused by their biological fathers.

Therefore, one of the reasons why these 18 participants reportedly beat up stranger-"rapists" and woman beaters was because they defined these perceived abusers as having no moral authority to enforce their male dominance over females who were not their girlfriends. Comparable to how they portrayed their mothers' abuse by social fathers as unjustified (these participants didn't identify these father-figures as the legitimate rulers of their homes), they likewise presented the abuse of females by male strangers as unjustified, since these male strangers did not have a natural and moral authority over those females. In the same way that they viewed their social fathers as interlopers, they portrayed these stranger-"rapists" and woman beaters to be interlopers as well. In contrast, they justified their own abusive behaviour with their girlfriends.

The peer groups/gangs provided an important site of influence for these ideological assumptions about family and gender. These assumptions were developed in early childhood and helped the participants make sense of their worlds. In most of the accounts, they intersect; for example, many of the participants considered it to be a direct challenge to their own patriarchal-authoritarian concept of masculinity if they could not be the "breadwinner."

The peer groups/gangs also provided an important social setting to develop, negotiate, and express their masculinities. In two cases, these settings also provided the two young men with "negative" masculinities an opportunity to resist the dominant, traditional form of masculinity. Chapter 4 showed that the participants' masculine identities were influenced by their familial and gender beliefs. Almost all exhibited a common type of masculinity in which they pursued the traditional male attributes of toughness, competitiveness, and dominance. As a protest against their marginalization, their abusive behaviour compensated for and masked their economic powerlessness and sexual anxieties. With the exception of the two youth with "negative" masculine types, their common type of masculinity was a natural extension of their patriarchal-authoritarian model of family and gender. These 28 young men embraced rigid ideological assumptions about family and gender to varying degrees. Defining their world from this viewpoint, they did not verbalize the apparent inconsistency of their abusive behaviour. They were engaging in behaviour that in most contexts would be defined as criminal, yet they presented their actions as moral and righteous. They had learned to protect their own self-image and overcome challenges to their masculine identities by picking on the less powerful.

Within this group of 28 youth with "protest" masculine types, there was no homogenous degree of adherence to a patriarchal-authoritarian model of family and gender. Those who collectively beat upon gays and/or other perceived woman abusers adhered most rigidly to this model. They also committed the most severe types of girlfriend abuse.

Don was the only participant who verbalized insight into his seemingly incongruous behaviour. Nonetheless, I suggest that his identification of the apparent conflict between beating up unfamiliar "rapists" and woman beaters, while at the same time perpetrating girlfriend abuse, is applicable to other participants as well. Like Don, almost all were scared young people who referred to their lives as worthless. They routinely exhibited defensive posturing, indicating that they had to constantly protect themselves from the outside world. Their masculine identity was reaffirmed and expressed by exerting raw power over the less powerful. In order to construct who and what they were, the participants had to draw the line with what they were not. Expanding upon Albert Cohen's concept of reaction formation,[8] these participants presented their behaviour as being exactly the opposite to the behaviour of the stranger-"rapist" and woman beater. They recognized too much of themselves in these interlopers and were afraid that they were going to become just like them.

Cohen's analysis of reaction formation hinges upon his assumption that working-class juvenile delinquents, having internalized middle-class cultural standards, protect their self-image from failure to achieve these standards. They deny any attachments to the material benefits of middle-class success. Deep down inside, these 28 participants in my study recognized that they were like the "rapists" and woman beaters they claimed to be hunting, while attempting to convince themselves and others that they were exactly the opposite. They had accepted conventional values and norms and had feelings of guilt and shame resulting from status problems. They may have been experiencing "strain":[9] their abusive and violent behaviour had to compensate for and cover up whatever could not be realized.

All participants were asked if the members of their male peer group/gang held beliefs supporting abusive behaviour, pressured them to have sex, if they had been told by these members to abuse their girlfriends in certain situations, and if their male friends were abusive. The majority of these young men had received instructions to physically and sexually abuse, had attachments to abusive peers, and had peers who held pro-abuse beliefs.

What is most striking about the data in this area are the differences between the small subgroup which did not have abusive peers and the remaining 27 young men. The youth with no abusive peers were far more likely than the other youth to not adhere to familial patriarchal beliefs or attitudes supporting physical girlfriend abuse, to not have received family support to abuse, and to not have used severe violence and forced sexual intercourse. These data point to the powerful impact of social learning from abusive peers about patriarchal-authoritarian models of family and gender. Twenty-seven of these youth witnessed and/or participated in collective acts of abuse. Accordingly, this qualitative data provides limited support for the assumptions made by the handful of quantitative researchers working in this area.[10] My data provide detail regarding the dynamics of peer support outlined by these authors and suggest a more dynamic, complex role played by these groups/gangs.

There are striking parallels between the instructions to abuse females received from male peers and those received from father-figures of the participants in early childhood, and there is a remarkable similarity between the socialization into patriarchal-authoritarian models of familial and gender of the participants as children and their socialization into their groups/gangs as adolescents. Recall that in Chapter 3 I reported that 27 participants described to me rigid, patriarchal gender roles of their mothers and father-figures in their natural families. Eleven of these youth reported that their peers adhered to at least one belief supporting physical girlfriend abuse. Thus, the male peer group/gang provided a significant space for the influence and expression of ideological assumptions about family and gender. This directly challenges hypotheses that the male peer group is the primary source of male patriarchal practices.[11] Instead, my data suggest that the adherence to patriarchal-authoritarian models of family and gender by the participants was grounded in their families of origin.

Further, I argue that the male peer group/gang also reinforced the participants' individual usage of a vocabulary of adjustment, in which they denied their socially unacceptable behaviour through the sophisticated usage of justifications. The individual participants' denial of wrongdoing regarding their abusive behaviour was reinforced in their peer groups/gangs through the informational support, abusive behaviour, and pressure to have sex by group/gang members. Attachments to abusive peers and the participation in collective assaults on females also played a key role in buttressing individual accounts of denial of wrongdoing.

Support is found for Fred Mathews' youth groups/gangs continuum.[12] Of the 23 participants who routinely engaged in criminal activities (auto theft, drug-dealing, aggravated and common assault, weapons trafficking, robbery, break and enter), 17 belonged to gangs which engaged in collective violence and crime. The remaining 13 participants belonged to school and neighbourhood-based male peer groups. Six of these youth also engaged in collective violence with their peer group, although criminal activity was not the motive for this violence.

Many of the participants were engaging in defensive posturing and self-protection from the outside world. In their male peer groups/gangs, they found a haven of moral superiority, reinforced by peer group/gang members and the status derived from participation in group/gang activities. The gang members had few choices and opportunities for education and employment. Their experiences of abuse in their families of origin, the virtual absence of effective social institutions in their communities, and a lack of realistic job options contributed to their attraction to gangs.[13]

However, these very same peer groups/gangs were also very threatening social settings for many of these same youth. Many who participated in collective gay-bashing and violent assaults against ethno-racial minorities were minority members themselves. Many of the young men in this study broke down and cried about the peer group/gang pressures around "compulsory" heterosexuality. These participants were invoking in their peer groups/gangs the very situations which characterized their families of origin.

Notes

1. See Chambliss, 1973; Willis, 1977; Messerschmidt, 1986, 1993; Schwendinger and Schwendinger, 1985; Connell, 1991.
2. These findings support the work of Katz, 1988.
3. For example, see DeKeseredy, 1988; DeKeseredy and Kelly, 1993a.
4. For example, see Kanin, 1967; Cohen, 1955; Cloward and Ohlin, 1960; McRobbie and Garber, 1976; Hall and Jefferson, 1976; Brake, 1980, 1985.
5. See Willis, 1977; Schwendinger and Schwendinger, 1983; Campbell, 1984; Fishman, 1988; DeKeseredy and Kelly, 1993a.
6. Katz, 1988.

7. For example, see DeKeseredy, 1988; DeKeseredy and Schwartz, 1991, 1998; DeKeseredy and Kelly, 1993b; Johnson, 1996.

8. Cohen, 1955.

9. See Broidy and Agnew, 1997, for an interesting discussion on the applicability of general strain theory to the explanation of male and female involvement in criminal behaviour.

10. For example, see DeKeseredy and Kelly, 1993b.

11. Kanin, 1967; DeKeseredy and Schwartz, 1991.

12. Mathews, 1993.

13. See Reister and Deegear, 1996, for further exploration on these issues.

conclusion

Summary of Findings and Directions for Future Research and Policy Initiatives

Summary of Findings

This project was undertaken with the objective of addressing some of the limitations of existing studies on girlfriend abuse, which rely mainly upon the reports of females who have been victimized by males. The collection of incidence and prevalence data has been their main goal. There are no qualitative, in-depth interviews with abusive male youth. In particular, the intentions, meanings, and motives of abusive male youth, from their perspective, are not researched.[1] To remedy this gap, this study asked abusive male youth why they do what they do and what their behaviour means.

The purpose of this research was to explore how marginal male youth who are abusive make sense of their behaviour, and how we can understand their behaviour as a social phenomenon. In other words, how we, as outside observers, can better analyze their world from their definition of the situation. In the analysis of how these males defined their situation, our comprehension of their behaviour in a social context is enhanced. This study focused on the development and impact of familial and gender ideologies among these young men in two distinct sites: their families and male peer groups/gangs. A multi-method research design was employed which identified three key concepts in the literature: familial patriarchal ideology, masculine identity, and male peer group/gang affiliation. The concepts were tested in the initial set of 90 screening interviews using standardized scales. In addition to verifying these concepts, the screening interviews were used to develop a definition of abuse, assess the schedule of interview questions, and select a sample of 30 marginal, abusive male youth for in-depth interviews. Following the screening interviews, the following research questions were developed: How do marginal males make sense of their participation in their abusive behaviour? What insights can be derived from the key concepts that will help us analyze the participant's behaviour in a broader social context? In the exploration of these research questions, three major themes were identified.

1. Developing familial and gender ideologies in the home

The findings indicate that many of the participants were beaten and emotionally abused, and witnessed their mother's beatings and emotional abuse, by father-figures. Most did not say that their own victimization by father-figures was wrong. Just under one-half of these 30 participants were routinely instructed by father-figures to abuse women. Almost all of those who witnessed their biological fathers abuse their mothers said these assaults were justifiable and caused by their mother. In contrast, almost all of those youth who saw their mothers being abused by non-biological father figures said these assaults were unjustified. One-half of the 12 participants who witnessed their mothers abused by non-biological father-figures stated that they used violence to protect their mothers from abuse. None of the 12 youth who witnessed their biological fathers abuse their mothers reported that they attempted to stop their father's abusiveness.

The data on the participants' development of familial and gender ideologies in the home suggest that for many of these young men, their ideological assumptions provided them with a patriarchal-authoritarian lens through which to understand their childhood. Within the context of rigid gender roles, abusive behaviour in the home was, for the most part, perceived to be a legitimate way to ensure that family members stayed within their prescribed roles. The participants acquired this rigid belief system at an early age for a number of reasons: they modelled the patriarchal and/or abusive behaviour of their care givers; for those who experienced abuse, these beliefs helped them understand the traumatic home environment; and some received explicit instructions from male family members to abuse women if they stepped outside of their expected roles. It made some sense to participants that their biological fathers, whom they indicated to be the legitimate rulers of their home, beat and degraded their mothers for not obeying house rules. The participants who witnessed their mothers being abused by non-biological fathers considered those assaults to be unjustified. They indicated that these men, not being their biological fathers, could not be the "natural" heads of their families. However, regardless of whether they defined their mother's victimization to be right or wrong, many of these youth internalized patriarchal beliefs and/or attitudes supporting abuse against women who violated these beliefs.

Further, the majority of the participants did not indicate that their own beatings and emotional abuse by father-figures was unjustified or had negative consequences for themselves. Their description of their own victimization makes sense when we consider that most of these adolescents saw their father-figures as being the "natural" rulers of their families who had to be obeyed at all costs. These issues directly relate to some of the fundamental assumptions of the familial and gender ideologies of these youth: biological fathers were the "natural" breadwinners, and their abusive behaviour was a legitimate method to deal with conflict and keep their wives and children "in line." As such, social learning, sex/gender roles, and socialization theories are useful in exploring how these young men developed their ideological beliefs.

However, adherence to patriarchal-authoritarian models of family and gender was not uniform in the sample. The following differences among these young men account for variations in the extent to which they embraced these rigid ideologies: one-third of the sample were either ethno-racial or sexual minorities; just under one-third were told by abusive fathers not to abuse women; the majority reported that they did not support using physical violence against girlfriends in any situations, and nine said that they did not adhere to familial patriarchal beliefs; seven said that they did not adhere to any of these patriarchal beliefs and pro-abuse attitudes, whereas eight told me that they did; six came from harmonious families; and two youth said that they resisted their father's violence by becoming gay or seriously questioning their sexual orientation. Accordingly, some of these youth developed their ideological assumptions about family and gender through different processes.

One of the key processes which likely distinguished the youth from harmonious families (HF) compared to those from abusive families (AF) relates to the two main sites of ideological influence: families and the male peer groups/gangs. How did the six HF young men learn to abuse? Some of the primary extra-familial agents of socialization (the media, sports, military, and peer group) probably played important roles in constructing masculinities conducive to their abusive behaviour. HF youth were much more likely to have been raised and to be living with biological parents. None of the HF young men were told by fathers to abuse, whereas one-half of the AF youth received these instructions from fathers. The AF youth were much more likely to have used the most serious types of physical and sexual violence, as well as being gang members.

Therefore, it is probable that the AF youth likely learned their abusive behaviour both at home and in violent peer groups/gangs. Given the importance of both of these sites in the development of rigid, patriarchal-authoritarian beliefs, it is not surprising that the AF youth committed the most severe forms of abuse. The existence of two sites for the development and expression of these beliefs probably resulted in a greater degree of adherence to these rigid models of thinking. As well, many of the AF young men experienced two sets of instructions to abuse females: from fathers and from male peers. These young men likely were more receptive to acting on this encouragement to abuse, having been supported to do so by many of the most significant males in their lives.

By contrast, the HF youth learned their abusive behaviour primarily outside of their families, from one or more of the primary, extra-familial agents of socialization. HF youth were much more likely to be ethno-racial minorities, and all were heterosexual. It may have been the case that the norms around wife assault, child abuse, and divorce were stronger in these ethno-racial minority families, possibly contextualized within their religious practices (all three of these families were devout Muslims, and all parents were biological). However, all three of these young men reported that their parents adhered to rigid gender and family roles in the home. Related to the issue of sexual orientation, it has been argued in the existing literature that gay/lesbian/bisexual/transgendered youth and youth questioning their sexual orientation are much more likely to have experienced abuse, serious conflict, and/or family breakdown than heterosexual youth.[2] Therefore, the finding of this study – that all sexual minority youth reported experiencing abuse at home – is consistent with this literature.

The differentiation within the group of 30 young men who comprised the in-depth interview sample is again apparent when the "believers" (the eight youth who both had patriarchal beliefs and supported physical girlfriend abuse) are compared to the "nonbelievers" (the seven youth who held neither of these beliefs). Both of these groups of young men became abusers, yet had very different experiences. The believers were much more likely to have used severe violence, to be physical/sexual/emotional abusers, to have come from an abusive family, and to have been directed by fathers to abuse their girlfriends. Therefore, the more serious abusers embraced most strongly patriarchal-authoritarian models of family and gender. Those young men who did not hold rigid ideological assumptions about family and gender engaged in the least serious forms of abuse.

There was also an intergenerational transmission of abuse and patriarchal-authoritarian beliefs: those youth who most strongly adhered to these rigid models of family and gender were most likely to have been told by fathers to abuse females and to have experienced abuse at home. Social learning and resource theories are helpful here in exploring how these youth became abusers. These believers were most likely to have witnessed their fathers' violence at home, and probably modelled this behaviour in their relationships with peers. This social learning interacted with any feelings of inferiority associated with their masculine identity.

2. Developing familial and gender ideologies outside of the home and coping with challenges to masculine identities

Data suggest that the participants' masculine identities were intertwined with their ideological assumptions about family and gender. Most of these young men negotiated their identities through protesting against and compensating for their perceived masculine deficits. Two negotiated their identities by taking a pathway out of traditional masculine identity.

The findings suggest that almost all participants used similar imagery to describe a common set of masculine ideals, which are comparable to those identified in the literature on middle- and upper-class youth and most closely reflect those masculine values described in the literature on working-class and marginal male youth. Most characterized themselves as powerful, sexual, fighting machines. They spoke about being "King Shit" in a hierarchy of the powerless, a hierarchy made up of girls, gays, and ethno-racial minorities. When initially speaking about their masculine identities, therefore, none of the participants talked about personal feelings of inadequacy or failure regarding the difficulties they faced in acquiring material wealth and good jobs.

However, when questioned about their lack of economic future, one-half of the participants broke down and cried. It was as if an emotional floodgate had opened. Nine of these participants were questioned regarding past suicide attempts and present plans to kill themselves because of their apparent hopelessness and despair.

These young men made use of a common set of symbols when talking about their future expectations. Twenty-eight clearly stated that, due to their lack of economic opportunity, their future would be defined by economic powerlessness: no job or a "shit" job; little money, forcing a dependence on welfare or crime; and few material possessions. Usually in the same breath, most said, "but I still have my balls and my fists." These participants clearly articulated their lack of an economic future. This finding – that these participants expressed feelings of powerlessness, despair, and humiliation regarding their economic futures – expands on previous work in this area, which focused on an adult population.[3] The data from my research on a group of youth aged 13-17 years suggest that the realities of a life based upon a dismal economic future can be identified at an early age by marginal male youth.

Most of the participants spoke about their anxieties and fears surrounding their sexuality. Twenty-nine of the participants admitted their need to have frequent sexual intercourse to prove that they were heterosexual. Eight said that they regularly beat up gays to protect themselves from being raped and to demonstrate that they were not gay. All but one of them employed defensive posturing when questioned about their sexual orientation. Data analysis indicates that they were acting in self-defense.

One of the most striking examples of the interconnectedness of familial and gender beliefs characteristic of many of the accounts is found in their definition of the "breadwinner": these youth indicated that in the absence of a good job, breadwinner status could still be achieved through heterosexuality, physical toughness, and the protection of families from harm. For these young men, their gender was inseparable from being the breadwinner: all but two said that they had to support their wives and children in the future. As well, gay males and females with power posed a direct affront to the masculinity of these 28 young men.

Variation within the sample is revealed in the comparison of the eight gay-bashers with the others. Bashers were most likely to have used severe physical violence against girlfriends, probably due to their strong adherence to patriarchal-authoritarian models of family and gender. As well, they were most likely to have experienced abuse at home and to have been told by fathers to abuse females.

Bashers were over four times as likely than non-bashers to be gay, bisexual, or have serious questions about their sexual orientation. This may be related to the difficulties inherent in negotiating masculinity in a gang context for sexual minority male youth. Many of the bashers were gang members and had not disclosed their sexual orientation to anybody. Any such disclosure probably would have resulted in victimization by severe violence. As well, the concept of "reaction formation" is applicable here.[4] Only one of the sexual minority young men (the one who was gay) indicated that he was completely comfortable with his sexual orientation. The remaining four youth (one bisexual, three questioning their orientation) were confused and somewhat afraid of their orientation. One of the ways that they dealt with this confusion and fear was to participate in a collective, public beating of someone whom they closely resembled.

How did the participants make sense of challenges to their masculine identities? They negotiated and constructed their identities on a daily basis, using the available resources given their "social space location" and social setting. Most compensated for, protested against, and masked their lack of economic future and sexual fears by engaging in a common set of behaviours with girlfriends. Their masculine identities were the direct impact of their ideological assumptions about family and gender. The lives of 28 of these young men were characterized, in varying degrees, by a pursuit of the traditional male attributes of toughness, competitiveness, and dominance. Building upon the work of other researchers in this area, the behaviour of the participants was in part a response to their blocked access to the traditional institutional benefits of patriarchy.[5] The physical, sexual, and emotional abuse of girlfriends by these participants compensated for the perceived threat to their masculine identities. The construction of masculinity was an ongoing process for these marginal male youth, and the practice of girlfriend abuse was an aspect of their identity construction.

Despite the fact that the majority of these young men exhibited "protest" masculine types, they did not all embrace this patriarchal-authoritarian model of gender with the same degree of rigidity. This is in part due to the fact that almost one-third of these 28 youth were sexual and ethno-racial minorities. Further, both of the youth categorized as having "negative" masculine types were sexual minorities. The process involved in the acquisition of masculine identities for these two youth was extremely different than those processes involved in the development of the identities for the others. Both these young men told me that they had consciously chosen a sexual orientation different than that of their fathers to take a pathway out of violence.

As well, neither of these two young men adhered to a patriarchal-authoritarian model of family and gender, belonged to gangs, had engaged in the most severe forms of physical or sexual abuse, or had been told by their fathers to abuse females. Further, they were the only two youth who had jobs at the time of the study. The presence of daytime structure (through employment) influenced their process of identity construction. Perhaps they envisaged a more secure economic future for themselves by virtue of the fact that they were able to partially support themselves through part-time work.

Again, considerable evidence supports the assumption that the sample of 30 youth was not a homogeneous group. Important intra-group differences explain the variation in the degree to which they embraced patriarchal-authoritarian models of family and gender and variation in the forms and seriousness of their abusive behaviour. They did not all define their masculinities in the same fashion.

This variation is clearly evident when the 22 youth who reported the most serious forms of physical and/or sexual abuse (SV/FI) are compared with the eight youth who reported having used minor violence and/or forced sexual contact (MV/FSC). The largest variation in processes related to learning abusive behaviour appears when the severe and minor physical abusers are compared. Severe physical abusers were over seven times more likely than minor physical abusers to have rigid, patriarchal-authoritarian models of family and gender, and minor physical abusers were over three and one-half times as likely to come from harmonious families. When sexual abuse severity is compared, the largest difference again relates to adherence to familial patriarchal beliefs and attitudes supporting physical abuse: the FI youth were twice as likely compared to the FSC youth to have rigid, patriarchal-authoritarian beliefs about family and gender. When the SV/FI and MV/FSC groups of young men are compared, the most severe physical and sexual abusers were over three times as likely to have used all three forms of abuse (physical, sexual, and emotional), and the least severe abusers were over four times as likely to be sexual minorities. The MV/FSC youth were almost three times as likely to have come from harmonious families.

Twenty-nine of these young men did not say that their abusive behaviour was inconsistent nor harmful. They were engaging in behaviour that in most contexts would be defined as criminal, yet they interpreted their actions as moral and righteous. Evidence suggests the existence of two interrelated value sets or planes of reality for most of them. The first plane was characterized by boredom, drudgery, powerlessness, and a preoccupation with daily living. The second plane was defined by a hierarchy of the powerless. Feelings of moral superiority were evoked in the participants when abusing the less-powerful.

3. Groups/gangs as important sites of ideological influence

The family of origin did not exist as a viable place for almost all of the participants. These youth had little or no contact with their families due to the abuse at home. All participants reported that they spent at least 4-5 hours each day with their male peer groups/gangs, which provided them with acceptance and identity and also threatened these very same masculine identities.

Almost all of the 30 young men reported that the members of their male peer group/gang held beliefs supporting abusive behaviour, pressured them to have sex, and told them to abuse their girlfriends in certain situations. There are striking parallels between the instructions to abuse females received from male peers and those received from father-figures. There are also distinct parallels between the development of familial and gender ideologies inside and outside of the home. The male peer group/gang further developed the patriarchal-authoritarian value-set of those participants who initially acquired them in early childhood. The data suggest that the adherence to patriarchal-authoritarian beliefs by many of the participants was grounded in the rigid gender roles in their families of origin.

Perhaps one of the most significant findings in this area relates to the social learning of abusive behaviour in these collectivities. All of the 27 young men who reported that they had male peers who were physically and/or sexually abusive had witnessed and/or taken part in at least one collective act of girlfriend abuse with these friends (they also had engaged in individual acts of girlfriend abuse). Modelling of abusive behaviour in a peer group setting is a powerful influence upon the development of patriarchal-authoritarian beliefs and the subsequent expression of these beliefs as harmful behaviour. Those young men who associated with abusive peers committed the most severe forms of abuse and embraced most strongly rigid ideological assumptions about family and gender (compared to the three youth who reported that their peers were not physically or sexually abusive). Lifestyle/routine activities theory is helpful in analyzing the reasons why these young men were abusive.

Further, important differences were found when gang members were compared to peer group members. These differences explain in part the variance in the extent to which these youth adhered to patriarchal-authoritarian beliefs and the forms and extent of abuse inflicted. Gang members were over six times more likely than peer group members to be gay-bashers and twice as likely to report participating in the collective beatings of suspected stranger-"rapists" and woman beaters. As well, both youth with "negative" masculine types were peer group members. Gang members were much more likely to use violence in a public fashion (all 17 gang members reported collective gay-bashing and/or woman abuser bashing) against individuals they considered to be lower than themselves on the hierarchy of the powerless than were male peer group members. This public face of the gang members' collective violence was a method by which these young men actively negotiated their identities. This is representative of how all participants actively constructed their masculinities within a specific social space and setting.

In addition, male peers played a significant role in threatening as well as reinforcing the construction of male identity in opposition to females, gays, and minorities: if these adolescents did not dominate these people, they were perceived to be less of a man. These young males attached significant meaning to humiliating each other. Being able to put down others elevated the status of those who could do it successfully.

Further, the male peer group/gang reinforced all but one of the participants' individual usage of a vocabulary of adjustment, in which they denied their socially unacceptable behaviour through the sophisticated usage of justifications.[6] The individual participants' denial of wrongdoing regarding their abusive behaviour was reinforced in their peer groups/gangs through the informational support and pressure to have sex by group/gang members. Attachments to abusive peers and the participation in collective assaults on females also played a key role in buttressing individual accounts of denial of wrongdoing. Finally, support is found for a youth group/gang continuum.[7]

An intriguing finding of this study is that most participants did not talk about the incongruity between their abusive behaviour and their mission to rid their community of perceived "rapists" and woman beaters. How could the participants present such similar behaviour so differently? Of the 18 participants who reported that they beat up stranger-"rapists" and woman beaters, 10 witnessed their mothers being abused by social fathers (including six who used violence to protect their mothers), five denied that their mothers were abused or refused to discuss this issue, and only three witnessed their mothers being abused by their biological fathers. One of the reasons why these 18 participants reportedly beat up stranger-"rapists" and woman beaters was because they believed these perceived abusers to have had no moral authority to enforce their dominance over females who were not their girlfriends.

Comparable to how they presented their mother's abuse by social fathers to be unjustified (these participants said that these father-figures were not the legitimate rulers of their homes), they likewise said the abuse of females by male strangers was wrong. They reported that these male strangers did not have a natural and moral authority over those females. Alternatively, these adolescents may have identified with their biological fathers, and it may have been easier to dissociate from social fathers.

4. Masculine identity

The findings of this study highlight the interactive effects of rigid familial and gender ideologies upon masculine identity. The lives of the participants were raw; the niceties of middle-class culture were stripped away. James Messerschmidt writes:

> Boys will be boys differently, depending upon their position in social structures and, therefore, upon their access to power and resources. Social structures situate young men in a common relation to other young men and in such a way that they share structural space. Collectively, young men experience their daily world from a particular position in society and differentially construct the ideals of hegemonic masculinity.[8]

Class deprivation, "where the claim to power that is central to hegemonic masculinity is *constantly* negated by facts of economic and cultural weakness"[9] has blocked access by these marginal males to the institutional benefits of patriarchy. The girlfriend abuse they inflicted is a microsocial expression of the broader stratified gender order, and in part served to maintain consensus and achieve masculinity. These youth were engaging in ongoing tactics to define themselves *vis à vis* the broader structure of power and were compensating for their failure to achieve popular masculine ideals.

The individual behaviour of the participants was shaped by their relationship to their families and peers and was constrained by their economic and social marginalization. Their abusive behaviour cannot be explained by individual personality factors or unique situations alone. These adolescents all shared a common structural space and shared a common world view. The similarity in their masculine identities is striking. As such, their behaviour can be considered as social. These youth had a shared definition of their situation; their reality was negotiated and challenged regularly; they created meaning out of what they believed to be hopeless lives. The social conditions of patriarchy and marginalization shaped their values and beliefs, which in turn shaped their behaviour. As such, their behaviour was socially conditioned, and can be explained by examining their common definition of their situation. These adolescents constructed their behaviour from a limited range of possibilities. Unable to meet the social obligations of the successful male, many defined themselves and derived meaning from a different set of criteria. Their masculine identities were acquired and negotiated through their relationships with peers and can therefore be viewed as social phenomena.

In addition, the findings inform feminist theory on familial patriarchal ideology. This concept has been widely used in the literature without being empirically grounded.[10] The participants' familial patriarchal beliefs, grounded in their families of origin, were translated into concrete, harmful actions.

Not only were the participants protesting against the unattainable imperatives of the masculine ideal; they simply were using the only means that they had to defend themselves. If these adolescents truly "protested" this much, surely they must have been uncertain about their behaviour. Only one participant showed an awareness of the inconsistencies in his account. However, it must be remembered that these adolescents were for the most part school dropouts and were lacking in literacy skills. The fact that they did not articulate an awareness of the incongruous nature of their narratives does not necessarily mean that they were unaware of these conflicts. They struggled to make sense of their lives, as all of us do. While their discourse may indicate a firm commitment to what they were saying, some of their behaviour and dialogue indicates doubt, uncertainty, and at times horror and fear. In many instances they were putting on an act for themselves and others to mask these feelings. This supports the existence of two reality planes.

Directions for Future Research

There is a need to qualify the relationship between poverty and abuse by focussing on ideologies. My data indicate that males who rigidly adhere to a patriarchal-authoritarian model of family and gender are most likely to use direct physical force to keep females "in line." If this is the case, then this finding should be applicable to any such men, regardless of their social class position. By focusing on familial and gender ideologies, there is an opportunity to explain the abusive behaviour of both marginal and high status males, as well as the non-abusive behaviour of all types of males. This is supported by the data from the 90 screening interviews. Of the 30 young men who were not abusive, approximately one-third adhered to at least one familial patriarchal belief and/or at least one attitude supporting physical girlfriend abuse. However, just under two-thirds of the sixty abusive screening sample youth adhered to at least one of these beliefs and/or attitudes.

The findings generated in this study are valid and reliable and should be generalizable to similar groups of marginal youth. The sampling procedures used are solid. Despite the fact that the findings are reported from a sample that was not randomly selected, they are nonetheless considered to be valid and representative of the marginal male youth population in a large, urban centre. Following grounded theory, the findings suggest testable hypotheses. For example, the more marginal the male youth and the higher the degree of adherence to patriarchal-authoritarian models of family and gender, the greater the expression of violent patriarchy. The pre-constructed scales tested in the screening interviews have high validity and reliability. The findings of both the screening and in-depth interviews have a high degree of consistency, suggesting that the data are credible. The findings support and expand upon the data in the existing literature, suggesting conceptual validity. The reliability or repeatability of the measures should be good. These measurements should consistently yield similar results in comparable samples.

Further research should follow up on a number of important questions raised in this project. Both qualitative and quantitative research designs would be useful in addressing these issues. First, qualitative study using similar methods is necessary on a sample of non-marginal male adolescents who are abusive. This would permit further investigation into the role marginalization may play in abuse perpetration. For example, one might expect the masculine identities of non-marginal youth to be different than those of marginal youth. Similarly, a comparable research design can be used on a sample of marginal male youth who are not abusive. This would permit study of how these young men deal with issues of marginalization without resorting to abusive behaviour. After all, it is only a minority of these youth who actually are abusive.

In addition, future research should include the girlfriends of these youth in the sample. By so doing, it would be possible to compare data from perpetrators and victims, and examine the role played by females in abusive behaviour. This may increase the accuracy of the data, and would shed important light on the following questions: Do girlfriends defend themselves during assaults? If so, how? What forms of violence (physical and sexual) do abusive female youth use? How do females make sense of their victimization by males? Are the concepts of familial patriarchal ideology, feminine identity, and peer group/gang affiliations useful in understanding their behaviour as a social phenomenon?

Similar research is necessary with a sample of younger males. The data in this current project suggest that abusive behaviour is learned at a young age, and that familial and gender ideologies are developed both inside and outside of the family. Rigid adherence to these ideologies can result in abusive behaviour of pre-adolescent males. Additional investigation of these issues with a sample of boys as young as eight years of age is warranted.

Social Policy and Practice Implications

1. Early identification of boys at risk of becoming abusers

The findings in this study suggest that boys at risk of becoming abusive can be identified at an early age. The risk-markers identified for predicting adolescent abusive behaviour include victimization by child abuse and witnessing wife assault; adherence to a rigid patriarchal-authoritarian model of gender and family; affiliations with violent peer groups/gangs; and marginalization. Early identification, monitoring and treatment of these children can prevent the future victimization of gays, girlfriends, ethno-racial minorities, and intimate partners in adult relationships. Outreach to young abused women in school settings is also necessary. Primary, elementary, and secondary school teachers and social service professionals can play key roles concerning this issue. No longer can we afford to ignore the developmental precursors to serious violence in adolescence.

Current research on the effectiveness of violence prevention programs that have been integrated into the core curriculum of primary and secondary schools for all students indicates that this method is successful in decreasing school-based violence and in linking students requiring more intrusive social service interventions with relevant community resources. Further, given the widespread nature of this type of intervention (all students are required to participate), particular students are not stigmatized due to being identified as "abusers" or "victims." The most successful of these programs are those which are initiated in kindergarten or in the elementary school grades (grades 1-6). Should there be any disclosures of abuse in the family or in peer relationships, these issues are dealt with in a confidential manner. Any necessary counselling interventions are arranged outside of the larger group in the classroom. In addition, early intervention with children at risk would also address one of the fundamental problems of working with marginal youth: many do not go to school regularly. Early intervention may remedy the high absenteeism rates of these adolescents in secondary school. Research has shown that one of the most important predictors of a healthy transition from adolescence into adulthood is staying in school.[11]

Findings in this study suggest that some abusive males do not define their behaviour to be harmful or wrong. Likewise, many social work practitioners (myself included) suggest that abused females define many of these abusive behaviours as justified and caused by their own wrongdoing. These issues point to a need for abuse education to be incorporated into primary and high school core curriculum. Sporadic attempts have been initiated by some local school boards in Canada to address this issue. If abuse education were to be implemented as part of the core curriculum for primary and secondary students, young people would be in a much better position to define certain behaviour as abusive. Using a school safety model based upon a prevention and developmental approach, there are select examples of how schools with high rates of violence have successfully been transformed into safe, welcoming, nurturing environments.[12]

On a related theme, the issue of sexual harassment and abuse against female students in primary and secondary schools should be explored. The participants reported numerous instances of abuses against female students, which had gone undetected. Although some schools are to be congratulated on their peer conflict resolution programs and zero tolerance policies on violence, these initiatives may not be effective in dealing with abuses against female and ethno-racial minority students and students with issues regarding their sexual orientation. Successful programs have been designed for the prevention of sexual assault in university and college settings. These include interventions to change the pro-abuse beliefs of male students and peer-facilitated sexual assault education workshops.[13]

2. Family support programs, child abuse and wife abuse prevention initiatives

The findings from this study, along with the many other studies referred to in this book, suggest a strong link between abuse victim- ization and perpetration in males. Again, this hypothesis does not seek to excuse abusive behaviour; instead, it may be helpful in explaining and reducing it. The youth in this project were not given the opportunity to develop their identities in supportive, nurturing, abuse-free families. Children who grow up in healthy environments have a better chance of developing into healthy adolescents and making a smooth transition into adulthood. The participants were robbed of their childhood, which was characterized by terror and trauma. They never experienced the warmth and love of caring familial relationships. Until this cycle of abuse and neglect is stopped, youth violence will continue to be a major social problem. This study suggests that abusive behaviour is learned in part through parental modelling. Unless parents model alternative behaviour, chil- dren will learn that solving problems by means of force is acceptable and desirable.

Compared to existing family support programs, the type of inter- vention recommended here is radical and intrusive. However, child abuse and wife assault will not be confronted without this kind of fundamental rethinking of social policy and practice. The answer is not for child protection agencies to take all abused and neglected children into residential care, nor should all abused women have to take refuge in shelters. These solutions are expensive, disruptive, and have not been effective in combating child abuse and wife assault.[14] Many of the participants had been taken into the care of the CAS or had received community-based child protection services. These interventions did not protect them from being beaten and witness- ing the beatings of their mothers. Likewise, many of the participants' mothers had taken refuge in shelters for battered women. Although these shelters provided temporary relief from the beatings, they could not prevent nor provide long-term solutions to wife assault.

Instead, fundamental changes are required in the way we raise our children and respond to situations of child abuse and neglect and wife assault. An effective system for identifying, supporting, and monitoring parents at high risk for abusing or neglecting their children must be implemented. There is growing evidence in the United States (St. Louis, Missouri; Louisville, Kentucky; Cedar Rapids, Iowa; and Jacksonville, Florida) that community child protection strategies, in which child protection agencies share their limited resources with schools, police, recreational organizations, parents, health professionals, other community agencies, and any other relevant community stakeholders, can effectively manage and protect children at risk of being abused in the community and result in a significantly lower incidence of child abuse and neglect. As well, there is promising new evidence regarding the effectiveness of home visitation services (intensive, home-based services with new, at-risk young parents, which focus on child-rearing education and enhancement of parent-child interaction) in the prevention of child abuse and neglect. These interventions are particularly effective with young families who refuse more traditional support services, and serve in part to link up these families with other relevant community services.[15]

Data generated in this project also suggest that the young men involved in the study experienced significant difficulties related to their socialization. For almost all of these adolescents, many of the primary agents of socialization had *failed* to instill values of self-respect and esteem, equality, compassion, and skills for violence-free relationships. Instead, most of these young men had been bombarded with images which glorified violence. Family, the media, sports, the military, and the male peer group helped construct an identity which relied upon the expression of violence for self-affirmation for most of these youth. They did not have exposure to alternative adult role models. Current literature indicates that mentoring programs for at-risk children and youth can effectively counteract the negative impact of growing up with the daily modelling of violence. New research suggests that these low-cost programs can be enough to help these high-risk children and youth make a successful transition into late adolescence and adulthood. One of the primary impacts of such programs is the consistent message that there is more than one way to "be a man."[16]

The findings of some studies, along with this one, suggest that in addition to the reasons mentioned above, some young people form gangs because of unmet needs related to status, identity, and acceptance. By strengthening support services to families, the numbers of youth involved in gangs may be reduced. If families are able to meet these basic human needs, it is logical to assume that some youth may not seek out gangs to replace their biological families.

3. Poverty and unemployment issues

The findings suggest that economic and social marginalization was a key factor related to abusive behaviour. With two exceptions, the participants identified their future to be hopeless; they believed that their chances of securing a meaningful, average-wage job were minimal. Most grew up with unemployed, working-poor or dependent-poor caregivers. They felt helpless and humiliated about their future employment prospects. Abusive behaviour was the currency of trade for these youth. These future expectations reported by the participants were, for the most part, realistic.

It is necessary to help marginal people find a viable future. Poverty and hopelessness about future in the labour market are related to abusive behaviour through their threats to masculine identity.[17] Adherence to rigid ideological assumptions about family and gender is a predictive factor in abuse perpetration severity and abuse type. Although these factors cannot excuse abusive behaviour, they help explain it.

Many studies conclude that the most effective way to reduce youth crime is to combat its root causes: poverty, unemployment, and child abuse.[18] This fact is also reflected in the Department of Justice Canada's proposed legislation to replace the Young Offender's Act, the new Youth Criminal Justice Act. Accordingly, coordinated national, provincial, and municipal youth employment strategies may aid in confronting the social problem of male perpetrated abusive behaviour. These strategies would include the creation of meaningful and adequately paying jobs for all youth and effective employment and educational programs for marginal youth. Through the provision of meaningful and adequately paying work, levels of youth violence and crime may decrease. Through employment, marginal males may be provided the opportunity to achieve those masculine ideals they so desperately want. These youth should be given the option to control their own destiny and plan a meaningful career. Employment, instead of abusive behaviour, may become central in constituting their masculine identity. Through the process of realizing their own potential, positive feelings of self-worth can emerge. Given the opportunity to make a contribution to their community and have these contributions valued may instill a sense of belonging. Since feelings of hopelessness and humiliation can contribute to abusive behaviour, youth must be given concrete proof that there is reason to be hopeful about their futures.

One of the primary reasons youth join gangs and engage in criminal behaviour lies in the context of poverty and ethno-racial minority segregation in which many of them live. However, the reader cannot generalize from this small sample that abusive behaviour is more concentrated among certain ethno-racial groups. I highlighted the different experiences of these minority youth only to help explain how different processes can lead to the development of familial and gender ideologies.

The sense of social and academic failure, rooted in their home lives and experiences at school, led many of the young men in this study to search out acceptance in "alternative" male peer groups and gangs. In the absence of strong, meaningful bonds with family and teachers, there was nothing to counteract the negative peer associations in many of the lives of these young men. With the provision of choices and opportunities for jobs and education, many of these youth would not seek out gangs.[19] The participants in this study were compelled to create violent peer groups/gangs in which they found their sense of belonging.

These strategies and programs should also be directed at adults. Those individuals who are unable to work should be guaranteed adequate rates of social assistance or a guaranteed annual income. Radical social policy changes like adequate income maintenance programs for the unemployable and single parents with young children would confront the grinding poverty which characterized the childhood of many of the research participants. Basic needs – such as food, clothing, shelter, and medical services – must be provided. Basic needs, if left unmet, can contribute to abusive behaviour. This does not mean that wealthy males are not physically abusive; clearly, some are. Males with more resources can commit different forms of abuse and may choose to direct this behaviour at different individuals. The point here is that poverty and unemployment can be contributing factors to abusive behaviour in some males. A key predictor of whether a male is abusive is the degree to which he embraces a patriarchal-authoritarian model of family and gender.

As well, poverty has been linked to a host of other serious physical and mental health problems, academic failure, and employability barriers. Individuals who grow up in the context of economic marginalization are at high risk for not making a successful transition into adulthood, thereby becoming a costly burden unto society. If for no other reason, it makes good economic sense to invest early in the lives of these individuals to prevent the costly care which may become necessary in their adult lives. There are successful models of intervention for addressing the many risks faced by children living in poverty.[20]

4. The criminal justice system

The vast majority of the participants had never been charged (nor convicted) of any of the many serious assaults they committed against their girlfriends. Most of these youth could be charged with a variety of offenses, including common assault, aggravated assault, assault with a weapon, assault causing bodily harm, uttering threats of physical violence or death, sexual assault, aggravated sexual assault, sexual assault with a weapon, and sexual assault causing bodily harm. How can so many serious crimes go undetected? According to many social workers and victims, female survivors of these assaults are often reluctant to lay complaints with the police for fear of retaliation by the perpetrator. As well, current policing practices do not make it easy for such complaints to be laid. Without a mandatory charge policy for such cases, an abused girlfriend must testify against the alleged perpetrator in court if there is to be any reasonable chance of conviction.

The presence of mandatory charge policies, however, has not been enough to ensure that wife assault charges will proceed through the legal system in a timely and efficient manner. For example, Ontario has had a mandatory charge policy for "domestic violence"[21] cases since the mid-1980s. At this time, the Ontario government initiated a strategy to criminalize "spousal violence" through mandatory charge policies, more vigorous prosecution of "domestic assault" cases, and the funding of some community-based services for survivors and treatment programs for male batterers. Despite these measures, and in the face of subsequent large government cuts and across-the-board reductions in funding to community agencies, it was evident that the justice system was not achieving effective outcomes with these domestic violence cases.[22]

Instead, considerable evidence has shown that mandatory charge policies, in combination with a comprehensive system of Domestic Assault Courts, can achieve substantially better rates of conviction and lower rates of recidivism for adult male batterers. For example, Winnipeg and Duluth have been leaders in the implementation of a coordinated and systematic response to domestic violence. The Winnipeg community moved from a coordinated community response to the development of the first criminal family violence court in North America. Data on the outcomes of the Winnipeg Family Court in successfully changing the processing of cases have been published. The Domestic Abuse Intervention Project (DAIP) in Duluth, Minnesota, has gained international reputation for its comprehensive community and judicial response to domestic assault. DAIP originated in 1981 with the collaboration of nine different agencies in the adoption of written guidelines, policies, and procedures. Both of these programs have demonstrated considerable success in the effective prosecution of batterers and the reduction of domestic violence cases in their respective communities. Evidence is mounting regarding the positive impact of such comprehensive community responses to male violence against women.[23]

Due to the fact that almost all of the assaults committed by the participants went undetected by the criminal justice system, it is evident that there are currently few sanctions against these types of behaviour. If these youth understand that their abusive behaviour is unlikely to be made public, there is little incentive to stop. Related to this issue is the fact that even when caught, abusive males have very little motivation to change their abusive behaviour. Despite being confronted about their abuse perpetration, very few participants followed up on referrals made for counselling. Therefore, any youth convicted on a charge related to girlfriend abuse should have to participate in a mandatory, therapeutic-educational group for perpetrators of woman abuse. The content of this type of group has been developed. Positive results have been found with these groups for abusive male adolescents.[24]

Sanctions for child abuse, child neglect, and wife assault must result in more positive outcomes. Existing studies and practice suggest that effective sanctions are those which are certain, immediate, and part of a comprehensive, community-based response to male violence against women and children. Court ordered, effective treatment must be pursued for convicted abusers.[25]

The types of issues raised here point to the necessity of addressing fundamental problems with the nature of our social order. The social problems of child abuse, wife assault, youth violence, poverty, and unemployment cannot be effectively confronted without making basic changes to the social relations of power in patriarchal-capitalist society. To the extent to which these social relations of gender, class, and race continue to be translated into power differences, these social problems will persist. However, these proposed initiatives, if undertaken in a comprehensive manner, may begin to chip away at patriarchal structures and ideologies. Practical steps can go a long way in confronting the social problem of girlfriend abuse. These small steps can result in longer-term social change.

Notes

1. Ptacek, 1988, and Scully, 1990, provide some of the only examples of qualitative work with abusive males. However, their samples are comprised of adults.

2. For example, see O'Brien, Travers, and Bell, 1993.

3. For example, see Stinchcombe, 1964; Sennett and Cobb, 1972; Rubin, 1983; and Connell, 1991.

4. Cohen, 1955.

5. For example, see Rubin, 1976; Klein, 1982; Connell, 1991; and Messerschmidt, 1993, 1997.

6. Kanin, 1967.

7. Mathews, 1993.

8. Messerschmidt, 1993, p.131.

9. Connell, 1991, p. 32.

10. For example, see Brownmiller, 1976; Walbee, 1990; DeKeseredy and Kelly, 1993a; Daley, 1978; Eisenstein, 1979; Firestone, 1974.

11. For example, see Wolfe et al., 1995, 1997; Astor, 1995; Borland, 1996; Straussner and Straussner, 1996; Guterman, 1997; Peled, 1997; Walker, Stieber, and Bullis, 1997; Sudermann and Jaffe, 1997; Morrison and LeBlanc, 1998; Ballantyne and Raymond, 1998.

12. See Dupper, 1995.

13. See Schewe and O'Donohue, 1996; Lonsway et al., 1998.

14. For example, Ballantyne and Raymond, 1998, in an important Ontario Ministry of Community and Social Services funded project, convincingly argue in an exhaustive review of the outcomes literature on effective strategies for adolescents at risk of out-of-home placement, that residential care for the vast majority of youth does not work. Only in the most severe cases of abuse (in particular, sexual abuse), self-harm, risk of harm to others, and neglect should adolescents be taken from their own homes. In most other cases, residential care may achieve worse outcomes compared to no intervention at all. Also, see James Madison University, Department of Psychology, 1996.

15. See Center for the Study for Social Policy, 1996; Frank Farrow Center for the Study of Social Policy, 1997; Mulroy, 1997; Daro, 1996; Morrison and LeBlanc, 1998.

16. For example, see Freedman, 1993; Big Brothers and Sisters of Canada, 1996; Totten, 1998; DeRosenroll et al., 1993. As well, the YSB, in partnership with Big Brothers and Big Sisters, delivers a Mentoring-in-School program for 8- to 14-year-olds who live in poverty, have experienced violence in the home, and who are experiencing significant problems at school related to attendance, learning, and behaviour. Preliminary outcomes are very positive on issues related to violence and aggression, school learning and attendance, and self-esteem.

17. For more discussion on these issues as they relate to violence perpetration, see Natale, 1994.

18. For example, see Currie, 1985; National Crime Prevention Council, 1995; Department of Justice Canada, 1999.

19. Cullingford, 1997; Reister and Deegear, 1996.

20. For example, see Danzig, 1996; Gonzales-Ramos, 1996; Halpern, 1997.

21. The terms "domestic violence," "spousal violence," and "domestic assault" are gender-neutral terms applied by the Ontario government (and many other governments, organizations, and individuals as well). I do not use these terms because they leave one with the impression that the prevalence of abusive behaviour and consequences thereof are equal among males and females. As discussed in the Introduction, males are much more likely than females to commit the most severe forms of abusive behaviour, thereby resulting in the

most serious injuries. When females use violence, it is much more likely to be minor and to be used in the context of self-defense or anticipation of another assault by a male (for example, see Totten and Reed, 2000).

22. For example, see Gill, 1998.

23. For example, see Ursel, 1994; Dobash et al., 1996.

24. For example, see Gondolf, 1987; Ptacek, 1988; Adams, 1988; Totten et al., 1995a, 1995b.

25. For example, see Lundy et al., 1996; Gill, 1998; Dobash et al., 1996.

appendix a

Screening Interview Questions

First/Street Name:
Interview Number:
Date:
Start/Finish Time:
Ethno-Racial Minority (self-identified):   yes   no

My name is Mark Totten. I am a Ph.D. student in Sociology. I also work for the Youth Services Bureau. I am doing research on problems in male-female dating relationships. Please answer each question as honestly as you can. All of your answers will be kept strictly confidential. However, if you tell me that any child under the age of 16 years is being abused or is currently at risk of being abused, I must report this to the CAS by law.

     If you do not wish to answer a particular question, tell me; we will go on to the next question. The consent form states that you understand what you are being asked to do in this interview and that you understand that your answers will be kept confidential.

     You will be paid $10.00 for this interview.

Informed Consent Form

I hereby give my informed consent to be interviewed. I understand the nature of my involvement, and I have been assured that my answers will be kept strictly confidential. At no point during future analysis will I be identified by name. I further understand that the questionnaire and the information recorded from these question-naires will be destroyed after the information has been used in the study for which it was intended. Any quotations from this interview will appear without anything which identifies who I am.

I am also aware that I have the right to refuse to answer any ques-tions and that I may withdraw at any time. I agree that the researcher may also terminate this survey with me at any time.

Finally, I understand that there is no risk to me, my friends or my relatives stemming from my involvement in this study.

Please initial or make your mark:
Date:

I want to begin with some general background questions.

1. How old are you?

2. Where are you currently living?

3. What is the highest school grade you have completed? (If still in school, indicate grade type).

4. Did your parent(s) bring you up? __yes __no

    If yes, which parent?

    If no, who brought you up?

    Any other siblings/relatives in your home?

5. What was the main source of income in your family (i.e., wel-fare, alimony, disability, work)? Who provided most of the income in your family while you were growing up?

6. When you were growing up, was your _____ usually working?

If no, probe for duration of unemployment, reasons why.

__ dependent poor

If yes, was s/he self-employed or working for someone else?

Probe: Self-employed: Did s/he usually have paid employees working for her/him, or did s/he usually work by her/himself?

___ capitalist
___ old middle class

Probe: Someone else: Did s/he usually work as a manager or supervisor?

___ new middle class
___ working class

7. What is the highest level of school completed by your parent(s)/person(s) who brought you up?

8. What would the total income/earnings (before taxes) of your parent be for last year?

9. If you support yourself, what was your total income/earnings (before taxes) for last year?

10. What kind of place (i.e. residence) did you grow up in (i.e., apartment, public housing, owned home)?

11. Are you straight/gay/bisexual?

The next questions are about the things you do with your friends and relatives, and what they think about females.

12. Of all your friends, who do you spend more time with:

___ female friends
___ male friends
___ mixed group of friends

Probe: For how much time each week?

13. Of all your relatives, who do you spend more time with:

___ female relatives
___ male relatives
___ male and female relatives together

Probe: For how much time each week?

14. Describe for me three things which you do with your male friends that take up most of this time:

1.
2.
3.

15. Describe for me three things which you do with your male relatives that take up most of this time.

1.
2.
3.

16. As far as you know, how many of your male friends (all, most, a few, none) have forced sex on girls/women?

Probe: Relation to victim, frequency, description of incident(s).

17. As far as you know, how many of your male relatives (all, most, a few, none) have forced sex on girls/women?

18. As far as you know, how many of your male friends (all, most, a few, none) have used physical force on girls/women?

Probe: Relation to victim, frequency, description of incident(s).

19. As far as you know, how many of your male relatives (all, most, a few, none) have used physical force on girls/women?

20. As far as you know, how many of your male friends (all, most, a few, none) have insulted, put down or threatened girls/women?

Probe: Relation to victim, frequency, description of incident(s).

21. As far as you know, how many of your male relatives (all, most, a few, none) have insulted, put down or threatened girls/women?

22. How many of your male friends (all, most, a few, none) have ever told you that it is all right for a male to use physical force against girls/women in certain situations?

Probe: Against which girls/women, what kinds of situations.

23. How many of your male relatives (all, most, a few, none) have ever told you that it is all right for a male to use physical force against girls/women in certain situations?

Probe: Against which girls/women, what kinds of situations.

24. How many of your male friends (all, most, a few, none) have ever told you that girls/women should have sex with you when you want?

Probe.

25. How many of your male relatives (all, most, a few, none) have ever told you that girls/women should have sex with you when you want?

Probe.

26. How many of your male friends (all, most, a few, none) have ever told you that if a male spends money on a date, she should have sex with him in return?

Probe.

27. How many of your male relatives (all, most, a few, none) have ever told you that if a male spends money on a date, she should have sex with him in return?

Probe.

28. How many of your male friends (all, most, a few, none) have ever told you that it is all right for a guy to insult/put down girls/women in certain situations?

Probe: Which girls/women, what situations.

29. How many of your male relatives (all, most, a few, none) have ever told you that it is all right for a guy to insult/put down girls/women in certain situations?

Probe: Which girls/women, what situations.

30. How much pressure, if any, have male friends placed on you to have sex with females?

31. How much pressure, if any, have male relatives placed on you to have sex with females?

32. Some people think it is all right for a male to slap a female in certain situations. Other people think it is not all right. For each of the following situations, please tell me if your male friends, female friends, male relatives, and female relatives would strongly agree, agree, disagree, strongly disagree with a male slapping a female if ...

Male Friends   Fem. Friends   Male Relatives   Fem. Relatives

a) she won't do what he tells her to do
b) she insults him when they are alone
c) she insults him in public
d) she gets drunk during an evening out together
e) she is sobbing hysterically
f) she won't have sex with him
g) he learns that she is dating another man
h) she hits him first when they are having an argument.

33. For each of the following situations, please tell me if you would strongly agree, agree, disagree, strongly disagree with a male slapping his girlfriend if …

a) she won't do what he tells her to do
b) she insults him when they are home alone
c) she insults him in public
d) she comes home drunk
e) she is sobbing hysterically
f) she won't have sex with him
g) he learns that she is dating another male
h) she hits him first when they are having an argument

34. For each of the following statements, please tell me if you strongly agree, agree, disagree, or strongly disagree.

a) A male and his wife/girlfriend should have equal say in deciding how to spend the family income.
b) A male and his wife/girlfriend should share the household chores if they are both working outside the home.
c) A male has the right to decide whether or not his wife/girlfriend should go out in the evening with her friends.
d) A male has the right to decide whether or not his wife/girlfriend should work outside the home.
e) Sometimes it is important for a male to show his wife/girlfriend that he is the head of the house.
f) Any woman who is raped is at least partly to blame.

g)   A male has the right to have sex with his wife/girlfriend when he wants, even though she may not want to.

h)   If a male hits his wife/girlfriend, it is because he's lost his temper and gone out of control.

35.   Next, I would like you to give me 10 quick answers to the question, "What is the ideal man?"

1.

2.

3.

4.

5.

6.

7.

8.

9.

10.

36.   Now I am going to read you some more statements. Please tell me if you strongly agree, agree, disagree, or strongly disagree.

a)   A man is never justified in hitting his wife.

1. strongly agree 2. agree 3. disagree 4. strongly disagree

b)   Being roughed up is sexually stimulating to many women.

4. strongly agree 3. agree 2. disagree 1.strongly disagree

c)   Many times a woman will pretend she doesn't want to have sex because she doesn't want to seem loose, but she is really hoping the man will just take over.

4. strongly agree 3. agree 2. disagree 1. strongly disagree

d)   A wife should move out of the house if her husband hits her.

1. strongly agree 2. agree 3. disagree 4. strongly disagree

e) Sometimes the only way a man can get a cold woman turned on is to use some force.

4. strongly agree 3. agree 2. disagree 1. strongly disagree

f) Most women dislike men who try to be too physical with them.

1. strongly agree 2. agree 3. disagree 4. strongly disagree

g) Most men like a woman to put up a struggle before agreeing to have sex.

4. strongly agree 3. agree 2. disagree 1. strongly disagree

h) When a woman says no to sex, it doesn't mean the man should give up.

4. strongly agree 3. agree 2. disagree 1. strongly disagree

i) Some women like to be hit, they seem to think it means you care for them.

4. strongly agree 3. agree 2. disagree 1. strongly disagree

j) The woman should be in control during a sexual encounter.

1. strongly agree 2. agree 3. disagree 4. strongly disagree

37. Have you ever dated a girl/woman?

38. The next questions are about your sexual experiences with girlfriends.

Probe: Frequency, context. If no assaults, probe why.

a) Have you engaged in sex play (fondling, kissing, or petting, but not intercourse) with a female when she didn't want to by overwhelming her with continual arguments and pressure?

b) Have you engaged in sex play (fondling, kissing, or petting, but not intercourse) with a female when she didn't want to by threatening or using some degree of physical force (twisting her arm, holding her down, etc.)?

c) Have you attempted sexual intercourse (getting on top of her, attempting to insert penis) with a female when she didn't want it by threatening or using some degree of physical force (twisting her arm, holding her down, etc.) but intercourse did not occur?

d) Have you attempted sexual intercourse with a female (getting on top of her, attempting to insert penis) when she didn't want it because she was drunk or high, but intercourse did not occur?

e) Have you engaged in sexual intercourse with a female when she didn't want to by overwhelming her with continual arguments or pressure?

f) Have you engaged in sexual intercourse with a female when she didn't want to because she was drunk or high?

g) Have you engaged in sexual intercourse with a female when she didn't want to by threatening or using some degree of physical force (twisting her arm, holding her down, etc.)

h) Have you engaged in sex acts (anal or oral intercourse or penetration by objects other than the penis) with a female when she didn't want to by threatening or using some degree of physical force (twisting her arm, holding her down, etc.)?

39. Please tell me how many times, if any, you have done the following things to your girlfriends. (Frequency:)

a) Insulted or swore at her
b) Put her down in front of friends or family
c) Accused her of having affairs or flirting with other men
d) Did or said something to spite her

e) Threatened to hit or throw something at her
f) Threw, smashed, or kicked something
g) Threw something at her
h) Pushed, grabbed, or shoved her
i) Slapped her
j) Kicked, bit, or hit her with your fist
k) Hit or tried to hit her with something
l) Beat her up
m) Choked her
n) Threatened her with a knife or a gun
o) Used a knife or gun on her

40. I really appreciate the time you have taken to complete this interview. I'd like to assure you that everything you have told me will remain strictly confidential. I realize that the topics covered in this interview are sensitive and that many males don't want to talk about these issues. I'm also a bit worried that I haven't asked the right questions. Have you had any other experiences in which you physically, sexually, or emotionally harmed any girlfriends that you would like to talk about?

Is there anything that came up in this interview for which you would like counselling/support? If yes, provide relevant referral information.

appendix b

In-Depth Interview Questions

First/Street Name:
Interview Number:
Date:
Start/Finish Time:

My name is Mark Totten. I am a Ph.D. student in sociology. I also work for the Youth Services Bureau. I am doing research on problems in male-female dating relationships. You have agreed to let me interview you as a follow-up to the interview we did about one year ago. You understand that I will be contacting your (ex) girlfriend to explain what I am doing, and to make sure that she is safe. Please answer each question as honestly as you can. All of your answers will be kept strictly confidential. However, if you tell me that any child under the age of 16 years is being abused or is currently at risk of being abused, I must report this to the CAS by law.

If you do not wish to answer a particular question, tell me, and we will go on to the next question. The consent form states that you understand what you are being asked to do in this interview and that you understand that your answers will be kept confidential.

Informed Consent Form

I hereby give my informed consent to be interviewed. I understand the nature of my involvement, and I have been assured that my answers will be kept strictly confidential. At no point during future analysis will I be identified by name. I further understand that the questionnaire and the information recorded from these questionnaires will be destroyed after the information has been used in the study for which it was intended. Any quotations from this interview will appear without anything which identifies who I am.

I am also aware that I have the right to refuse to answer any questions and that I may withdraw at any time. I agree that the researcher may also terminate this survey with me at any time.

Finally, I understand that there is no risk to me, my friends or my relatives stemming from my involvement in this study.

Please initial or make your mark:
Date:

Begin with completed 1993 interview, probing at identified questions and inserting following questions.

Following # 11:

What do you think about your family?

How do you feel about the way they treat you?

Was/Is there any abuse between your parents? What type? How often?

Did/do you experience any abuse from your parents?

How have your parents influenced you?

What kinds of beliefs or values does your family have around male and female roles?

Following # 35:

What does it mean to you ... to be male?

Do you think this has anything to do with the way you get along with

___ females
___ gays
___ other guys

Following # 38:

I'd like to ask you some questions about your relationships with girl-friends over the past year.

Have you had a sexual relationship?

If yes: can you tell me about it? If no: go to number 26.

Probe: To assess whether sex was consensual or forced:

Was verbal pressure used to persuade female to have sex?

Were verbal threats used to force female to have sex?

Was physical force used to have sex?

Were drugs and/or alcohol used to overcome resistance?

After # 39:

Please tell me how many times, if any, you have done any of these same things to your girlfriends during the past year.

a)   Insulted or swore at her
b)   Put her down in front of friends or family

c) Accused her of screwing around
d) Did or said something to get back at her
e) Threatened to hit or throw something at her
f) Threw, smashed, or kicked something
g) Threw something at her
h) Pushed, grabbed, or shoved her
i) Slapped her
j) Kicked, bit, or hit her with your fist
k) Hit or tried to hit her with something
l) Beat her up
m) Choked her
n) Threatened her with a knife or a gun
o) Used a knife or gun on her

After # 40:

I'm a bit worried that I haven't asked the right questions. Have you had any other experiences in which you physically, sexually, or emotionally harmed a girlfriend during the past year?

41. I'd like to find out about the emotions and feelings you have/had about the abuse. How does/did it feel to be abusive in a relationship? What kinds of emotions did/do you experience at the time of the abusive incident(s)? Immediately after?

42. How do you feel about the abuse now?

43. What do you think led you to be abusive? Do you think that the way you see yourself as being a guy has anything to do with you being abusive?

44. What helped/would help you to stop being abusive?

45. What kinds of things do you think could have prevented you from being abusive?

Provide relevant referral info.

references

Aber, J.L., Allen, J.P., Carlson, V., and D. Cicchetti. (1989). The effects of maltreatment on development during early childhood: recent studies and theoretical, clinical and policy implications. In D. Cichetti and V. Carlson (Eds.), *Child maltreatment: theory and research on the causes and consequences of child abuse and neglect* (pp. 579-619). Cambridge, UK: Cambridge University Press.

Adams, David. (1988). Treatment models of men who batter: a pro-feminist analysis. In Kersti Yllo and Michele Bograd (Eds.), *Feminist Perspectives on Wife Abuse*. Beverly Hills, CA: Sage.

Allen, D., and K. Tarnowski. (1989). Depressive characteristics of physically abused children. *Journal of Abnormal Child Psychology*, 17, 1-11.

Alvi, Shahid, and Kevin Selbee. (1997). Dating status variations and woman abuse: a test of the dependency, availability, and deterrence (DAD) model. *Violence Against Women* 3(6), 610-28.

Astor, Ron A. (1995). School violence: a blueprint for elementary school interventions. *Social Work in Education* 17(2), 101-15.

Ballantyne, Mary, and Leslie Raymond. (1998). *Effective strategies for adolescents at risk of out-of-home placement*. Toronto: Ontario Association of Children's Aid Societies.

Bandura, Albert. (1973). *Aggression – a social learning analysis*. Englewood Cliffs, NJ: Prentice-Hall.

——. (1977). *Social learning theory*. Englewood Cliffs, NJ: Prentice-Hall.

Barash, David. (1987). Sociobiology and behavior. In Juanita Williams, *Psychology of women: behaviour in a biosocial context*. New York: W.W. Norton.

Barnes, Gordon E., Leonard Greenwood, and Renna Sommer. (1991). Courtship violence in a Canadian sample of male college students. *Family Relationships*, 40, 37-44.

Barrett, Michelle. (1980). *Women's oppression today: problems in Marxist feminist analysis*. London: Verso.

Barrett, Michelle and Mary McIntosh. (1982). *The anti-social family*. London: Verso.

Bass, Ellen, and Laura Davis. (1988). *The courage to heal*. New York: Harper and Row.

Beirne, Piers, and James Messerschmidt. (1995). *Criminology* (2nd ed.). San Diego, CA: Harcourt, Brace Jovanovich.

Benson, Dennis, Catherine Charleton, and Fern Goodhart. (1992). Acquaintance rape on campus: a literature review. *College Health*, 40, 157-65.

Bergman, L. (1992). Dating violence among high school students. *Social Work*, 37, 21-27.

Bersani, Carl, and Huey-Tsy Chen. (1988). Sociological perspectives in family violence. In Vincent Van Hasselt, Randall Morrison, and Allan Bellack (Eds.), *Handbook of family violence* (pp. 57-86). New York: Plenum Press.

Besharov, Douglas J. (1990). *Family violence: research and public policy issues*. Washington, DC: AEI Press.

Big Brothers and Sisters of Canada. (1995). *The in-school mentoring program*. Burlington, ON: BBSC.

Bograd, Michele. (1988). Feminist perspectives on wife abuse: an introduction. In Kersti Yllo and Michele Bograd (Eds.), *Feminist perspectives on wife abuse*. Beverly Hills, CA: Sage.

Borland, Carole J. (1996). *Conflict "cans": schoolwide conflict resolution training program for grades K-6, trainer packet*. Oak View, CA: self-published.

Brake, Michael. (1980). *The sociology of youth culture and youth subcultures: sex, and drugs and rock'n'roll*. London: Routledge.

———. (1985). *Comparative youth culture: the sociology of youth cultures and youth subcultures in America, Britain, and Canada*. London: Routledge and Kegan Paul.

Breines, Winni, and Linda Gordon. (1983). The new scholarship on family violence. *Signs: Journal of Women in Culture and Society*, 8(3), 490-531.

Breslin, F., D. Riggs, K. Daniel O'Leary, and Leana Arias. (1990). Family precursors: expected and actual consequences of dating aggression. *Journal of Interpersonal Violence*, 5(2), 247-58.

Brinkerhoff, M.B., and E. Lupri. (1988). Interspousal violence. *The Canadian Journal of Sociology*, 13, 407-34.

Broidy, Lisa, and Robert Agnew. (1997). Gender and crime: a general strain theory perspective. *Journal of Research in Crime and Delinquency*, 34(3), 275-306.

Browne, Angela. (1987). *When battered women kill.* New York: Free Press.

Brownfield, David, and Kevin Thompson. (1991). Attachment to peers and delinquent behaviour. *Canadian Journal of Criminology,* Jan., 45-60.

Browning, James and Donald Dutton. (1986). Assessment of wife assault with the conflict tactics scale: using couple data to quantify the differential reporting effect. *Journal of Marriage and the Family,* 48, 375-79.

Brownmiller, Susan. (1976). *Against our will: men, women and rape.* Harmondsworth: Penguin.

Brush, Lisa. (1990). Violent acts and injurious outcomes in married couples: methodological issues in the national survey of families and households. *Gender and Society,* 4, 56-67.

Burt, Martha. (1980). Cultural myths and supports for rape. *Journal of Personality and Social Psychology,* 38(2), 217-30.

Calhoun, Karen S., et al. (1997). Sexual coercion and attraction to sexual aggression in a community sample of young men. *Journal of Interpersonal Violence,* 12(3), 392-406.

Caputo, Tullio. (1994). *Youth violence and youth gangs in Canada. Background document for conference participants.* Ottawa: Richard Weiler and Associates.

Center for the Study of Social Policy. (1996). *Community partnerships for protecting children.* New York: Edna McConnell Clark Foundation.

Cernkovich, Stephen A., and Peggy C. Giordano. (1992). School bonding, race, and delinquency. *Criminology,* 30(2), 261-91.

Chambliss, William J. (1973). The saints and the roughnecks. *Society,* 11(1), 24-31.

Chodorow, Nancy (1974). Family structure and feminine personality. In M. Rosaldo and L. Lamphere (Eds.), *Women, culture and society* (pp. 43-66). Standford, CT: Standford University Press.

———. (1979). Mothering, male dominance and capitalism. In Zillah Eisenstein (Ed.), *Capitalist patriarchy and the case for socialist feminism* (pp. 83-106). New York: Monthly Review Press.

Clement, Wallace. (1990). Comparative class analysis: locating Canada in a North American and Nordic context. *Canadian*

Review of Sociology and Anthropology, 27(4).

Cloward, Richard, and Lloyd Ohlin. (1960). *Delinquency and opportunity.* New York: Free Press.

Coffey, Patricia, et al. (1996). Dating violence: the association between methods of coping and women's psychological adjustment. *Violence and Victims,* 11(3), 227-38.

Cohen, Albert. (1955). *Delinquent boys: the culture of the gang.* New York: Free Press.

Coleman, Wil. (1990) Doing masculinity, doing theory. In J. Hearn and D. Morgan (Eds.), *Men, masculinities and social theory.* London: Unwin Hyman.

Comstock, Gary D. (1991). *Violence against lesbians and gay men.* New York: Columbia University Press.

Connell, Robert W. (1989). Cool guys, swots and wimps: the interplay of masculinity and education. *Oxford Review of Education,* 15(3), 291-303.

———. (1991). Live fast and die young: the construction of masculinity among young working-class men on the margin of the labour market. Unpublished paper.

Cooley, Charles Horton. (1922). *Human nature and the social order.* New York: Scribner's.

Cullingford, Cedric, Jenny Morrison. (1997). Peer group pressure within and outside the school. *British Educational Research Journal,* 23(1), 61-80.

Currie, Elliot. (1985). *Confronting crime.* New York: Pantheon.

Daley, M. (1978). *Gyn/Ecology: the metaethics of radical feminism.* London: Woman's Press.

Danzig, Rivka Ausubel. (1996). Children in homeless families. In Norma Kolko Phillips and Shulamith Lala Ashenberg Straussner (Eds.), *Children in the urban environment: linking social policy and clinical practices* (pp. 191-208). Springfield, IL: Charles C. Thomas.

Daro, Deborah. (1996). New dimensions in preventing child sexual abuse-home visitations. *NRCCSA News,* 5(4).

DeKeseredy, Walter S. (1988). *Woman abuse in dating relationships: the role of male peer support.* Toronto: Canadian Scholar's Press.

DeKeseredy, Walter S., and Ronald Hinch. (1991). *Woman abuse: sociological perspectives.* Toronto: Thompson Educational Publishing.

DeKeseredy, Walter S., and Katharine Kelly. (1993a). Woman abuse in university and college dating relationships: the contributions of the ideology of familial patriarchy. *Journal of Human Justice*, 4(2), 25-52.

——. (1993b). The incidence and prevalence of woman abuse in Canadian university and college dating relationships. *Canadian Journal of Sociology*, 18(2), 137-59.

DeKeseredy, Walter S. and Brian MacLean. (1990). Researching women abuse in Canada: a realist critique of the conflict tactics scale. *Canadian Review of Social Policy*, 25, 19-27.

DeKeseredy, Walter S., and Martin D. Schwartz. (1991). *Rethinking the relationship between male peer support and woman abuse in university dating relationships.* Paper presented at the annual meetings of the Academy of Criminal Justice Sciences, Nashville.

——. (1994). Locating a history of some Canadian woman abuse in elementary and high school dating relationships. *Humanity and Society*, 18(3), 49-63.

——. (1998). *Woman abuse on campus: results from the Canadian National Survey.* Thousand Oaks, CA: Sage Publications.

DeKeseredy, Walter S., Martin D. Schwartz, and Karen Tait. (1992). Sexual assault and stranger aggression on a Canadian university campus. *Sex Roles*, 28(5/6), 263-77.

DeMaris, A. (1987). The efficacy of a spouse abuse model in accounting for courtship violence. *Journal of Family Issues*, 8(3), 291-305.

DeMontigny, Gerald. (1995). *Social working: an ethnography of frontline practice.* Toronto: University of Toronto Press.

Department of Justice Canada. (1999). *Canada's Youth Criminal Justice Act: a new law, a new approach.* Ottawa: Minister of Public Works and Government Services, Canada.

DeRosenroll, David, Greg Saunders, and Rey Carr. (1993). *Stay in school mentoring strategy resource kit.* Victoria, BC: Systems Consulting Group, Inc.

Deykin, E., J. Alpert, and J. McNamara. (1985). A pilot study of the effect of exposure to child abuse or neglect on adolescent suicidal behaviour. *American Journal of Psychiatry*, 142, 1299-1303.

Dobash, Rebecca Emerson and Russell Dobash. (1979). *Violence against wives.* New York: Free Press.

Dobash, Russell and Rebecca Emerson Dobash. (1988). Research as social action: The struggle for battered women. In Kersti Yllo and Michelle Bograd (Eds.), *Feminist perspectives on wife abuse* (pp. 51-74). Newbury Park, CA: Sage.

Dobash, Russell, R. Emerson Dobash, Margo Wilson, and Martin Daly. (1992). The myth of sexual symmetry in marital violence. *Social Problems*, 39, 71-91.

Dobash, Russell, R. Emmerson Dobash, K. Cavanagh, and R. Lewis. (1996). *Research evaluation of programmes for violent men.* University of Manchester, Violence Research Centre: Manchester, England.

Dupper, David R. (1995). Moving beyond the crime-focused perspective of school violence. *Social Work in Education*, 17(2), 71-72.

Dutton, Donald G. (1984). Interventions into the problem of wife assault: therapeutic, policy and research implications. *Canadian Journal of Behavioural Science*, 16(4), 281-97.

Edleson, Jeffrey and Mary Pat Brygger (1989). Gender differences in reporting of battering incidences. *Family Relations*, 35, 377-82.

Eisenstein, Zillah R. (1979). Developing a theory of capitalist patriarchy and socialist feminism. In Zillah Eisenstein (Ed.), *Capitalist patriarchy and the case for socialist feminism* (pp. 5-40). New York: Monthly Review Press.

Elliot, Susan, Dave Odynak, and Harvey Krahn. (1992). *A survey of unwanted sexual experiences among University of Alberta students.* Research report prepared for the Council on Student Life. University of Alberta: Population Research Laboratory.

Elliot, Frank. (1977). The neurology of explosive rage: the dyscontrol syndrome. In Maria Roy (Ed.) *Battered women: a psychosocial study of domestic violence* (pp. 98-109). New York: Van Nostrand Reinhold.

———. (1982). Biological contributions to family violence. In Lawrence Barnhill (Ed.), *Clinical approaches to family violence: the family therapy collection* (pp. 36-58). Rockville, MD: Aspen Publications.

Ellis, Desmond, and L. Wright. (1987). Post separation woman abuse: the contribution of lawyers. *Victimology*, 12, 14-21.

Fantuzzo. J.W., and C.V. Lindquist. (1989). The effects of observing conjugal violence on children: a review and analysis of research methodology. *Journal of Family Violence*, 4, 77-94.

Fantuzzo, J.W., L.M De Paola, L. Lambert, T. Marturo, G. Anderson, and S. Sutton. (1991). Effects of interparental violence on the psychological adjustment and competencies of young children. *Journal of Consulting and Clinical Psychology*, 59, 258-65.

Finkelhor, David (1983). Common features of family abuse. In David Finkelhor, Richard Gelles, Gerald Hotaling, and Murray Straus (Eds.), *The dark side of families: current family violence research* (pp. 17-28). Newbury Park, CA: Sage.

Firestone, Shulamith. (1974). *The dialectic of sex: the case for feminist revolution.* New York: Morrow.

Fishman, Laura. (1988). *The vice queens: an ethnographic study of black female gang behaviour.* Paper presented at the Annual Meeting of the American Society of Criminology.

Foo, Louise and Gayla Margolin. (1995). A multivariate investigation of dating aggression. *Journal of Family Violence*, 10(4), 351-77.

Forsstrom-Cohen, B., and A. Rosenbaum. (1985). The effects of parental marital violence on young adults: an exploratory investigation. *Journal of Marriage and Family*, 47, 467-72.

Frank Farrow Center for the Study of Social Policy. (1997). *Building community partnerships for child protection.* Harvard Executive Session on New Paradigms for Child Protective Services Forum.

Franken, Robert. (1988). *Human motivation.* Pacific Grove, CA: Brooks/Cole.

Frazier, Patricia A., and Lisa M. Seales. (1997). Acquaintance rape is real rape. In Martin D. Schwartz (Ed.). *Researching sexual violence against women: methodological and personal perspectives* (pp. 54-64). Thousand Oaks, CA: Sage Publications.

Freedman, Marc. (1997). *The kindness of strangers: reflections on the mentoring movement.* Portsmouth, NH: Dare Mighty Things.

Gelles, Richard J. (1979). *Family violence.* Beverly Hills, CA: Sage.

———. (1983). An exchange/social control theory. In David Finkelhor, Richard Gelles, Gerald Hotaling, and Murray Straus (Eds.), *The dark side of families: current family violence research* (pp. 151-165). Newbury Park, CA: Sage.

Gelles, Richard J. and Claire P. Cornell. (1985). *Intimate violence in families.* Beverley Hills, CA: Sage.

Gelles, Richard J., and Murray A. Straus. (1988). *Intimate Violence.* New York: Simon and Schuster.

Gill, Richard. (1998). *An evaluation of two domestic violence courts in*

Ontario. Internal working document. Toronto: Ministry of the Attorney-General.

Glaser, Bernie, and Anselm Straus. (1967). *The discovery of grounded theory*. Chicago: Aldine.

Gondolf, Edward W. (1987). Evaluating programs for men who batter: problems and prospects. *Journal of Family Violence*, 2(1), 95-108.

Gonzales-Ramos, Gladys (1996). Children living in poverty. Norma Kolko Phillips and Shulamith Lala Ashenberg Strassner (Eds.). *Children in the urban environment: linking social policy and clinical practices* (pp. 27-42). Springfield, IL: Charles C. Thomas.

Greenberg, David F. (1977). Delinquency and the age structure of society. *Contemporary Crises*, 1(2), 189-224.

Grossman, S. (1988). A textbook of physiological psychology (New York: Wiley 1967), cited in Robert Franken, *Human motivation* (p. 316). Pacific Grove, CA: Brooks/Cole.

Guterman, Neil B. (1997). Early prevention of physical child abuse and neglect: existing evidence and future directions. *Child Maltreatment*, 2(1), 12-34.

Gwartney-Gibbs, Patricia, Jean Stockard, and S. Bohmer. (1987). Learning courtship aggression: the influence of parents, peers, and personal experiences. *Family Relations*, 36, 276-82.

Hall, S., and T. Jefferson (Eds.). (1976). *Resistance through rituals*. London: Hutchinson.

Halpern, Robert. (1997). Good practice with multiply vulnerable young families: challenges and principles. *Children and Youth Services Review* (UK), 19(4), 253-75.

Hammersley, M. (1992). *What's wrong with ethnography: methodological explorations*. London: Routledge.

Harry, Joseph. (1992). Conceptualizing anti-gay violence. In Gregory Herek and Kevin Berril (Eds.), *Hate crimes: confronting violence against lesbians and gay men*. Newbury Park: Sage.

Hershorn, M., and A. Rosenbaum. (1985). Children of marital violence: a closer look at the unintended victims. *American Journal of Orthopsychiatry*, 55, 260-66.

Heward, Christine. (1988). *Making a man of him*. London: Routledge.

Hill, Stuart, and Ron Santiago. (1992). *Tragic magic: the life and crimes of a heroin addict*. Chicago: Nelson Hall.

Holden, G.W., and K. L. Ritchie. (1991). Linking extreme marital discord, child rearing, and child behaviour problems: evidence from battered women. *Child Development, 62*, 311-27.

Hotaling, Gerald T., and David Sugarman. (1986). An analysis of risk markers in husband to wife violence: the current state of knowledge. *Violence and Victims, 1*, 101-24.

Huesmann, L. Rowell, and Neil Malamuth. (1986). Media violence and anti-social behaviour: an overview. *Journal of Social Issues, 42*(3), 1-6.

Hughes, H. (1988). Psychological and behavioural correlates of family violence in child witnesses and victims. *American Journal of Orthopsychiatry, 58*(1), 77-90.

Jaffe, Peter, David Wolfe, S. Wilson, and L. Zak. (1986a). Family violence and child adjustment: a comparative analysis of girls' and boys' behavioural symptoms. *American Journal of Psychiatry, 143*, 74-77.

———. (1986b). Similarities in behavioural and social maladjustment among child victims and witnesses to family violence. *American Journal of Orthopsychiatry, 56*, 142-46.

Jaffe, Peter, and D. Reitzel. (1990). Adolescents' views on how to reduce family violence. In R. Roesch, Donald G. Dutton, and V.F. Sacco (Eds.), *Family violence: perspectives on treatment, research and policy* (pp. 51-66). Burnaby, BC: Simon Fraser University.

Jaffe, Peter, David Wolfe, and Susan K. Wilson. (1990). *Children of battered women.* Newbury Park, CA: Sage.

Jaffe, Peter, Marlies Sudermann, Deborah Reitzel, and Steve M. Killip. (1992). An evaluation of a secondary school primary prevention program on violence in intimate relationships. *Violence and Victims, 7*, 129-46.

James Madison University, Department of Psychology. (1996). Treatment outcome part III: intervention for the child. *Virginia Child Protection Newsletter, 48*(1-2).

Johnson, Holly. (1990). Wife abuse. In Craig McKie and Keith Thompson (Eds.), *Canadian social trends* (pp. 173-76). Toronto: Thompson Educational Publishing Inc.: 173-76.

———. (1996). *Dangerous domains: violence against women in Canada.* Toronto: Nelson Canada.

Kalmuss, Deborah. (1984). The intergenerational transmission of marital aggression. *Journal of Marriage and the Family, 46*(11), 11-

19.

Kanin, Eugene J. (1967). Reference groups and sex conduct norm violation. *Sociological Quarterly*, 8, 495-504.

Katz, Jack. (1988). *Seductions of crime: moral and sensual attractions in doing evil.* New York: Basic Books.

Kaufman, Joan. (1991). Depressive disorders in maltreated children. *Journal of American Academic Child and Adolescent Psychiatry*, 30, 257-65.

Kaufmann, Joan, and Edward Zigler. (1987). Do abused children become abusive parents? *American Journal of Orthopsychiatry*, 57, 186-92.

———. (1993). The intergenerational transmission of abuse is overstated. In Richard J. Gelles and D. R. Loseke (Eds.), *Current controversies on family violence.* Newbury Park, CA: Sage.

Kennedy, Leslie, and Donald G. Dutton. (1989). The incidence of wife assault in Alberta. *Canadian Journal of Behavioural Science*, 21, 40-54.

Kessler, S., D. Ashenden, Robert Connell, and G. Dowsett. (1985). Gender relations in secondary schools. *Sociology of Education*, 58(1), 34-48.

Kivel, Paul. (1992). *Men's work.* CA: Hazelden/Ballantine.

Klein, Dorie. (1982). Violence against women: some considerations regarding its causes and elimination. In Barbara Price and Natalie Sokaloff (Eds.), *The criminal justice system and women* (pp. 83-96). New York: Clark Boardman.

Koss, Mary P., and C. J. Oros. (1982). Sexual experiences survey: a research instrument investigating sexual aggression and victimization. *Journal of Consulting and Clinical Psychology*, 50, 455-57.

Koss, Mary P., and C.A. Gidycz. (1985). Sexual experiences survey: reliability and validity. *Journal of Consulting and Clinical Psychology*, 53, 422-23.

Koss, Mary P., C.A. Gidycz, and N. Wisniewski. (1987). The scope of rape: incidence and prevalence of sexual aggression and victimization in a national sample of higher education students. *Journal of Consulting and Clinical Psychology*, 55(2), 162-70.

Koss, Mary P. and Hobart H. Cleveland. (1997). Stepping on toes: social roots of date rape lead to intractability and politicization. Martin D Schwartz (Ed.). *Researching sexual violence against women: methodological and personal perspectives* (pp. 4-21). Thousand Oaks, CA: Sage.

Kreuz, L. and R. Rose. (1972). Assessment of aggressive behaviour and plasma testosterone in a young criminal population. *Psychosomatic Medicine*, 34 (1972), 321-32, cited in Robert Franken (1988), *Human motivation* (p. 322). Pacific Grove, CA: Brooks/ Cole.

Lane, Katherine E., and Patricia Gwartney-Gibbs. (1995). Violence in the context of dating and sex. *Journal of Family Issues*, 6, 45-49.

Langhinrichsen-Rohling, Jennifer, and Peter Neidig. (1995). Violent backgrounds of economically disadvantaged youth: risk factors for perpetrating violence? *Journal of Family Violence*, 10(4), 379-97.

Langhinrichsen-Rohling, Jennifer, P. Neidig, and G. Thorn. (1995). Violent marriages: gender difference in levels of current violence and past abuse. *Journal of Family Violence*, 10, 159-76.

Lonsway, Kimberly A., et al. (1998). "No means no": outcomes of an intensive program to train peer facilitators for campus acquaintance rape education. *Journal of Interpersonal Violence*, 13(1), 73-92.

Lundy, Colleen, Linda Davies, Mark Holmes, and Lynn Urquhart. (1996). Re-Education for men abusive to women. *Canadian Social Work Review*, 13(2).

Lundy, Colleen and Mark Totten. (1997). Youth on the fault line. *The Social Worker*, 65(3), 98-106.

Lupri, E. (1990). Male violence in the home. In C. McKie and K. Thompson (Eds.), *Canadian social trends*. Toronto: Thompson Educational Publishing.

Maiuro, R., T. Cahn, P. Vitaliano, B. Wagner, and J. Zegree. (1988). Anger, hostility and depression in domestically violent versus generally assaultive men and nonviolent control subjects. *Journal of Consulting and Clinical Psychology*, 56(1), 17-23.

Makepeace, James M. (1986). Gender differences in courtship violence victimization. *Family Relations*, 35, 383-88.

Mangold, W., and P. Koski. (1990). Gender comparisons in the relationship between parental and sibling violence and nonfamily violence. *Journal of Family Violence*, 5, 225-35.

Margolin, Gayla, Linda Gorin Sibner, and Lisa Gleberman. (1988). Wife battering. In Vincent Van Hasselt, Randall Morrrison, and Alan Bellack (Eds.), *Handbook of family violence* (pp. 89-117). New York: Plenum Press.

Marshall, L., and P. Rose. (1987). Gender, stress and violence in the adult relationships of a sample of college students. *Journal of Social and Personal Relations*, 4, 299-316.

Martin, Del. (1981). *Battered wives*. San Francisco: Volcano Press.

Mathews, Frederick. (1993). *Youth gangs on youth gangs*. Ottawa: Solicitor General of Canada.

Matza, David. (1964). *Delinquency and drift*. New York: John Wiley and Sons.

McKendy, John P. (1997). The class politics of domestic violence. *Journal of Sociology and Social Welfare*, 24(3), 135-55.

McLaren, Peter. (1986). *Schooling as a ritual performance: towards a political economy of educational symbols and gestures*. London: Routledge and Kegan Paul.

McRobbie, Angela. (1980). Settling accounts with subcultures: a feminist critique. *Screen Education*, 34, 37-49.

McRobbie, Angela, and Jenny Garber. (1983). Girls and subcultures. In Stuart Hall and Tony Jefferson (Eds.), *Resistance through rituals: youth subcultures in post-war Britain* (pp. 209-22). London: Hutchinson.

Mead, George Herbert. (1934). *Mind, self and society*. Chicago: University of Chicago Press.

Mercer, Shirley L. (1988). Not a pretty picture: an exploratory study of violence against women in high school dating relationships. *Resources for Feminist Research*, 17, 15-23.

Messner, Michael. (1989). Masculinities and athletic careers. *Gender and Society*, 3(1), 71-88.

Messerschmidt, James W. (1986). *Capitalism, patriarchy and crime*. New Jersey: Rowman and Littlefield.

———. (1993). *Masculinities and crime: critique and reconceptualization of theory*. Maryland: Roman and Littlefield.

———. (1997). *Crime as structured action: gender, race, class and crime in the making*. Thousand Oaks, CA: Sage Publications, Inc.

Morrison, Margaret M., and Terry LeBlanc. (1998). *Effective services for young children with conduct problems*. Toronto: Ontario Association of Children's Aid Societies.

Muehlenhard, Charlene and Melaney Linton. (1987). Date-rape and sexual aggression in situations: incidence and risk factors. *Journal of Counselling Psychology*, 34(2), 186-96.

Mulroy, Elizabeth. (1997). Building a neighbourhood network:

inter-organizational collaboration to prevent child abuse and neglect. *Social Work*, 42(3), 255-65.

Natale, Jo Anna. (1994). Roots of violence. *American School Board Journal*, 181(3), 33-40.

National Crime Prevention Council. (1995). *Clear limits and real opportunities – the keys to preventing youth crime*. Ottawa: NCPC.

O'Brien, Carol-Ann, Robb Travers and Laurie Bell. (1993). *No safe bed: lesbian, gay and bisexual youth in residential services*. Toronto: Central Toronto Youth Services.

Offord, Dan, Mike Boyle, and Yvonne Racine. (1990). *Ontario child health study: children at risk*. Toronto: Queen's Printer for Ontario.

O'Keefe, Maura. (1997). Predictors of dating violence among high school students. *Journal of Interpersonal Violence*, 12(4), 546-68.

——. (1998). Factors mitigating the link between witnessing inter-parental violence and dating violence. *Journal of Family Violence*, 13(1), 39-57.

O'Neil, James M., and Michel Harway. (1997). A multivariate model explaining men's violence against women. *Violence Against Women*, 3(2), 182-203.

Okun, Lewis (1986). *Woman abuse: facts replacing myths*. New York: State University of New York Press.

Pagelow, Mildred D. (1981). *Woman-battering: victims and their experiences*. Beverly Hills, CA: Sage.

Peled, Einat. (1997a). Intervention with children of battered women: a review of current literature. *Children and Youth Services Review* (UK), 19(4), 277-99.

——. (1997b). The Battered Women's Movement response to children of battered women. *Violence Against Women*, 3(4), 424-46.

Persky, H., K. Smith, and G. Basu. (1971). Relation of psychologic measures of aggression and hostility to testoterone production in man, *Psychosomatic Medicine*, 33 (1971), 265-77, cited in Janet Shibley Hyde (1980). *Half the human experience: the psychology of women* (p. 316). Lexington, MA: D.C. Heath.

Ptacek, James. (1988). Why do men batter their wives? In Kersti Yllo and Michele Bogard (Eds.), *Feminist perspectives on wife abuse*. Newbury Park, CA: Sage.

Reinharz, S. (1979). *On becoming a social scientist*. San Francisco: Jossey-Bass.

Reister, Albert E., and James Deegear. (1996). Urban youth gangs: ecological intervention strategies. Norma Kolko and Shulamith Lala Ashenberg Straussner (Eds.). *Children in the urban environment: linking social policy and clinical practices* (pp. 798-790). Springfield, IL: Charles C. Thomas.

Rich, Adrienne. (1980). Compulsory heterosexuality and lesbian existence. *Signs* 5(4), 631-60.

Rodgers, Karen. (1994). Wife assault: the findings of a national survey. *Juristat Service Bulletin,* 14(9).

Rosenbaum, Alan, and Daniel O'Leary. (1981). Marital violence: characteristics of abusive couples. *Journal of Consulting and Clinical Psychology,* 49, 63-71.

Rubin, Lillian B. (1976). *Worlds of pain: life in the working class.* New York: Basic Books.

———. (1983). *Intimate strangers: men and women together.* New York: Harper Colophon.

Sacco, Vincent F. and Leslie W. Kennedy. (1994). *The criminal event.* Scarborough, ON: Nelson.

Sappington, A.A. et al. (1997). Relationships between child abuse, date abuse, and psychological problems. *Journal of Clinical Psychology,* 53(4), 319-29.

Sarbin, Theodore R. and Bernard G. Rosenberg. (1955). Contributions to role-taking theory. *Journal of Social Psychology,* 42, 71-81.

Saunders, Daniel G. (1988). Wife abuse, husband abuse, or mutual combat: a feminist perspective on the empirical findings. In Kersti Yllo and Michele Bograd (Eds.), *Feminist perspectives on wife abuse* (pp. 90-113). Beverley Hills, CA: Sage.

———. (1989). *Who hits first and hits most? Evidence for the greater victimization of women in intimate relationships.* Paper presented at the annual meeting of the American Society of Criminology, Reno, Nevada.

Schechter, Susan. (1982). *Women and male violence: the visions and struggles of the battered women's movement.* Boston, MA: South End Press.

Schwendinger, Herman, and Julia Schwendinger. (1983). *Rape and inequality.* Beverly Hills, CA: Sage.

———. (1985). *Adolescent subcultures and delinquency.* New York: Praeger.

Scott, M., and S. Lyman. (1968). Accounts. *American Sociological Review*, 33, 46-62.

Scully, Diana. (1990). *Understanding sexual violence*. Boston: Unwin Hyman.

Sennett, Richard, and Jonathon Cobb. (1972). *The hidden injuries of class*. New York: Vintage.

Shapiro, Brenda L., and J. Conrad Schwartz. (1997). Date rape: its relationship to trauma symptoms and sexual self-esteem. *Journal of Interpersonal Violence*, 12(3), 407-19.

Schewe, Paul A., and William O'Donohue. (1996). Rape prevention with high-risk males: short-term outcome of two interventions. *Archives of Sexual Behavior*, 25(5), 455-71.

Shibley Hyde, Janet. (1980). *Half the human experience: the psychology of women*. Lexington, MA: D.C. Heath.

Silverman, D. (1993). *Interpreting qualitative data*. London: Sage.

Smith, Michael D. (1986). *Patriarchy and violence against women*. Unpublished manuscript. Department of Sociology, York University, Ontario, Canada.

———. (1987). The incidence and prevalence of woman abuse in Toronto. *Violence and Victims*, 2(3), 173-87.

———. (1990a). Patriarchal ideology and wife beating: a test of a feminist hypothesis. *Violence and Victims*, 5, 257-73.

———. (1990b). Sociodemographic risk factors in wife abuse: results from a survey of Toronto women. *Canadian Journal of Sociology*, 15(1), 39-58.

Smith, J.P., and J.G. Williams. (1992). From abusive household to dating violence. *Journal of Family Violence*, 7(2), 153-65.

Spender, Dale. (1982). *Invisible women: the schooling scandal*. London: Writers and Readers Publishing Cooperative Society.

Statistics Canada. (1993). The violence against women survey. *The Daily*, November 18.

———. (1994). *Violence against women survey*. Microdata file. Ottawa.

Stearns, Frederic. (1972). *Anger: psychology, physiology, pathology*. Springfield: Charles C. Thomas.

Steinmets, Suzanne, (1981). A cross-cultural comparison of marital abuse. *Journal of Sociology and Social Welfare*, 8, 404-14.

Stets, Jan E. (1990). Verbal and physical aggression in marriage. *Journal of Marriage and the Family*, 52, 501-14.

Stets, Jan E., and Murray A. Straus. (1989). The marriage license as a hitting license: a comparison of assaults in dating, cohabiting and married couples. In Murray A. Straus and Richard J. Gelles (Eds.), *Physical violence in American families* (pp. 227-44). New Brunswick, NJ: Transaction.

Stets, Jan E., and D.A. Henderson. (1991). Contextual factors surrounding conflict resolution while dating: Results from a national study. *Family Relations*, 70, 29-36.

Stinchcombe, Arthur L. (1964). *Rebellion in a high school*. Chicago: Quadrangle Books.

Straus, Murray. (1990a). Ordinary violence, child abuse, and wife-beating: What do they have in common? In Murray A. Straus and Richard J. Gelles (Eds.), *Physical violence in American families* (pp. 403-24). New Brunswick: Transaction.

——. (1990b). Social stress and marital violence in a national sample of American families. In Murray Straus and Richard Gelles (Eds.), *Physical violence in American families: risk factors and adaptations to violence in 8,145 families* (pp. 181-201). New Brunswick, NJ: Transaction.

Straus, Murray A., and Richard J. Gelles (1986). Societal changes and change in family violence from 1975 to 1985 as revealed by two national surveys. *Journal of Marriage and the Family*, 48, 465-79.

Straus, Murray A., Richard J. Gelles, and Suzanne Steinmetz. (1980). *Behind closed doors: violence in the American family*. Garden City, NY: Doubleday.

Straussner, Joel H., and Shulamith L.A. Straussner. (1996). Impact of community and school violence on children. In Norma Kolko Phillips and Shulamith Lala Ashenberg Straussner (Eds.). *Children in the urban environment: linking social policy and clinical practices* (pp. 61-77). Springfield, IL: Charles C. Thomas.

Sudermann, Marlies, and Peter Jaffe. (1997). Children and youth who witness violence: new directions in intervention and prevention. In David A. Wolfe, Robert J. F. McMahon, and Ray D. Peters (Eds.). *Child abuse: new directions in intervention and treatment across the lifespan*. Thousand Oaks, CA: Sage Publications.

Sugarman, David, and Gerald Hotaling. (1989). Dating violence: prevalence, context, and risk markers. In Maureen A. Pirog-Good and Jan E. Stets (Eds.), *Dating violence: emerging social issues* (pp. 3-32). New York: Praeger.

Swift, Karen. (1995). *Manufacturing bad mothers: a critical perspective on child neglect*. Toronto: University of Toronto Press.

Sykes, Gresham, and David Matza. (1957). Techniques of neutralization: a theory of delinquency. *American Sociological Review*, 22, 664-70.

Szinovacz, Maximiliame. (1983). Using couple data as a methodological tool: the case of marital violence. *Journal of Marriage and the Family*, 45, 633-44.

Thiessen, D. (1976). *The evolution and chemistry of aggression*. Springfield: Charles C. Thomas.

Thorne-Finch, Ron. (1992). *Ending the silence: the origins and treatment of male violence against women*. Toronto: University of Toronto Press.

Tolman, Richard M., Jeffrey L. Edleson, and Michael Fendrich. (1996). The applicability of the theory of planned behaviour to abusive men's cessation of violent behaviour. *Violence and Victims*, 11(4), 341-54.

Tolson, Andrew. (1977). *The limits of masculinity*. London: Tavistock.

Totten, Mark. (1998). *Youth and Violence — Fact Sheet*. National Clearinghouse on Family Violence, Family Violence Prevention Division, Health Programs and Services Branch. Health Canada: Ottawa.

Totten, Mark. (2000). *The special needs of females in Canada's youth justice system: an account of some young women's experiences and views*. (draft document). Ottawa: Department of Justice Canada.

Totten, Mark and Colleen Lundy. (1999). Monitoring agency effectiveness: the use of outcome measures. *Canadian Social Work Review* 16(1).

Totten, Mark, Louise Manton, and Don Baker (1995a). *Alternatives to violence: a therapeutic group manual for abusive male youth*. Ottawa: Youth Services Bureau of Ottawa-Carleton.

——. (1995b). *The reduction of abusiveness in male youth as a result of pro-feminist group intervention: An exploratory study*. Unpublished paper.

Totten, Mark and Paul Reed. (2000). *Serious youth violence in Canada*. Ottawa: Youth Services Bureau of Ottawa-Carleton.

Ursel, Jane. (1994). The Winnipeg family violence court. *Juristat Service Bulletin* 14(12).

Walby, Sylvia. (1990). *Theorizing patriarchy*. Oxford: Basil Blackwell.

Walker, Hill M., Steve Stieber, and Michael Bullis. (1997). Longitudinal correlates of arrest status among at-risk males. *Journal of Child and Family Studies*, 6(3), 289-309.

Walker, Lenore. (1979). *The battered woman.* New York: Harper Colophon.

———. (1989). *Terrifying love: why battered women kill and how society responds.* New York: Harper Perennial.

Wallace, R., D. Wallace, and H. Andrews. (1997). Aids, tuberculosis, violent crime, and low birthweight in eight U.S. metropolitan areas: public policy, stochastic resonance, and the regional diffusion of inner-city markers. *Environment and Planning A* (UK), 29(3), 525-55.

Weissman, Eric. (1992). Kids who attack gays. In Gregory Herek and Kevin Berrill (Eds.), *Hate crimes: confronting violence against lesbians and gay men* (pp. 170-78). Newbury Park: Sage.

Wharf, Brian. (1993). *Rethinking child welfare in Canada.* Toronto: McClelland and Stewart.

White, J., and Mary Koss. (1991). Courtship violence: incidence in a national sample of higher education students. *Violence and Victims*, 6, 247-56.

Willis, Paul. (1977). *Learning to labour.* Farnborough, England: Saxon House.

Wilson, Margo, and Martin Daly. (1985). Competitiveness, risk taking and violence: the young male syndrome. *Ethology and Sociobiology*, 6(1), 59-73.

Wind, T., and L. Silvern. (1992). Type and extent of child abuse as predictors of adult functioning. *Journal of Family Violence*, 7, 261-81.

Wofford Mihalic, Sharon, and Delbert Elliott. (1997). A social learning theory model of marital violence. *Journal of Family Violence*, 12(1), 21-47.

Wolfe, David A., Peter Jaffe, Susan Wilson, and Lidia Zak. (1985). Children of battered women: the relation of child behaviour to family violence and maternal stress. *Journal of Consulting and Clinical Psychology*, 53, 657-65.

———. (1986). Child witnesses to violence between parents: Critical issues in behavioural and social adjustment. *Journal of Abnormal Psychology*, 14, 95-104.

Wolfe, David, Christine Wekerle, Deborah Reitzal, and Robert Gough. (1995). Strategies to address violence in the lives of high-risk youth. In Einat Paled, Peter Jaffe, and Jeffrey Edelson (Eds.), *Ending the cycle of violence* (pp. 255-74). Thousand Oaks, CA: Sage.

Wolfe, David A. et al. (1997). Interrupting the cycle of violence: empowering youth to promote healthy relationships. In David A. Wolfe, Robert J McMahon, and Ray D. Peters (Eds.), *Child abuse: new directions in prevention and treatment across the lifespan* (pp. 102-29). Thousand Oaks, CA: Sage Publications.